COLLOQUIAL
RUSSIAN

COLLOQUIAL
RUSSIAN

By

MARK SIEFF

Published by THE BLAKISTON COMPANY, Philadelphia

Distributed by E. P. DUTTON & CO., INC. New York

CONTENTS

GRAMMATICAL NOTES

SECTION I—SOUNDS

SECTION II—PARTS OF SPEECH

1. говори́ть	— -каза́ть.	2. дава́ть	— дать.
3. брать	— взять.	4. -става́ть	— стать.
5. быва́ть	— быть.	6. дева́ть	— деть.
7. -има́ть	— -ять.	8. ходи́ть	— итти́.
9. е́здить	— е́хать.	9a. бежа́ть	— -бега́ть.
10. носи́ть	— нести́.	11. вози́ть	— везти́.
12. води́ть	— вести́.	13. па́дать	— пасть.
14. кла́дывать	— класть; -лага́ть — -ложи́ть.		

SECTION III—SYNTAX

Essentials of Russian Syntax: PAGES

Introduction, § 99. *The Sentence*, § 100. *Relation
between Words in the Sentence*, § 101. *The* Subject,
§ 102. *The* Predicate, §§ 103-104. *Irregular use of
Tenses in Sentences*, § 105. *Peculiarities in the
use of Moods*, § 106. *The* Object, §§ 107-108.
Direct object in the Genitive in Negative Sentences,
§ 108*a*. *Indirect object in the Nominative plural*,
§ 108*b*. Qualifying Words, § 109. *The* Apposition,
§ 110   182-192

Adverbial Expressions :

Of place, § 111 ; *of* time, § 112 ; *of* manner, § 113 ;
of cause, § 114 ; *of* purpose, § 115 . .   193-194

Co-ordination and Subordination :

(1) *Co-ordination*, § 117. (2) *Subordination*, § 118.
1. *Peculiar cases of Co-ordination between Subject
and Predicate*, § 119. 2. *Peculiar cases of Co-
ordination between Qualifier and Qualified word*,
§ 120   194-199

Personal and Impersonal Sentences :

Personal Sentences, § 121. *Impersonal Sentences*,
§ 122   199-202

Negative Sentences   202-203

Use of the Infinitive as Object . . .   203

Use of the Imperative   203-204

LESSONS

PREFACE

THIS manual has been written expressly for adult students who are unable to attend Russian classes, but who would like to acquire a knowledge of the language by self-tuition. As such students will experience greater difficulty in comprehending the elements of Russian than those who are instructed by a tutor, the author has endeavoured to present the subject-matter as lucidly as possible.

As the book is not intended for school use, the arrangement of its material differs from the usual pattern of a school manual, i.e. :

(1) It does not contain translation-work.

(2) The Grammatical Notes are set out in a compact and concise form, rather than dealt with piecemeal.

Experience has convinced the author that translation-work is not always conducive to the mastery of colloquial, everyday speech. Colloquial Russian does not always fit in with literal translations of English expressions. A 'translation bias' may prevent the student from assimilating idiomatic Russian in a natural way.

The compact arrangement of the Grammatical Notes will enable the student to acquire the indispensable minimum of grammar in an orderly way and will help him to gain quickly some insight into the 'mechanism' of Russian construction before taking up more advanced reading.

When he has learnt to wade through simple Russian, the student can attempt to master the **Essentials of Syntax,** which comprise a minimum of the most important elements of Syntax as they apply to the construction of a simple sentence, and the simpler forms of a **complex sentence.**

Russian **impersonal** and **negative** constructions, which present some difficulties to a foreigner, and which are not always easily explained by grammar, have been adequately treated in the **Syntax-Section**. Once the student has mastered these two characteristic modes of construction of a Russian sentence, he will have no difficulty in finding his way through more advanced Russian, or in comprehending spoken Russian.

In the **Lessons-Section** simple basic words and colloquial expressions are used which deal with the everyday round in the home and in the country.

The **Vocabulary**, though limited, includes the most important words in current use.

The **Verbs**, on the other hand, have been treated comprehensively. The conjugation-pattern of each verb is given throughout. The functions of **passive participles**, and the use of the **passive voice** in all its prevalent forms, have been adequately treated.

In both the **Grammar-Section** and the **Lessons-Section** are given selected examples which illustrate grammatical rules, and which exemplify the use of cases of declinable parts of speech. A complete statement of the **Governance of cases** is given in the **Syntax-Section**, which is reiterated in the **Lessons-Section**. The framework of a Russian sentence is made very clear and accessible to the student.

The general aim of this book is not so much to provide a full range of vocabulary and expressions, or a complete course of grammar, as to give comprehensive treatment to each essential peculiarity of the Russian language, and to consider the essential basic expressions that go to make up Russian everyday speech.

Both the Grammar- and Lessons-Sections have been amply provided with cross-references, and grammatical indexes in Russian and English are appended.

The book will thus help to lay a solid foundation for the student's knowledge of Russian, and will serve as a ' jumping-off ground ' for further study.

The **stress-accent** presents some difficulties to students of Russian. As some knowledge of its vagaries is indispensable, a few pointers are given here and there. Although the rules relating to the accent cannot be conveniently classified, or easily remembered by the student, they will, nevertheless, be found useful. The student is advised to take up at an early stage some accented (and annotated) reading matter to supplement his studies.

Phonetics.—The author has avoided illustrating Russian sounds by phonetic transcriptions. Not many students are acquainted with the accepted symbols. But, apart from this, the terminations and inflexions are learnt all the quicker in their natural Russian appearance. Garbed in phonetic symbols they will only be the more perplexing to the student. The **alphabet** is easily learnt, and the letters themselves are better suited to give the value of Russian sounds than are the best phonetic transcriptions.

In conclusion, the author would advise the student never to let himself be perplexed over the seeming difficulties of Russian. These are as easily overcome as in other languages. When he has mastered the initial difficulties, he will find that the construction of Russian is both lucid and exact. The verbal system, apart from the aspects and the personal terminations, which are easily learnt, is not so involved as is, for example, the verbal system of German. In Russian there is no subjunctive mood for all the tenses; there is no treble past tense, and no complicated future tenses. The simplicity of the Russian verb gives to the language elasticity and clarity. The Russian tongue has the sonorous grandeur of a classical language, and its vigour, grace, and flexibility combine to make it a great modern language.

MARK SIEFF.

SUGGESTIONS TO THE STUDENT

(1) Master chapter on Sounds (§§ 1-14), and learn to read the words in §§ 14a-14d.

(2) After 2 to 3 weeks' study of the chapters dealing with nouns, adjectives, pronouns, and numerals, and the paragraph on the conjugation of verbs (§ 70), start on **Lessons-Section** (pp. 241-307).

(3) All vocabularies must be thoroughly mastered. The Russian words to be read aloud, and written out *several times* to fix them in the mind.

(4) Grammatical forms (declensions and conjugations) must be assimilated by constant practice and ' drill,' and must keep pace with the vocabulary and the phrases of the **Lessons-Section.**

(5) The Les**s**ons to be learnt *as Russian* without any mental reference to their English translation. The English columns are merely intended to help the student to understand the Russian columns *as Russian.* Having thoroughly mastered a page, the student can check up his knowledge by means of the English column.

(6) Note the fitness of prepositions as used in Russian expressions, without attempting to find their exact equivalent in English. (See Note on the vagaries of some prepositions at the end of the Russian Index, p. 318.)

(7) The student should master the material of the 12 Lessons before taking up Russian reading matter.

(8) Acquire the habit of thinking in Russian within the limits of what has been learnt, but not in terms of words translated from the English.

b

(9) The chapters on the Conjugation of Verbs (§§ 71-88) are to be taken up at the next stage of study when the student has gained some knowledge of the construction of simple Russian.

(10) Syntax can be taken up a little later. The beginner need only take up the paragraphs dealing with a simple sentence (§§ 99-115); those on co-ordination and sub-ordination (§§ 116-120); on the Impersonal and Negative Sentences (§§ 121-123); on the verbs быть and имѣть (§§ 134-134a); on Expressions, etc. (§§ 135-136), and on the Governance of Cases (§§ 137-141). Complex Sentences, Clauses, the Passive Voice, etc., the student need not take up until he has learnt to read freely. The same applies to the paragraphs on the Stress-Accent, which are intended as a guide, but not as a subject of study. A closer acquaintance with the Stress-Accent can be made later.

(11) At a later stage the student can attempt to compile ' his own Russian Dictionary ' of all the words contained in the book, particularly the verbs, giving their conjugation-patterns.

(12) As the Indexes (pp. 316-323) contain only those words which have some grammatical significance, the student is advised to compile ' his own Index ' of the various subjects and expressions treated in the book. This will be of great benefit to his studies.

Of the Russian reading-books that have come under his notice, the author can recommend with confidence the following :

'Elementary Russian Reader,' by G. Z. PATRICK. (For beginners, published by Pitman.)

PUSHKIN's ' The Captain's Daughter,' edited with Notes and Vocabulary, by ANNA H. SEMEONOFF. (For more advanced students, published by Dent.)

BIBLIOGRAPHY

The following works have been chiefly consulted in the compilation of this manual:

В. А. Богородицкий, «Общий курс русской грамматики,» 4th edition. (Kazan, 1913.)

Ѳ. Буслаев, «Учебник русской грамматики,» 11th edition. (Moscow, 1913.)

В. Нифонтов, «Синтаксис.» (Yuriev, 1915.)

E. Berneker, 'Russische Grammatik.' (Leipzig, 1897.)

S. C. Boyanus, 'A Manual of Russian Pronunciation.' (Sidgwick and Jackson, London, 1935.)

P. Boyer et N. Spéranski, 'Manuel pour l'étude de la Langue Russe.' (Paris, 1905.)

Henry Sweet, 'A New English Grammar.' (Clarendon Press, London, 1900.)

The Notes on the Stress-Accent are from the author's book, 'A Guide to the Russian Accent.' (David Nutt, London, 1919.)

THE RUSSIAN ALPHABET.

Ordinary Characters.	Italic.	Written.	Russian Name.	Normal Corresponding Sound in English.	Accidental Sound.
А а	Аа	*А а*	ah	a *in* "father"	e, o
Б б	Бб	*Б б*	beh	**b**	p
В в	Вв	*В в*	veh	**v**	f
Г г	Гг	*Г г*	geh	g *in* "gate"	v, h, k, kh
Д д	Дд	*Д д*	deh	d	t
Е е	Ее	*Е е*	(y)eh	ye *or* e *in* "yet"	yo, o[1]
Ж ж	Жж	*Ж ж*	zheh	s *in* "leisure" (French j)	sh
З з	Зз	*З з*	zeh	z	s
И и	Ии	*И и*	ee	ee	yee
I i	Ii	*I i*	ee (съ то́чкою, with a dot)	ee	yee
Й й	Йй	*Й й*	и кра́ткое (short ee)	ee (short)[2]	
К к	Кк	*К к*	kah	c *in* "cat"	

[1] When e is printed ё, it is pronounced as *yo* or *o*.
[2] A very short i(ee).

Ordinary Characters.	Italic.	Written.	Russian Name.	Normal Corresponding Sound in English.	Accidental Sound.
Л л	Лл		el	l	
М м	М м		em	m	
Н н	Нн		en	n	
О о	Оо		o	o in "pot"	a
П п	Пп		peh	p	
Р р	Рр		er	r (emphatic)	
С с	С с		ess	s in "seat"	z
Т т	Тт		teh	t	
У у	у у		oo	oo	
Ф ф	Фф		ef	f	
Х х	Хх		kha	ch in Scotch "loch"	
Ц ц	Цц		tseh	ts	

Ordinary Characters.	Italic.	Written.	Russian Name.	Normal Corresponding Sound in English.	Accidental Sound.
Ч ч	Ч ч		cheh	ch in "church"	sh
Ш ш	Ш ш		shah	sh	
Щ щ	Щ щ		shchah	sh + ch	
Ъ ъ	Ъ ъ		yer		
Ы ы	Ы ы		yerü[1] (еры)	See Notes on Pronunciation.	
Ь ь	Ь ь		yer'[2] (ерь)		
Ѣ ѣ	Ѣ ѣ		yat' (ять)	yeh, eh	yo
Э э	Э э		eh	ay in "nay"	
Ю ю	Ю ю		yoo	u in "use"	
Я я	Я я		yah	ya in "yard"	ye, yi, e, i
Ѳ ѳ	Ѳ ѳ		feetáh	f	

[1] German *ü* followed by a short *i*, or *y* in *pity* sharply pronounced.

[2] The *r* is to be pronounced softly and followed by a short *i-* or *y*-sound, indicated by *'*.

Ѵ ѵ (the so-called ижица) is now rarely used, being replaced by и. It was only employed in words borrowed from the Greek, to represent υ (upsilon). Care should be taken not to confuse в, н, р, с, у, х with the similarly formed letters of the English alphabet.

NOTE. In the new Russian Orthography the letters I, Ѣ, Ѳ have been discarded. И, Е, Ф now take their place respectively.

In the prefixes из, воз (вз), раз (роз), низ, без, the з is commuted into с if they are prefixed to a word beginning with a voiceless consonant. (See § 63, note 1.)

The terminations аго, яго in the genitive of adjectives, participles, pronouns, and numerals, are now replaced by ого, его.

The feminine and neuter terminations ыя, ія in the nominative and accusative of adjectives, participles, pronouns and numerals, are now replaced by ые, іе (to conform to the masculine terminations).

ея (genitive of она́, and when used as a possessive pronoun) is now replaced by её.

The hard sign (ъ) is no longer used at the end of a word terminating in a hard consonant.

GRAMMATICAL NOTES

SECTION I

SOUNDS

Pronunciation of Russian Sounds

§ **1.** 1. *The Vowels.*

> **a** sounds as the English *a* in *far.*
> **э** „   „   „   *e* in *emblem.*
> **ы** (For pronunciation see next page.)
> **o** sounds as the English *aw* in *raw.*
> **y** „   „   „   *u* in *put.*
> **и** „   „   „ $\begin{cases}(1)\ ee\ \text{in}\ eel\ \text{and}\\ (2)\ yea\ \text{in}\ yeast.\end{cases}$

> **я** sounds as a $\left.\begin{matrix}\\ \\ \\ \\ \end{matrix}\right\}$ but with a fleeting 'jot' or **и**
> **e** „ э element fused with these sounds,
> **ё** „ o that is as :
> **ю** „ y

$$\left.\begin{matrix}{}^{j}a\\ {}^{j}\vartheta\\ {}^{j}o\\ {}^{j}y\end{matrix}\right\} \text{ or } \left\{\begin{matrix}{}^{и}a\\ {}^{и}\vartheta\\ {}^{и}o\\ {}^{и}y\end{matrix}\right. \quad \text{(See § 4.)}$$

The Russian **a** is produced with the mouth wide open ; the sound is articulated at the back of the mouth ; voiced breath is sent upwards.

For the pronunciation of the **o** the lips are protruded forward but in a downward movement, and the sound (also produced at the back of the mouth) is sent through the protruded lips downwards.

For the **y** the lips are well protruded in a forward movement, and the sound, produced at the back of the mouth,

A

is driven right forward. Care must be taken not to give
the Russian **у** the slightly composite ' off-glide ' quality of
the English *oo* in the words *food, good, moon*.[1]

The **и** is produced near the middle of the hard palate
with the co-operation of the middle part of the tongue,
with the mouth slightly open. It is a deep, close sound.
The ' jot,' which is the phonetic term for the **и**, is not
used in Russian as a separate letter.

The **э** is a middle sound between **а** and **и**. To produce
this sound the mouth is opened a little wider than for the
и. The position of the middle part of the tongue is much
lower than for the **и**. This letter appears only in a few
Russian pronouns, such as : э́тот, э́та, э́то, э́ти, э́такой
-ая -ое -ие, э́так. It is mainly used in borrowed foreign
words with an open **е** : эконо́мия, эта́ж, эма́ль, etc.
When not stressed it sounds almost as an indistinct **и**.

The **ы** is produced with the central part of the tongue
poised against the hard palate. The lips are even less open
than for the **и**. At the place where the **ы** is articulated
no **и** sound would be possible. It is not a deep sound as the
и, and is pronounced almost as *y* in *pity*. It is suggested
that the student should begin with the Russian **у** sound,
but right at the start, without protruding the lips forward
as for an **у** sound, end the half-begun **у** with an **и**.
The articulation thus begun of the hard, open **у** will not
allow the sound to finish with a close, deep **и** (as the
Russian **у** does not readily *fuse* with an **и**), and so the
correct sound **ы** will be the result. The student will get
better results if he tries at first to produce the sound **ы**
with labials (**б, п, м, ф, в**). The combination **муи, пуи,
буи, фуи, вуи**, quickly pronounced will produce the sound
ы. The vowels **уи** must be well joined. (This experimental
' sound-trick ' must not be confused with the legitimate
diphthongs : **пуй, суй, куй, муй, буй**, etc., where the **у**
sound is well completed and the short **й** (see p. 4) just
tacked on without any attempt at *fusing*.)

[1] As sometimes pronounced in the Midlands and in the North.

лы—this syllable is the easiest to pronounce if the sound of the hard л has been mastered (see p. 5).

The e is the soft (jotated) counterpart of the hard э. Frequently, when stressed, the open e[1] sounds as ё (yo): (1) initially ; (2) in the middle of words after a vowel, or after ь and ъ; (3) before a hard consonant in purely Russian words.

Rule (3), however, admits of many exceptions. To give a list of these exceptions would be too confusing to the beginner. The student is advised to form the habit of pronouncing the correct ё sound through practice, and from texts provided with the diaeresis. Often after the non-palatalized ж, ш, ц and also after the soft ч, щ, the ё sounds as an o. An accented ё after these five consonants usually turns into an o automatically, with the exception of personal terminations of verbs, where the ё is retained, but is sounded as an o.

(1) ёж, hedgehog
ёлка, Christmas tree

(2) наём, hire, loan
моё, mine
житьё, living
объём, size

(3) лёд, ice
мёд, mead
овёс, oats
шёпот [шópot], whisper
жёлоб [жóлоб], trough
течёт, runs
печёт, bakes
жжёт, burns

NOTE. There are no mute vowels in Russian. Every vowel is sounded.

§ 2. *The letters* ь, ъ, й.

The ь (soft sign) indicates that the preceding consonant is palatalized. (See § 8.)

Examples :

дань, tribute
день, day
пень, stump of tree

дверь, door
соль, salt
коньяк, brandy

[1] See § 10.

The consonants ж, ш are never palatalized by the soft sign, or soft vowels.

ц is never followed by ь, и, ю, я ; it can be followed by е, but is not made soft by this vowel.

The ъ (hard sign) indicates that the preceding consonant is hard (non-palatalized). It can now be found in the middle of a word only, before a soft vowel (in compound words), where it shows that this soft vowel is sounded as a pure vowel, and that its softness (jotation) has not been absorbed by the consonant before the ъ :

объяснить, to explain
объём,   size, dimension
субъéкт,   worthless individual ; subject

In some texts this ъ is replaced by an apostrophe (').

Before the New Orthography came into force, the ъ always stood at the end of every word which ended in a hard consonant. It has now been discarded.

NOTE. Soft vowels, standing after ь or ъ, do not lose their ' jot ' element. (See § 9e.)

The short и. This is marked й. It is used only for forming diphthongs in combination with other vowels :

чай,	tea	лей,	pour
мой,	mine	бей,	beat
сарáй,	shed	бéдный,	poor
читáй,	read	грóмкий,	loud
дуй,	blow		

§ 3.   2. *The Consonants.*

(*a*) The hard consonants : п, б, м, ф, в, к, г are similar to the English   *p, b, m, f, ·v, k, g.* (See § 9.)

(*b*) The hard т, д, н, л, although broadly similar to the English   *t, d, n, l,* yet have a shade of difference which makes them fit better into the ' vocal mechanism ' of Russian. They are dental and are formed with the tip of the tongue *against the upper teeth*, and not against the teeth-ridge. (See § 9*a*.)

The sound of the hard л is removed further from the sound-value of the English *l* by the characterístically Russian hollow sound (see § 9*a*). The nearest approximation to the sound of the Russian hard л is that of the English *l* in *apple, bubble, sample, purple*. But the Russian sound is more expanded and hollow.

(*c*) The hard с, з also deviate slightly from the English *s, z*. They are produced between the tip of the tongue and the upper teeth (by narrowing the air-passage), and not between the tip *and* blade, and the teeth-ridge. The Russian с, з are more sharply outlined than the English *s, z*. (See § 9*b*.)

(*d*) The hard р is similar to the English ' rolled ' *r* as sounded in the north of England, but the ' trill ' is a moderate one. (See § 9*a*.)

In рот, mouth⎱ the р sounds as⎱ in *ring, rotter,*
    руká, hand ⎰ the English *r* ⎰   *rubbish.*

(*e*) The hard х is similar to the Scottish and German sound *ch* in *loch*. It is produced with very weak friction, and sounds almost as a voiceless *h*. Its sound has no harsh, rasping quality (see § 9*c*):

хам (ill-bred fellow) sounds almost as a slightly thicker English *h* would sound in *hard*.

The г has a voiced[1] counterpart which sounds as *h*. It is used in a few words mainly of scriptural origin, such as :

Бóга, of God ; Гóсподи ! Oh Lord ! блáго, good ; etc.

It is also used in a few foreign proper names which contain an *H*, such as :

Гáмбург, Hamburg ; Гéйне, Heine ; etc.

As there is no special letter in Russian for the aspirate sound, г is used in such words.

---

[1] aspirate.

(*f*) The hard ж, ш, ц are pronounced : -

> ж as *s* in *measure* ;
> ш as *sh* in *harsh* ;
> ц as *ts* in *rats* (but more closely fused). ·

These three consonants have no palatalized counterparts. They are never followed by ю, я. They can be followed by и, е, and ё, but these sound as ы, э, о after them, and they impart no softened quality to the consonant.

(*g*) The ч and щ are always soft ; they have no hard counterparts ; ч sounds as *ch* in *church*, щ is a combination of ш and ч (finely fused), and sounds as *shch* in fre*sh* *ch*eese. It must be pronounced as one sound. ·

ч and щ are never followed by ю, я, ы. They have a palatalized sound even when followed by а, о, у.

CLASSIFICATION OF RUSSIAN SOUNDS

§ 4. *The Vowels.*

Hard and Soft Vowels :

$$\text{Pure} \begin{cases} \text{а, э, ы, о, у} = \text{hard,} \\ \text{я, е, и, ё, ю} = \text{soft (jotated).} \end{cases}$$

The soft (jotated) vowels, while having the same fundamental sound as their corresponding hard vowels, have the element of a ' jot ' [1] preceding them.

Thus the sound of я corresponds to that of *ya* in *yard* ;

,,	,,	е	,,	,,	,,	*ye* in *yes* ;
,,	,,	и	,,	,,	,,	{(1) *ee* in *eel* ; {(2) *yea* in *yeast* ; [2]
,,	,,	ё	,,	,,	,,	*yo* in *yonder* ;
,,	,,	ю	,,	,,	,,	*yu* in *yuletide*.

But in the Russian soft vowels the ' jot ' element is not so open or pronounced as in analogous English sounds : it is more closely fused with the fundamental sound of the

[1] ' jot ' is the term adopted in phonetics for the и element [or of a very close English *y*].

[2] Initially (stressed) in : их, им, ими (gen., dat., instr. of они, *they*). ·

corresponding hard vowel, and thus forms a pure sound of its own.

The soft vowel retains its softness only if it stands as an initial syllable at the beginning of words, or when it follows another vowel (or ъ, ь) in the middle of a word :

яма, pit   моё, mine (*neuter*)
éду, I go (travel)   мо́ю, I wash
и́ва, willow tree   мою́, mine (*acc. fem.*)

But in

ря́дом, abreast   слепо́й, blind   сли́ва, plum

the я, е, и have given up the ' jot ' element to their preceding consonants. (See § 9e.)

Both hard and soft vowels retain their pure fundamental sound only when stressed (accented). Some of the vowels, when not stressed, sound fainter and become almost indefinite, and they deviate from their original cardinal sound-value, thus :

an unstressed a sounds as an indistinct ə (or the short unstressed English *a* in the words *alone, mortal*).

Example : кни́га, book,   sounds as кни́гə,
         ба́ба,   peasant woman,   „   ба́бə ;

an unstressed я sounds as an indistinct е :

за́яц,   sounds as за́ец,   hare,
мясни́к,   „   месни́к, butcher ;

an unstressed е often sounds as и : ·

поезда́ sounds almost as поизда́, trains ;

an unstressed о sounds as an indistinct unstressed a :

молоко́ sounds as малако́, milk.

The vowels ы, и, у, ю, when not stressed, do not very markedly differ from their cardinal sound-values.

It will be seen that the stress-accent plays a very important part in deciding how the vowels should be sounded in both *stressed* and *unstressed syllables.*

§ 5. *Effect of the Stress-Accent on the Pronunciation of Vowels.* (See § 11.)

It has been established by phonetic research that vowels, when removed from the stressed syllable in the Russian word, both before and after the accented vowel, have a tendency to be further modified into slightly different variations of their original sound, in accordance with the respective distance from the stress-centre. Phoneticians have provided these variations with appropriate symbols ; but for the beginner the multiplication of sounds and sound-symbols will only be confusing. The Russian sounds are best learned from a native, and the broad values of the fundamental vowel-sounds (and the few above-mentioned deviations) must always be borne in mind. By acquiring and fostering the habit of pronouncing the stressed syllables with a heightened tone and due resonance, the student will imperceptibly learn to pronounce the unstressed vowels almost as a native. In this connection three points must be remembered :

(1) The accented syllable is the most important part of a Russian word. It must be pronounced vigorously and with resonance. If all the 'vocal light' is focussed on the stressed syllable, the other syllables will automatically be left in the shade, and thus the unstressed vowels will assume their natural sound without the student being aware of it.

(2) There can only be one accented syllable in a Russian word. The student must aim at acquiring and fostering the habit of putting the proper stress on the accented syllable without giving vocal prominence to any other syllable in the word, that is to say : he must not create two stress-centres. A wrongly accented vowel will upset the pronunciation of the whole word.

(3) If the word ends in a consonant and the accent is on the last syllable, the student should take great care not to

' hit ' that consonant : he should just pronounce the
accented vowel with due resonance and then tack on the
consonant lightly. Consonants when hit are usually doubled,
and Russian does not tolerate doubled consonants. The
only exceptions to this rule in Russian words are a double н
and a double с, where the second н and с are inserted for
morphological reasons.

(Further hints on the value and importance of the stress-
accent will be given as we go along.)

§ 6. *Length of Stressed Vowels.*

There are no long or short vowels in Russian. Normally
all vowels are of a medium length, that is to say : half-way
between the English long and short vowels. But a stressed
vowel sounds a little longer, owing to the extra strength of
the stress. In a word pronounced with special *emphasis-
intonation* the stressed syllable will, naturally, sound much
longer than usual.

§ 7. *Diphthongs* (two vowels representing the sound of a single vowel).

All Russian vowels can form diphthongs by taking a
short н (written : й), which is placed after the vowel. The
result is a new sound, which resembles in some ways the
English diphthong formed by a vowel when it is followed
by a *y*. The Russian diphthongs are not so broad and open
as the English variety, and they are shorter, when not
stressed. They are really vowels to which has been added
half of the sound-value of the н together with half of its
' jotation.' This makes the principal-vowel element of
the diphthong very much closer than that of an English
diphthong.

Compare : май, May, with *my*

пей, drink, with *hey*

бой, battle, with *boy*, etc.

(See § 14c.)

A *

§ 8. *Soft Vowels and Palatalized Consonants.*

Soft vowels affect very strongly the consonants which precede them by giving them a modified, soft, character. The 'jot'-element of the soft vowel is communicated to the consonant, making it soft or palatalized. All such consonants receive a sound, slightly crushed, somewhat liquefied in some districts, and almost inwardly directed, with the element of a fleeting 'jot' lent to it. The initial consonants in the English words, *pew, few, tune, league, duty* can give some approximation to the pronunciation of Russian palatalized consonants. But the Russian palatalized consonants are much softer and closer. It would be very difficult to give precise guidance how to produce this soft (palatalized) variety of Russian consonants in one or two paragraphs : a whole booklet would be needed in order to give in detail the structure of the vocal organs, position of the tongue when uttering any given sound, etc. And even then the student would be much perplexed, and would never be certain whether he had pronounced this or that sound correctly or not. As the mastery of the soft consonants is of the utmost importance in learning Russian, the student is advised to learn the sounds from a native. For those who have already assimilated the vocal-value and functions of every Russian sound, a few hints about the palatalized consonants may be useful. These are set out in §§ 9-9e.

§ 9. *Pronunciation of Soft (palatalized) Consonants.*

The broad distinction between the pronunciation of hard consonants and their soft counterparts is this : that while the hard consonants are produced *without the participation of the middle part of the tongue*, those of the palatalized variety are pronounced *with the active participation of the middle part of the tongue* (nearer the front in the case of some consonants, and nearer the back in the case of others, as will be specified in each case). We will begin with the sounds produced with the participation of the lips (labials), п, б, м, ф, в. The hard п, б, м (full-labials) are produced with both lips compressed, the sound going outwards. The hard ф, в (half-labials) are produced by the lower lip touching the tips of the upper teeth, the sound going outwards. In the case of the *palatalized* variety of these five labials, the sound, as it were, goes inwards, as if to pick up the 'jot' (or й) sound which makes them soft, while the middle part of the tongue (middle-front) simultaneously moves towards that spot of the hard palate where the 'jot' is produced.

The vocal organs of a Russian perform all these nice functions automatically. The English student will need some 'mouth-drill' at the beginning. When this 'trick' is learnt the student will have no further difficulty with the soft consonants. But learn it he must, otherwise his spoken Russian will never be really intelligible, or, at best, it will have a marked un-Russian flavour.

§ 9a. Next come the *dentals* : т, д, н, л, and the trilled (or rolled) р. The hard (non-palatalized) т, д, н are formed with the tip of the tongue against the upper teeth, the sound going outwards. For the palatalized set the lips are spread, the tip of the tongue is slightly lowered, leaving a clearance between tip of tongue and upper teeth, and the front of the tongue is simultaneously raised towards the hard palate (to infuse the 'jot' element into the consonant). In this process the blade of the tongue presses firmly against the teeth-ridge.

To produce a hard л the tip of the tongue is placed against the upper teeth, the middle of the tongue is lowered ; the sound is produced by the back of the tongue against the soft palate. The soft л is produced in the same way as the soft т, д, н.

The non-palatalized hard р is produced by holding the tongue loosely near the teeth-ridge (of the upper teeth). The air stream causes the tip of the tongue to vibrate, and produces the right trill. The soft (palatalized) **p** is produced by raising the tongue higher in the direction of the hard palate, with the mouth opened wider. The trill should not be overdone : just a momentary soft-pedalled vibration will do.

§ 9*b*. The hard **c** and **з** are produced by bringing the tip of the tongue very close to the upper teeth (without touching them).

For the soft **c** and **з** it is necessary to raise the front of the tongue towards the hard palate.

Thus the soft consonants **т, д, н, л, р, c, з**, have a middle-front (tongue) palatalization.

§ 9*c*. We now come to the *back-consonants* (usually called gutturals). They are formed between the back of the tongue and the soft palate :

к, г, х. Hard **к** is pronounced as the English *c* before a hard vowel (as in *cat*).

Hard **г** is pronounced as the English hard *g* in *go*.

Hard **х** is pronounced as *ch* in Scottish and German *loch*; but the Russian **х** is not so harsh, it almost sounds as a thick English *h*.

The palatalized variety of these three back-consonants is produced by endeavouring to articulate them a little forward in the direction where the **и** is articulated.

The soft back-consonants can be described as having a middle-back (tongue) palatalization.

§ 9*d*. There remain **ж, ш, ц**, which are not capable of palatalization, and **ч, щ**, which are pre-eminently soft (palatalized).

The student could practise the pronunciation of the soft consonants (except **ж, ш, ц**) by pronouncing them together with an **и**. Having obtained a satisfactory result, he can drop the **и** and try to experiment without any vowel at

all. He will find that a soft б is really б^u with only the
fleeting ' jot ' element of the и sounded, etc.

The palatalization of к, г, х is not so pronounced as in
the other consonants.

> NOTE. The position of the front part of the tongue,
> when producing a palatalized consonant, should always be
> close to the hard palate, except in the case of *labials*,
> when this is not quite possible.

§ 9e. It will be seen that the soft vowels create a new set
of soft consonants which are distinct in pronunciation from
the corresponding hard set. But having performed the
function of palatalizing the preceding consonant the soft
vowel has given up its ' jot ' element (which has now
been absorbed by the preceding consonant), and has only
retained its cardinal sound-value, thus :

> няня, nurse, is pronounced as н'а́н'а ; [1]
> дядя, uncle, is pronounced as д'а́д'а.

It would be impossible to pronounce a palatalized consonant with the soft vowel retaining its ' jot ' element.
In cases where such retention is needed, the palatalized
consonant is separated from the soft vowel by ь. (See
§ 2.)

A few examples of words, with both hard and soft consonants, are given below (see §§ 14a and 14b). After a
little practice the pronunciation of palatalized consonants
should become quite easy.

§ 10. *Open and Close Vowels.*

All vowels, both soft and hard, when they stand immediately before a palatalized consonant have a close, almost
contracted, sound. This is effected automatically by the
correct pronunciation of the palatalized consonant that
follows the vowel. In the act of correctly fusing the
vowel and the consonant, an almost new vowel is pro-

---

[1] The apostrophe indicates the softened, palatalized consonant.

duced which has a resemblance to a very close diphthong, with an imperceptible ' jot '-quality. By a process of assimilation the vowel absorbs a part of the palatalization of the soft consonant, and it now takes a shade of the ' jot ' on the side nearest to the soft consonant. The following examples will illustrate this process of vocal fusion and assimilation :

Open vowels before hard consonants :	*Close (contracted) vowels before soft consonants :*	
брат, brother	брать, [браʲть]	to take
дан, given	дань, [даʲнь]	tribute
лён, flax	лень, [л'еʲнь]	state of laziness
кол, pile (pointed stake)	коль, [коʲль]	if
дал, he gave	даль, [даʲль]	distance
надут, inflated	надуть, [надуʲть]	to inflate, to cheat
мат, checkmate	мать, [маʲть]	mother

In all these examples the close vowels are produced by simply tacking on the well-articulated palatalized consonant, without any conscious effort being made by the student to render the vowel close. *The student's task is simply to sound the vowel correctly in accordance with its cardinal sound-value, and then to tack on, without any pause, the well-palatalized consonant.* The result will be the correct close vowel. If, however, he should aim at, or be conscious of, producing a close vowel, the result will be a *diphthong*, which will upset the euphony of the word.

§ 11. *The Stress-Accent.* (See § 5.)

One of the main difficulties in the study of Russian is the accent. It is a *stress*-accent, the accented (or stressed) syllable requiring a higher pitch, or ring, of the voice. As the accent is frequently shifted from one syllable to another in the declension, or conjugation, of the same word, or in the formation of derivatives, an early practical acquaintance with the position of the stress-accent in the word is necessary. As far as beginners are concerned there are no rigid rules that can be of any practical value, and so the student must form the habit of memorizing the place of the accent in the word from accented texts. This habit will help the learner to wade through the seemingly hopeless maze of the accent. It must be borne in mind that by putting the accent on the wrong syllable the meaning of the word is often altered. A few examples will illustrate this :

while	до́ма	means	at home,	дома́	means	houses ;
	за́мок	,,	a castle,	замо́к	,,	a lock ;
	му́ка	,,	torment,	мука́	,,	flour.

But, apart from this, unless the student has formed the habit of giving the accented syllable the proper stress, he will have greater difficulty in comprehending the sounds and meaning of Russian as spoken by a native, and his own Russian will not be easily understood.

The accented vowel should be stressed clearly and resonantly, without, however, lengthening the sound unduly. It must be remembered that there are no long or short vowel sounds in Russian (see § 6). If a stressed syllable ends in a consonant the full force of the stress should fall on the accented vowel, but never on the consonant. The consonant is tacked on lightly without being hit. It is alien to Russian to double a consonant by hitting it. (See § 5, note 3.)

Vowels without the stress-accent are almost reduced in

sound-value ; they remain in the shade, and are not so clearly pronounced (see § 5, note 1). Unstressed vowels which stand immediately before the accented syllable are not quite so much reduced in sound-value as those standing after the accented syllable. The latter are heard indistinctly and the sound is often not clearly defined.

All these observations on the accent can, of necessity, give only an approximate idea about the manifold changes which unstressed vowels undergo in the process of sound-formation. But a careful study and application of the few hints given above will enable the student to pronounce the various sounds as near as possible to the living sounds of spoken Russian. An approximation to the exact shading of sounds will come with practice and knowledge. The main thing is to stress the accented syllable correctly, and to pronounce the palatalized consonants properly. The rich expressiveness of Russian can only be attained through paying meticulous attention to these rules and hints about the sounds and the accent.

§ 12. *Voiced and Voiceless Consonants (Sonants and Surds).*[1]

(*a*) Voiced :　б, в, г, д, з, ж, м, н, л, р, —— —— ——

(*b*) Voiceless : п, ф, к, т, с, ш, —— —— —— —— ч, щ, х

(1) Voiced consonants are sounded as voiceless at the end of words after a vowel :

лоб,	forehead,	sounds as	лоп
кровь,	blood,	,,	крофь
мог,	could,	,,	мох
стог,	haystack,	,,	стох
ног,	feet (*gen. pl.*),	,,	нох
режь,	cut (*imp. 2nd pers. sing.*),	,,	решь
клад,	buried treasure,	,,	клат

(2) At the beginning of words, and often in the middle, consonants have a tendency to assimilate

---

[1] Voiced consonants are uttered with vocal vibration; voiceless consonants are uttered with the breath and not with the voice.

the voiced, or voiceless, quality of the preceding
consonant by lending to it their own vocal quality
(or timbre) :

(a) сдѣлать, to make, sounds as здѣлать
   про́сьба, request,   ,,   про́зьба
   та́кже, also,   ,,   та́гже
   (both consonants are rendered *voiced*).

(б) ла́вка, shop,   sounds as ла́фка
   вхо́д, entrance,   ,,   фхот
   (both consonants are rendered *voiceless*).

(c) з, с, before ж sound as ж :

сжечь, to burn,   sounds as жжечь
изжо́га, heartburn,   ,,   ижжо́га

з, с, before ш sound as ш :

сшить, to sew, sounds as шшить

с before ч sounds as ш :

счёт, account, sounds as шчёт [or щёт]

NOTE 1. If the second consonant in a word is р, л,
м, н, в, these, although voiced, *do not* turn a preceding voiceless consonant into a voiced one :

пра́вда, truth   снег, snow
пла́тье, dress   свой, one's own
смотрю́, I look

NOTE 2. Assimilation of consonants takes place
even if the respective consonants are in two different
words, if the first word has no stress of its own :

к дѣлу,   sounds as   г дѣлу,   to the point
с зо́лотом,   ,,   з зо́лотом, with gold

NOTE 3. In all cases of assimilation of consonants
the student should not make any conscious effort to
assist the natural tendency of the sounds themselves.
At the end of words, for example, all that he has to do
is to sound the stressed vowel with proper emphasis
and resonance, and then to tack on the final voiced

sound lightly, without any conscious effort. The result
will be a voiceless consonant of the proper effortless
quality, without unnatural exaggeration.

§ **13.** *Some Peculiarities in the Pronunciation of Consonants.*

(1) In the combinations здн, стн, the д and т are sounded
faintly, or not at all :

> поздно,   late,   sounds as пózно
> извéстно, it is known,   ,,   извéсно

(2) л is often sounded faintly, or not at all, particularly
at the end of words after labials :

> сóлнце, sun,   sounds as сóнце
> рубль, rouble,   ,,   рупь

(3) г before к, ч, sounds as х :

> легкó, light, easy,   sounds as лехкó
> мя́гко, softly,   ,,   мя́хко
> лéгче, lighter, easier,   ,,   лéхче
> мя́гче, softer,   ,,   мя́хче

(4) г sounds as в in the suffixes его, ого (terminations of
the genitive singular case for masculine and neuter of
adjectives, some pronouns, and ordinal numerals) :

> егó,   his,   sounds евó
> бéлого, of white,   ,,   бéлово

(5) ч before н is often sounded as ш :

> скýчно,   it's boring, sounds as скýшно
> конéчно,   of course,   ,,   конéшно
> прáчечная, laundry,   ,,   прáчешная

NOTE. In some words, however, the ч in чн retains its sound :

> тóчный,   exact, precise
> отлúчный, excellent
> конéчный, terminal, final
> востóчный, oriental, eastern
> беспéчный, carefree

(6) кто is sounded as хто
    что   ,,   ,,   што

§ 13a. *Commutation of Russian Sounds.*

In the process of forming new forms from stems (by declension and conjugation, etc.) and new words from roots (by derivation), all Russian vowels (except э), and many consonants, can be interchanged ; often they are inserted, or dropped, for euphony. These changes are effected in conformity with definite morphological laws and in consonance with the linguistic and phonetic tendencies of both Russian and Old Slavonic—the language from which modern Russian has evolved.

For practical purposes it will be sufficient for the beginner to be acquainted with only a few of these interchanges of sounds.

The most frequent changes of *vowels* are :

(*a*) ь into и or е   и into е
     е ,,   о   у ,,   ы
     о ,,   а   у and ы ,,   в, ав, ов, ва.

(*b*) о, е are dropped, or inserted, for euphony.

(*c*) и, у, а take the place of ы, ю, я after г, к, х, ж, ч, ш, щ
     а, у take the place of я, ю after ц.

Of the *consonant* changes the most frequent are :

(*a*) г} к} х}
     з} ц} с} change respectively into ж, ч, ш

       ск}
       ст} change into щ

       т   ,,   ,,   ч and щ
       д   ,,   ,,   ж and жд.

(*b*) The insertion of a euphonic л after labials б, в, м, п, ф before a ' jotated ' vowel (mainly ю, я, e).

(*c*) л preceded by a consonant is frequently dropped in the formation of the past tense of verbs if the л is not followed by a vowel.

NOTE 1. Besides the enumerated commutations of consonants, all consonants have a tendency to effect a change in the vocal quality of any other preceding consonant by assimilating it. This is explained in § 12.

NOTE 2. In this manual all the cases of commutation of sounds are clearly indicated throughout.

§ 14. *Stress.*

Having said all about the Russian sounds that the beginner will have to acquire before he sets out on his study of Russian, I must not omit to mention that a certain minimum knowledge of the simpler cases of sentence-stress will be useful to him. In the simplest sentence or word-group there are usually words of greater importance (head-words) and words of lesser importance, or what we shall call subordinate words. To such subordinate words belong prepositions (excepting those enumerated in § 96*f*), conjunctions, and many pronouns of the shorter type. These subordinate words are usually tacked on to the more important words, and in the process they lose their own stress. The same tendency also exists in English. But in Russian this is of greater importance, seeing that vowels which have no stress sound somewhat differently from the stressed variety. Apart from this, the law of assimilation, which makes a consonant sound either voiced or voiceless, in conformity with the type of consonant that follows it, will extend its operation also to consonants of a subordinate word in the sentence (see § 13). It is, therefore, not enough to pronounce a word with meticulous care, and hope that by uttering the correct words one after another the whole Russian sentence will turn out correct. If the less important words are given undue prominence the vowel-values will be distorted and the sentence will probably sound very un-Russian. The bare correctness of the pronunciation of individual sounds and single words, without the effort to unify them into a coherent whole, will bear no resemblance to the co-ordinated, well-modulated, and well-knit sounds of living Russian speech.

Until the beginner has learnt a little more Russian it will be safe for him to assume that sentence-stress and sentence-intonation of a simple sentence are much alike in both Russian and English. He will, no doubt, commit blunders, but this will not matter so much as far as sentence-stress is concerned.

The observations on Russian pronunciation in the preceding pages are necessarily of limited scope. For those students who wish to acquaint themselves with a wider scientific treatment of Russian sounds, the excellent 'Manual of Russian Pronunciation,' by S. C. Boyanus (Sidgwick and Jackson), is recommended. The subject-matter of the work is treated on phonetic principles and is phonetically transcribed. It contains useful hints on word stress and sentence intonation.

§ 14a. Hard Consonants and Open Vowels. (See §§ 9-10.)

ба	бо	бу	бы	ба́ба	ха́та	ма́ло
ва	во	ву	вы	бобы́	изба́	ло́ма
га	го	гу	—	губа́	па́па	са́жа
да	до	ду	ды	дубы́	ма́ма	коза́
жа	жо	жу	—	ду́ба	ма́ло	она́
за	зо	зу	зы	возы́	мы́ло	зако́н
ка	ко	ку	—	во́за	брат	па́ра

ла	ло	лу	лы	луга́	хват	пора́
ма	мо	му	мы	го́ды	ла́па	ра́на
на	но	ну	ны	—	ла́пы	ра́но
па	по	пу	пы	дуга́	па́ла	на́ра
ра	ро	ру	ры	дугу́	па́ло	нора́
са	со	су	сы	вода́	упа́ла	носу́
та	то	ту	ты	буза́	мука́	суда́
ха	хо	ху	—	ко́ла	кума́	суду́
ца	цо	цу	цы	колы́	му́ка	ма́ку

то́-то	на́до	ху́до	плы́ла	вожу́
са́ло	дано́	худа́	плы́ло	бужу́
лоса́	рука́	ножи́[ы́]	выл	дул
ра́ды	ку́ры	ножа́	слыл	гул
ра́да	худа́	кора́	ры́нок	тума́н
го́да	о́ба	ка́ра	пыла́л	болва́н
года́	жук	ра́са	пыла́ла	ко́локол
два	лук	роса́	куды́	колокола́ .
ры́ло	сук	суп	ра́ды	боло́то
мы́ло	хам	глуп	рад	мо́лот
вы́ла	нам	мы́за	ра́да	хо́бот
дыбы́	да́ром	мы́зы	кула́к	плуг
вы́бор	па́ром	копы́то	ду́мал	друг
двум	паро́м	лы́ко	ду́мала	слух
ры́ба	ду́ха	уны́ло	куда́	му́ха
дыра́	ду́ху	плыл	дура́к	дух

NOTE 1. Unstressed **a** and **o** have the indefinite
sound of the first *o* in the English word *Morocco*.
Unstressed **y** sounds as the English *u* in *put*. Stressed **a**
sounds as the English *a* in *ah*; stressed **o** sounds as the
English *aw* in *saw*; stressed **y** sounds as the English
oo in *doom*. For the correct sound of **ы** see § 1.

NOTE 2. It is essential that the student should become thoroughly acquainted with the pronunciation of
Russian sounds as set out in §§ 1-14 before he attempts
to read the reading exercises.

NOTE 3. There is only one stress-centre in a Russian word : the accented vowel. This should be vigorously and *resonantly* sounded.

§ 14*b*. *Palatalized Consonants with Open and Close Vowels.*
(See §§ 8-9.)

бя = б'а[1]	бе = б'э	бё = б'о	би = б'и
вя = в'а	ве = в'э	вё = в'о	ви = в'и
			ги = г'и
дя = д'а	де = д'э	дё = д'о	ди = д'и
			жи = жы
зя = з'а	зе = з'э	зё = з'о	зи = з'и
			ки = к'и
ля = л'а	ле = л'э	лё = л'о	ли = л'и
мя = м'а	ме = м'э	мё = м'о	ми = м'и
ня = н'а	не = н'э	нё = н'о	ни = н'и
пя = п'а	пе = п'э	пё = п'о	пи = п'и
ря = р'а	ре = р'э	рё = р'о	ри = р'и
ся = с'а	се = с'э	сё = с'о	си = с'и
тя = т'а	те = т'э	тё = т'о	ти = т'и
фя = ф'а	фе = ф'э	фё = ф'о	фи = ф'и
			хи = х'и
			ши = шы

бю = б'у	ча = ч'а ⎫
вю = в'у	ща = щ'а
дю = д'у	чо = ч'о
зю = з'у	що = щ'о
лю = л'у	чу = ч'у
мю = м'у	щу = щ'у
ню = н'у	че = ч'э
пю = п'у	ще = щ'э ⎭
рю = р'у	
сю = с'у	же = жэ ⎫
тю = т'у	ше = шэ ⎭
фю = ф'у	

These consonants are always soft.

Always hard.

[1] See footnote, p. 13.

бья = б'я	бьё = б'ё	бье = б'е	бью = б'ю
вья = в'я	вьё = в'ё	вье = в'е	вью = в'ю
дья = д'я	дьё = д'ё	дье = д'е	дью = д'ю
зья = з'я	зьё = з'ё	зье = з'е	зью = з'ю
лья = л'я	льё = л'ё	лье = л'е	лью = л'ю
мья = м'я	мьё = м'ё	мье = м'е	мью = м'ю
нья = н'я	ньё = н'ё	нье = н'е	нью = н'ю
пья = п'я	пьё = п'ё	пье = п'е	пью = п'ю
рья = р'я	рьё = р'ё	рье = р'е	рью = р'ю
сья = с'я	сьё = с'ё	сье = с'е	сью = с'ю
тья = т'я	тьё = т'ё	тье = т'е	тью = т'ю
фья = ф'я	фьё = ф'ё	фье = ф'е	фью = ф'ю
	чьё = ч'ё	чье = ч'е	чью = ч'ю

NOTE. The soft vowels in the above examples retain their ' jot ' element as the consonants derive their palatalization from the ь. (See §§ 4 and 9e.)

беру́	мя́со	берёза	дя́дю
беда́	мёд	бельё	дя́ди
ве́ра	мя́та	бедня́к	дя́де
бюро́	не́бо	беси́ть	тётя
идём	не́бо	бе́дность	тёти
де́да	нет	—	тёте
де́ду	ле́то	опёнки	тётю
зерно́	лета́	котёнок	ня́ня
зёрна	лёг	—	ня́ню
весна́	ряд	пятно́	ня́ни
верста́	подря́д	пять	ня́не
ведро́	ся́ду	опя́ть	тя́тя
вёдра	ре́дко	ведь	тя́тю
ковёр	врёт	ве́рить	тя́ти
метла́	тюк	ве́рю	тя́те

мётла	утю́г	ве́рят	би́ли	дробь
ме́на	Фёдор	мель	ли́ли	кладь
мелка́	фи́га	медь	ви́ли	лазь
ме́ла	фе́рма	лечь	зю́зя	

изме́на	фи́рма	лень	Фе́дя
	хил	вре́мя	фе́я
	брю́ки	весьма́	филе́й
	хрю́кать	ве́чер	пле́мя
		—	се́мя

стать	ста́ли	дари́ть	дари́т
моло́ть	мо́лот	вари́ть	ва́рит
коло́ть	ко́лот	варю́	ва́ришь⎫[1]
пу́ля	пу́лю	дарю́	дари́шь⎭
пу́ли	пу́ле	пали́ть	палю́
лупи́ть	луплю́	по́ле	поля́
купи́ть	куплю́	куре́ние	мо́ре
ку́пля	кури́	лече́ние	моря́
кури́ть	курю́	враньё	мытьё
люблю́	любя́		

пыль	ковы́ль
у́быль	при́быль

о́кунь	корь	знать	конь	мазь
дунь	гарь	па́дать	ось	даль
дуть	дурь	пасть	брось	тень
грудь	фона́рь	класть	кость	выпь
грусть	янта́рь	па́мять	боль	высь
пусть	грань	ло́шадь	жаль	лось
путь	ве́рьте	морко́вь	вдаль	хоть
мыть	ме́рьте	це́рковь	нельзя́	
ныть	цель	кровь		
плыть	мель			
	свире́ль			
	колыбе́ль			

[1] Pronounced as : ва́риш, дари́ш. (See § 9*d*.)

§ 14c. *Diphthongs.*
(See § 7.)

лай	дуй	дóлгий
май	куй	хорóший
пай	плюй	вечéрний
рай	жуй	сúний
лéй	ночýй	
пей	бýйный	
грей	густóй	
шей	пустóй	
брей	мéлкий	
мой	мéдный	
свой	плохóй	
твой	гóлый	
	уйтú	
	уйдý	

§ 14d. -ться *pronounced as* -тса.

мыться	=	мытса
брúться	=	брúтса
купáться	=	купáтса
одевáться	=	одевáтса
одéться	=	одéтса
обýться	=	обýтса

etc.

SECTION II

PARTS OF SPEECH

1. NOUNS

§ 15. *Genders, Numbers, and Cases of Nouns.*

1. There are three Genders of Russian nouns : Masculine ; Feminine ; Neuter.
2. Two Numbers : Singular ; Plural.
3. Six Cases : (1) Nominative ; (2) Genitive ; (3) Dative ; (4) Accusative ; (5) Instrumental ; (6) Locative (also called Prepositional).

The cases answer to the questions :

(1) *Nom.*	кто ? что ?	who ? what ?
(2) *Gen.*	кого ? чего ?	whom ? what ?
	от кого ? от чего ?	from whom ? from what ?
	у кого ? у чего ?	near [of] whom ? near what ?
(3) *Dat.*	кому ? чему ?	to whom ? to what ?
(4) *Acc.*	кого ? что ?	whom ? what ?
(5) *Instr.*	кем ? чем ?	by whom ? by what ?
	с кем ? с чем ?	with whom ? with what ?
(6) *Loc.*	в ком ? в чём ?	in whom ? in what ?
	на ком ? на чём ?	on whom ? on what ?

The nominative case is called the direct case ; all the other cases are called the oblique cases. The vocative, or exclamation case, has now been merged in the nominative. Only a few nouns have retained the vocative case :

Бог,	God,	Бо́же !
Госпо́дь,	Lord,	Го́споди !
Христо́с,	Christ,	Христе́ !

§ 16. *Functions of Cases.*

The nominative is the ' subject case,' its main function being to supply the subject of the sentence :

брат пи́шет письмо́　　brother writes a letter

The **accusative** is the 'direct object case'; it serves to complete the meaning of a transitive verb :

    я пишу́ письмо́   I write a letter

The **dative** serves as an indirect object, in the meaning of : where to, to whom, etc. :

    я пишу́ к бра́ту   I write to (my) brother

The **genitive** shows that the noun in this case is an adjunct to another noun :

    я получи́л письмо́   I have received (my) brother's
    бра́та   letter

The **instrumental** case expresses the instrument or manner of action :

    я пишу́ перо́м   I write with a pen

The **locative** case expresses place :

    я живу́ в го́роде   I live in town

Both the instrumental and locative cases can be regarded as '**adverb cases.**'

§ 17. *How to distinguish the Gender of Nouns.*

The gender of inanimate nouns [1] is distinguished by the termination of the nominative case :

Masculine nouns terminate : (*a*) in a consonant, (*b*) in ь, (*c*) in й :

    го́род, town   день, day   чай, tea

Feminine nouns terminate : (*a*) in a, (*b*) in я, (*c*) in ь :

    кни́га, book   земля́, earth   ло́шадь, horse

Neuter nouns terminate : (*a*) in o, (*b*) in e, (*c*) a few words in мя :

    окно́, window   мо́ре, sea   и́мя, name

Also the word :   дитя́, child

---

[1] Nouns denoting inanimate things.

Nouns of all genders can be either of the hard group, or of the soft group, according to their case-endings :

	Hard Group		Soft Group
Masculine, ending in a consonant ;		-ь	-й
Neuter, ,, -o ;		-e	-мя
Feminine, ,, -a ;		-я	-ь

§ 18. *Declension of Masculine Nouns.*

The terminations of the masculine nouns according to their cases are :

	Singular			*Plural*	
	Hard	*Soft*		*Hard*	*Soft*
Nom.	—	-ь, -й	*Nom.*	-ы	-и
Gen.	-a	-я	*Gen.*	-ов	-ей, -ев
Dat.	-у	-ю	*Dat.*	-ам	-ям
Acc.[1]	— or -a	-ь, -й or -я	*Acc.*[1]	-ы or -ов	-и, -ей, -ев
Instr.	-ом	-ем [-ём]	*Instr.*	-ами	-ями
Loc.	-e	-e	*Loc.*	-ах	-ях

[1] See note 1, p. 30.

Examples :

Singular

Nom.	стол (table)	замóк (lock)	кон-ь (horse)	сарá-й (shed)
Gen.	стол-á	замк-á	кон-я́	сарá-я
Dat.	стол-ý	замк-ý	кон-ю́	сарá-ю
Acc.	стол	замóк	кон-я́	сарá-й
Instr.	стол-óм	замк-óм	кон-ём	сарá-ем
Loc.	стол-é	замк-é	кон-é	сарá-е

Plural

Nom.	стол-ы́	замк-и́	кóн-и	сарá-и
Gen.	стол-óв	замк-óв	кон-éй	сарá-ев
Dat.	стол-áм	замк-áм	кон-я́м	сарá-ям
Acc.	стол-ы́	замк-и́	кон-éй	сарá-и
Instr.	стол-áми	замк-áми	кон-я́ми	сарá-ями
Loc.	стол-áх	замк-áх	кон-я́х	сарá-ях

NOTE 1. The accusative of inanimate nouns is the same as the nominative in both singular and plural:

	Singular	Plural
Nom. Acc.	стол	столы́

In animate nouns[1] the accusative has the same termination as the genitive in both singular and plural:

	Singular	Plural
Nom.	конь	ко́ни
Acc.	коня́	коне́й

But if the accusative of an inanimate noun forms the direct object in a sentence having a **negative** predicate, the genitive takes the place of the accusative:

Я не купи́л стола́   I did not buy the table

NOTE 2. Masculine nouns ending in ь have the termination ей in the genitive plural. But those ending in ай, яй, ой, ей, уй take the termination ев or ёв.

Example:

Masc. sing.	Gen. pl.
конь	коне́й
сара́й	сара́ев
чай	чаёв (of various sorts of tea)

NOTE 3. As г, к, х cannot be followed by ы, this vowel is changed into и in the declension of nouns ending in these three letters:

кни́га, book,   кни́ги $\begin{cases} Gen.\ sing. \\ Nom.\ pl. \end{cases}$

NOTE 4. Masculine nouns ending in ч, щ, although soft (ending in a soft consonant), cannot be followed by я, ю or ё. These are supplanted by а, у, о:

плащ, cloak,   плаща́, плащу́, плащо́м
врач, physician, врача́, врачу́, врачо́м

[1] Nouns denoting living beings.

All nouns ending in ж, ш, ч, щ have the termination ей in the genitive plural. They are never followed by ы, я, ю, ё. The place of these vowels is taken by и, а, у, о.

плащ,	плащи́, (*Nom. pl.*)	плащёй (*Gen. pl.*)
врач,	врачи́,	врачёй
нож, knife,	ножи́,	ножёй
шала́ш, hut,	шалаши́,	шалашёй

NOTE 5. Masculine nouns ending in ц have the genitive plural termination ев if this syllable is not accented, but ов if it is accented :

па́лец, finger, па́льцев [1]
коне́ц, end, концо́в [2]

§ 19. *Fleeting* o *and* e *in the Declension of Masculine Nouns.*

Very often the o or the e in the final syllable of the nominative singular disappears in the oblique cases. (See § 13a.)

па́лец		коне́ц	
Singular	*Plural*	*Singular*	*Plural*
Nom. па́лец	па́льц-ы	*Nom.* коне́ц	конц-ы́
Gen. па́льц-а	па́льц-ев	*Gen.* конц-а́	конц-о́в
Dat. па́льц-у	па́льц-ам	*Dat.* конц-у́	конц-а́м
Acc. па́лец	па́льц-ы	*Acc.* коне́ц	конц-ы́
Instr. па́льц-ем	па́льц-ами	*Instr.* конц-о́м	конц-а́ми
Loc. па́льц-е	па́льц-ах	*Loc.* конц-е́	конц-а́х

NOTE 1. The o and e are retained in declension in words which would be difficult to pronounce if these vowels were dropped, thus :

кузне́ц, blacksmith,	кузнеца́	-цу́, -цо́м, -це́
мертве́ц, dead body,	мертвеца́	
пото́к, stream,	пото́ка	-ку, -ком, -ке
уро́к, lesson,	уро́ка	

[1] The e of the nominative singular is changed into ь (after an л).
[2] The e of the nominative singular disappears altogether.

NOTE 2. The vowel e after л in the last syllable of the nominative singular usually changes into ь in the oblique cases.

If the vowel e in the last syllable of the nominative singular is preceded by another vowel, it changes into й in the oblique cases :

наём, hire, найма́ ⎫
заём, loan, займа́ ⎬ -у́, -о́м, -е́
боец, fighter, бойца́ ⎭

· заяц [за́ец],[1] hare, за́йца -у, -ем, -е

Nouns terminating in ей change the e into ь in the oblique cases :

воробей, sparrow, воробья́, -ью́, -ьём, -ьé
соловей, nightingale, соловья́, -ью́, -ьём, -ьé
ручей, stream, ручья́, -ью́, -ьём, -ьé
муравей, ant, муравья́, -ью́, -ьём, -ьé

§ 20. *Irregular Terminations in the Declension of some Masculine Nouns.*

(1) Some masculine nouns, such as :

чай, tea   табак, tobacco
сахар, sugar   миндаль, almonds

take an y or ю in the genitive singular if the noun is used in the sense of a portion of, or some of it :

some tea,   ча́ю   instead of ча́я
some sugar,   са́хару   ,,   са́хара
some tobacco, табаку́   ,,   табака́
some almonds, миндалю́   ,,   миндаля́

This 'quantitative' form is only used when the noun is used in a partitive sense. Otherwise the legitimate ending of a, я for the genitive singular is retained. .

---

[1] As an unaccented я sounds as e, this noun is classed in the same category by analogy.

A few other masculine nouns have also the tendency to take **y** in the genitive singular in the following expressions :

мно́го наро́ду,	many people
без то́лку,	without sense
с ве́рху,	from the top
с ни́зу,	from underneath

(hence the adverbs : сни́зу, све́рху)

(2) In a number of monosyllabic masculine nouns the locative case ends in **ý, ю́** instead of **e**, but only when they are preceded by the prepositions **в** and **на** :

в лесу́,	in the forest	на полу́,	on the floor
в году́,	in the year	на льду́,	on the ice
в саду́,	in the garden	на берегу́,	on the shore (of sea)
в снегу́,	in the snow		or bank of river
в бою́,	in battle		
в раю́,	in heaven (paradise)		

(3) A number of masculine nouns terminating in a consonant take an accented **á** as their case-ending for the nominative plural instead of **ы, и** :

Nom. Sing.		*Nom. Pl.*
рука́в,	sleeve	рукава́
бе́рег,	shore, bank of river	берега́
глаз,	eye	глаза́
рог,	horn	рога́
го́род,	town	города́
лес,	forest	леса́
го́лос,	voice	голоса́
дом,	house	дома́
ко́локол,	bell	колокола́

Also a few nouns of foreign origin :

до́ктор,	doctor	доктора́
профе́ссор,	professor	профессора́
ку́чер,	coachman	кучера́

в

(4) Some masculine nouns have both endings in the nominative plural : **ы** and **á**. The different endings usually denote different meanings :

хлéбы, loaves of bread	хлебá, grain (various kinds)
цветы́, flowers	цветá, colours
мехи́, bellows	мехá, furs

(5) Some masculine nouns take **ья** as the termination for nominative plural. The other cases also retain the **ь** :

Nom. -**ья**;   *Gen.* -**ьев**;   *Dat.* -**ьям**;

Instr. -**ьями**;   *Loc.* -**ьях**

брат,	brother,	брáт-ья,	брáт-ьев,	брáт-ьям
кáмень,	stone,	камéн-ья,	камéн-ьев,	камéн-ьям
стул,	chair,	стýл-ья,	стýл-ьев,	стýл-ьям
сук,	bough,	сýч-ья,	сýч-ьев,	сýч-ьям
ýголь,	coal,	ýгол-ья,	ýгол-ьев,	ýгол-ьев
лист,	leaf,	лúст-ья,	лúст-ьев,	лúст-ьям

Instr. -**ьями**,   *Loc.* -**ьях**

(6) The following masculine nouns are declined in the same manner, with the exception of genitive plural, which takes **ей** (not **ьев**) :

друг,	friend,	друз-ья́,	друз-éй,	друз-ья́м
князь,	prince,	княз-ья́,	княз-éй,	княз-ья́м
муж,	husband,	муж-ья́,	мýж-éй,	муж-ья́м
зять,	son-in-law,	зят-ья́,	зят-éй,	зят-ья́м

Instr. -**ья́ми**,   *Loc.* -**ья́х**

The nouns : сын (son), кум (godfather, gossip) take the suffix **ов** besides **ья** in the plural :

сын-ов-ья́, сын-ов-éй, сын-ов-ья́м

кум-ов-ья́, кум-ов-éй, кум-ов-ья́м

Instr. -**ов-ья́ми**,   *Loc.* -**ов-ья́х**

(7) The nouns сосéд (neighbour), чорт [чёрт] (devil),

are declined as hard nouns in the singular, but as soft
nouns in the plural :

Nom.	сосе́д-и,	че́рт-и
Gen.	сосе́д-ей,	черт-е́й
Dat.	сосе́д-ям,	черт-я́м
Acc.	сосе́д-ей,	черт-е́й
Instr.	сосе́д-ями,	черт-я́ми
Loc.	сосе́д-ях,	черт-я́х

(8) Most masculine nouns ending in **ин** (usually denoting
a person of a certain nationality or calling) drop this termination in all the cases of the plural, taking **e** or **a** for the
nominative plural (occasionally **ы**) :

		Nom.	*Gen.*
ри́млян-ин,	Roman	ри́млян-е	ри́млян
англича́н-ин,	Englishman	англича́н-е	англича́н
христиан-и́н,	Christian	христиа́н-е	христиа́н
гражда́н-ин,	citizen	гра́ждан-е [гражда́н-е]	гра́ждан
крестья́н-ин,	peasant	крестья́н-е	крестья́н
тата́р-ин,	Tartar	тата́р-ы [тата́р-е]	тата́р
болга́р-ни,	Bulgarian	болга́р-ы [болга́р-е]	болга́р
ба́р-ин,	squire	ба́р-е	бар
госпо́д-ин,	master gentleman	госпо́д-а́	госпо́д
хозя́-ин,	master	ᐧхозя́-ев-а [1]	хозя́-ев

Dat. -ам ; *Acc.* as *Gen.* ; *Instr.* -ами ; *Loc.* -ах

(9) A few masculine nouns have the same form in the
genitive plural as in the nominative singular :

Nom. Sing.		*Gen. Pl.*
во́лос,	hair	воло́с
драгу́н,	dragoon	драгу́н
ту́рок,	Turk	ту́рок

[1] The suffix ев is inserted throughout the plural.

Nom. Sing.		Gen. Pl.
солдáт,	soldier	солдáт
глаз,	eye	глаз
аршúн,	arshin (measure)	аршúн
сажéнь,	3 arshin measure	сáжен (also саженéй)
человéк,	man	человéк [1]
раз,	time (in the sense : once, twice, etc.)	раз
чулóк,	stocking	чулóк
цыгáн,	gipsy	цыгáн
кадéт,	cadet	кадéт

(10)	Nom.	Госпóд-ь (Lord)	Христ-óс (Christ)
	Gen.	Гóспод-а	Христ-á
	Dat.	Гóспод-у	Христ-ý
	Acc.	Гóспод-а	Христ-á
	Instr.	Гóспод-ом	Христ-óм
	Loc.	Гóспод-е	Христ-é

§ 21. *The Russian Accent as it affects the Parts of Speech.*

In the chapter on Russian sounds (§§ 5, 11, 14) the student's attention has been drawn to the importance of the accent for the correct pronunciation of Russian words, and for the correct fusing of the individual sounds that go to make up the words themselves. As the accent has a tendency to shift from one syllable to another in the declension of nouns and conjugation of verbs, the student will have to form the habit of pronouncing the words in each case with the right stress due to the respective form of the word. As it is impossible to give the numerous and various instances of accent-shifting within the scope of this work, the author has to confine himself to a few hints on the main types of accent-shifting, giving only a limited number

---

[1] This form of the genitive plural is used if it is preceded by a number: пять человéк, five people ; нéсколько человéк, a few people ; but : мнóго людéй, many people (*Nom.* лю́ди). (See § 54b.)

of examples. For the rest the student will have to fall back on accented texts, and to make a point of memorizing the diverse changes of accents in words. As a more detailed guide to the Russian accent, relating to all the parts of speech, and containing extensive lists of the most essential words used in the Russian language, the author would recommend his work, 'A Guide to the Russian Accent' (published by David Nutt). This work shows at a glance the manifold variations of the accent as they affect the morphological changes of all parts of speech.

§ 22. *The Accent in the Declension of Masculine Nouns.* (See §§ 18-20.)

A great number of masculine nouns retain the accent on the same syllable in all the cases of both singular and plural :

вóрон, raven,   вóрона, -у, -ом, -ы, etc.
вопрóс, question, вопрóса, -у, -ом, -ы, etc.

In many instances, however, the accent is shifted in declension from the stem to the case-endings. The shifting of the accent in such instances is usually effected in this manner :

(1) Shifting begins with the genitive singular and extends to all the cases of both singular and plural (excepting accusative singular where the noun denotes an inanimate object, in which case the accusative is the same as the nominative).

Singular

Nom.		Gen.	Dat.	Instr.	Loc.
топóр,	axe	топорá	-ý	-óм	-é
столя́р,	joiner	столярá	-ý	-óм	-é
плод,	fruit	плодá	-ý	-óм	-é

Plural

Nom.	Gen.	Dat.	Instr.	Loc.
топоры́	-óв	-áм	-áми	-áх
столяры́	-óв	-áм	-áми	-áх
плоды́	-óв	-áм	-áми	-áх

To this accent-type belong a number of simple, mainly monosyllabic, masculine nouns ; also nouns terminating in ун, ж, ч, ш ; and many nouns with an accented vowel before the final consonant, such as ending in : éц, úк, áк, я́к, éж, áч.

конéц, end	старúк, old man	дурáк, fool
морáк, sailor	мятéж, mutiny	богáч, rich man

(2) Shifting begins with the nominative plural, extending to all the cases of the plural (the accent of the oblique cases of the singular remains on the same syllable as in the nominative singular) :

	Nom. Pl.	*Gen.*	*Dat.*	*Instr.*	*Loc.*
дар, gift	дарú ⎫	-óв	-áм	-áми	-áх
вéчер, evening	вечерá ⎭				

NOTE. To this accent-type belong all the masculine nouns which take á, я́ as the termination of the nominative plural. (See § 20, group 3.)

(3) Shifting begins with the genitive plural, extending to the remaining cases of the plural. (All the cases of the singular, and nominative plural, have the accent on the stem ; if the noun denotes an inanimate object the accusative plural is the same as the nominative plural) :

Singular

	Gen.	*Dat.*	*Instr.*	*Loc.*
волк, wolf	-a	-y	-ом	-е
гóлубь, pigeon	-я	-ю	-ем	-е

Plural

	Nom.	*Gen.*	*Dat.*	*Instr.*	*Loc.*
вóлки		-óв	-áм	-áми	-áх
гóлуби		-éй	-я́м	-я́ми	-я́х

(4) Shifting begins with the genitive singular, extending to all the cases of singular and plural, *but with the exception of nominative plural* :

Singular

	Gen.	Dat.	Instr.	Loc.
гвоздь, nail } конь, horse }	-я́	-ю́	-ём	-é

Plural

	Nom.	Gen.	Dat.	Instr.	Loc.
гво́зди } ко́ни }		-éй	-я́м	-я́ми	-я́х

§ 23. *Declension of Neuter Nouns.*

Neuter nouns terminate in o, e, ê, and a few in мя :

	Singular		Plural	
	Hard	Soft	Hard	Soft
Nom.	-o	-e, -ê	-a	-я
Gen.	-a	-я, -я́	—	-eй
Dat.	-y	-ю, -ю́	-ам	-ям
Acc.	-o	-e, -ê	-a	-я
Instr.	-oм	-ем, -ём	-ами	-ями
Loc.	-e	-e, -é	-ах	-ях

Note that the terminations of the oblique cases of both singular and plural of neuter nouns are identical with those of masculine nouns.

Examples :

Singular

Nom.	дéл-о (affair)	пóл-е (field)	ружь-ê (rifle)
Gen.	дéл-а	пóл-я	ружь-я́
Dat.	дéл-у	пóл-ю	ружь-ю́
Acc.	дéл-о	пóл-е	ружь-ê
Instr.	дéл-ом	пóл-ем	ружь-ём
Loc.	дéл-е	пóл-е	ружь-é

Plural

Nom.	дел-а́	пол-я́	ру́жь-я
Gen.	дел	пол-е́й	ру́же-й
Dat.	дел-а́м	пол-я́м	ру́жь-ям
Acc.	дел-а́	пол-я́	ру́жь-я
Instr.	дел-а́ми	пол-я́ми	ру́жь-ями
Loc.	дел-а́х	пол-я́х	ру́жь-ях

§ 24. Note 1. *Fleeting* o, e.

The vowels o, e are occasionally inserted in the genitive plural before the end-consonant of the stem for the sake of euphony :

Nom. Sing.		*Gen. Pl.*
зло,	evil	зол
дно,	bottom	дон
кольцо́,	ring	ко́лец (note : ь changes into e)
окно́,	window	о́кон
се́рдце,	heart	серде́ц
око́шко,	window	око́шек
стекло́,	glass, pane	стёкол
кре́сло,	arm-chair	кре́сел
ведро́,	bucket	вёдер
письмо́,	letter	пи́сем (ь changes into e)

§ 25. Note 2.

Neuter nouns ending in ие (mainly belonging to the large class of abstract nouns derived from verbs) have the terminations ии for locative singular and ий for genitive plural :

		Loc. Sing.	*Gen. Pl.*
гуля́н-ие,	walk, promenade	гуля́н-ии	гуля́н-ий
име́н-ие,	estate	име́н-ии	име́н-ий
желáн-ие,	wish	желáн-ии	желáн-ий

Neuter nouns ending in ье have the termination of ьев for their genitive plural :

		Gen. Pl.
плáть-е,	clothes	плáть-ев
кýшань-е,	food	кýшань-ев

§ 26. Note 3.

Some neuter nouns take the termination of masculine nouns in the nominative plural :

плечó,	shoulder	плéчи, плеч, плечáм, -áми, -áх
дно,	bottom	дны [also дóнья]
я́блоко,	apple	я́блоки (gen. я́блок and я́блоков)
словéчко,	little word, mot	словéчки (gen. словéчек)
очкó,	eye, bud; point in games	очки́ (gen. очкóв), eyeglasses

Augmentative masculine nouns terminating in ище are treated as masculine nouns, and they follow the soft masculine declension. An exception forms the word клáдбище (churchyard), which is a pure neuter noun and belongs to the soft neuter class.

§ 26a. Note 4.

A few neuter nouns have some irregularities in the declension of their plural :

	Nom. Pl.	Gen. Pl.	Dat.	Inst.	Loc.
(1) óко, eye (only used in poetic expressions)	óчи	очéй,	-áм,	-áми,	-áх
ýхо, ear	ýши	ушéй,	-áм,	-áми,	-áх
колéно { 1. tribe	1. колéна	колéн,	-ам,	-ами,	-ах
{ 2. knee	2. колéни	колéней,	-ям,	-ями,	-ях
{ 3. link	3. колéнья	колéньев,	-ьям,	-ьями,	-ьях

в*

дéрево, tree	дерéвья	дерéвьев	⎫
перó, pen, nib	пéрья	пéрьев	⎬ -ЬЯМ, -ЬЯМИ, -ЬЯХ
крылó, wing	крьілья	крьільев	⎪
шйло, awl	шйлья	шйльев	⎭

(2) нéбо (heaven) and чýдо (miracle) have the suffix
ес inserted in all the cases of the plural :

	Singular		Plural	
Nom.	нéб-о	чýд-о	неб-ес-á	чуд-ес-á
Gen.	нéб-а	чýд-а	неб-éс	чуд-éс
Dat.	нéб-у	чýд-у	неб-ес-áм	чуд-ес-áм
Acc.	нéб-о	чýд-о	неб-ес-á	чуд-ес-á
Instr.	нéб-ом	чýд-ом	неб-ес-áми	чуд-ес-áми
Loc.	нéб-е	чýд-е	неб-ес-áх	чуд-ес-áх

(3) A few soft neuter nouns ending in мя, and дитя́
(child), have irregular case-endings both in the singular
and plural :

(a)	Sing.	Pl.	(b)	Sing.	Pl.
Nom.	дитя́	дéт-и		врéм-я	врем-ен-á
Gen.	дитя́-ти	дет-éй		врéм-ен-и	врем-ён
Dat.	дитя́-ти	дéт-ям		врéм-ен-и	врем-ен-áм
Acc.	дитя́	дет-éй		врéм-я	врем-ен-á
Instr.	дитя́-тею [дитéй]	дет-ьмй [дет-я́ми]		врéм-ен-ем	врем-ен-áми
Loc.	дитя́-ти	дéт-ях		врéм-ен-и	врем-ен-áх.

To group (a) can be added a number of nouns denoting
the young offspring of animals. They have the suffix
ёнок [or онок after a root ending in к or д, which are
commuted into ч or ж]. Their plurals take я́та or áта.
The singular is declined as a masculine noun, dropping
the o before the к; the plural is treated as that of a
neuter noun :

Singular

	(foal)	(wolf cub)	(bear cub)	(puppy)
Nom.	жереб-ёнок	волч-о́нок [1]	медвеж-о́нок [1]	щ-ено́к
Gen.	жереб-ёнк-а	волч-о́нк-а	медвеж-о́нк-а	щ-енк-а́
Dat.	жереб-ёнк-у	волч-о́нк-у	медвеж-о́нк-у	щ-енк-у́
Acc.	жереб-ёнк-а	волч-о́нк-а	медвеж-о́нк-а	щ-енк-а́
Instr.	жереб-ёнк-ом	волч-о́нк-ом	медвеж-о́нк-ом	щ-енк-о́м
Loc.	жереб-ёнк-е	волч-о́нк-е	медвеж-о́нк-е	щ-енк-е́

Plural

Nom.	жереб-я́т-а	волч-а́т-а	медвеж-а́т-а	щ-ен-я́та [щенки́]
Gen.	жереб-я́т	волч-а́т	медвеж-а́т	щ-ен-я́т
Dat.	жереб-я́т-ам	волч-а́т-ам	медвеж-а́т-ам	щ-ен-я́т-ам
Acc.	жереб-я́т	волч-а́т	медвеж-а́т	щ-ен-я́т
Instr.	жереб-я́т-ами	волч-а́т-ами	медвеж-а́т-ами	щ-ен-я́т-ами
Loc.	жереб-я́т-ах	волч-а́т-ах	медвеж-а́т-ах	щ-ен-я́т-ах

NOTE. By analogy a child is also called ребёнок, *pl.* ребя́та. It conforms to the above mode of declension.

To this class belong :

поросёнок,	sucking pig	цыплёнок,	chicken
ослёнок,	foal of an ass	телёнок,	calf
ягнёнок,	lamb	котёнок,	kitten
			etc.

According to group (3) (*b*) are declined the following neuter nouns ending in **мя** :

бре́мя,	burden (used only in the singular)
пле́мя,	tribe
те́мя,	crown of the head (used only in the singular)
се́мя,	seed (*gen. pl.* семя́н)
стре́мя,	stirrup (*gen. pl.* стремя́н)
зна́мя,	banner
пла́мя,	flame (used only in the singular)
и́мя,	name
вы́мя,	udder

[1] Also: волчёнок, медвежёнок.

§ 27. *The Accent as it affects the Declension of Neuter Nouns.*

(1) (*a*) Polysyllabic nouns terminating in o and e, with the last syllable unaccented, retain the accent of the nominative singular in all the cases of both singular and plural :

занятие,	occupation,	-я, -ю, -ем, -и
мужество,	manliness, courage	-а, -у, -ом, -е
жилище,	habitation,	-а, -у, -ем, -е
пространство,	space,	-а, -у, -ом, -е
зеркало,	mirror (shifts the accent to the case-ending in the plural)	
озеро,	lake (shifts the accent to the second syllable in the plural)	

Nom.	зеркала́	озёра
Gen.	зеркал	озёр
Dat.	зеркала́м	озёрам
Acc.	зеркала́	озёра
Instr.	зеркала́ми	озёрами
Loc.	зеркала́х	озёрах

(*b*) If the terminations o and e in polysyllabic neuter nouns are accented, the accent is on the case-endings in declension :

божество́, Deity	*Sing.* -а́, -у́, -о́м, -е̏
серебро́,[1] silver	*Pl.* -а́, -а́м, -а́ми, -а́х
лезвее̏, sharp edge	-я́, -я́м, -я́ми, -я́х

Exceptions are the following nouns, terminating in accented o and e, which shift the accent back by one syllable in the entire plural :

веретено́,	spindle,	веретёна,	веретён
долото́,	chisel,	долота,	доло́т
колесо́,	wheel,	колёса,	колёс
решето́,	sieve,	решёта,	решёт

-ам, -ами, -ах

ружье̏,	rifle,	ру́жья,	ру́жей

-ьям, -ьями, -ьях

---

[1] Has no plural.

(2) (a) Dissyllabic nouns in o and e, *with the accent on the first syllable in the nominative singular, retain the accent on the same syllable in all the cases of the singular ; in the plural the accent is shifted to the case-ending :*

Singular			Plural		
слóво, word, слóва	} -у, -ом, -е		словá, слов	} -áм, -áми, -áх	
мéсто, place, мéста			местá, мест		
пóле, field, пóля	} -ю, -ем, -е		поля́, полéй	} -я́м, -я́ми, -я́х	
мóре, sea, мóря			моря́, морéй		

(b) Dissyllabic nouns in o and e, *with the accent on the last syllable in the nominative singular, retain the same accent in all the cases of the singular ; in the plural the accent is shifted back to the first syllable :*

Singular		Plural	
селó, village	} -á, -ý, -óм, -é	сёла	} -ам, -ами, -ах
гнездó, nest		гнёзда	
лицó, face		лúца	

(3) Neuter nouns terminating in **мя** retain the accent of the nominative singular in all the cases of the singular ; in the plural the accent falls on the case-endings. (See § 26a.)

	Singular		Plural	
Nom.	úм-я	плéм-я	им-ен-á	плем-ен-á
Gen.	úм-ен-и	плéм-ен-и	им-ён	плем-ён
Dat.	úм-ен-и	плéм-ен-и	им-ен-áм	плем-ен-áм
Acc.	úм-я	плéм-я	им-ен-á	плем-ен-á
Instr.	úм-ен-ем	плéм-ен-ем	им-ен-áми	плем-ен-áми
Loc.	úм-ен-и	плéм-ен-и	им-ен-áх	плем-ен-áх

Exception :

Nom.	знáм-я (banner)	знам-ён-а
Gen.	знáм-ен-и	знам-ён
Dat.	знáм-ен-и	знам-ён-áм
Acc.	знáм-я	знам-ён-а
Instr.	знáм-ен-ем	знам-ён-ами
Loc.	знáм-ен-и	знам-ён-ах

§ 28. *Declension of Feminine Nouns.*

Feminine nouns terminating in **a**, **я** take the following case-endings in singular and plural :

	Singular		*Plural*	
	Hard	*Soft*	*Hard*	*Soft*
Nom.	-a	-я	-ы	-и
Gen.	-ы	-и	— [1]	-ь
Dat.	-e	-e	-ам	-ям
Acc.	-y	-ю	-ы	-и
Instr.	-ою [-ой]	-ею [-ей] -ёю [-ёй]	-ами	-ями
Loc.	-e	-e	-ах	-ях

Examples :

Nom.	вод-á (water)	бáн-я (bath)	вóд-ы бáн-и
Gen.	вод-ы́	бáн-и	вод бан-ь
Dat.	вод-é	бáн-е	вод-áм бáн-ям
Acc.	вóд-у	бáн-ю	вóд-ы бáн-и
Instr.	вод-óю [-ой]	бáн-ею [-ей]	вод-áми бáн-ями
Loc.	вод-é	бáн-е	вод-áх бáн-ях

NOTE 1. Animate feminine nouns have the same case-ending in the accusative plural as in the genitive plural :

бáба, peasant woman $\begin{cases} gen.\ pl. \\ acc.\ pl. \end{cases}$ баб

ры́ба, fish $\begin{cases} gen.\ pl. \\ acc.\ pl. \end{cases}$ рыб

козá, she-goat $\begin{cases} gen.\ pl. \\ acc.\ pl. \end{cases}$ коз

сестрá, sister $\begin{cases} gen.\ pl. \\ acc.\ pl. \end{cases}$ сестёр

NOTE 2. As no **ы** can stand after **г, к, х, ж, ч, ш, щ,** its place is taken by **и** in genitive singular and nominative plural :

[1] As the stem.

		Gen. Sing.	*Nom. Pl.*
рука́,	hand	руки́	ру́ки
нога́,	leg	ноги́	но́ги
руба́ха,	shirt	руба́хи	руба́хи
свеча́,	candle	свечи́	све́чи
но́ша,	load	но́ши	но́ши
ро́ща,	coppice	ро́щи	ро́щи

NOTE 3. Feminine nouns terminating in **ая**, **ея** have the case-endings **ай** and **ей** in genitive plural :

	Gen. Pl.
стáя, flock, esp. birds	стай
змея́, snake	змей
ше́я, neck	шей

NOTE 4. Instrumental terminations **ою**, **ею**, **е́ю** are frequently shortened into **ой**, **ей**, **е́й**, and are pronounced as a diphthong.

§ 29. *Fleeting* o *and* e *in the Declension of Feminine Nouns.*

If the stem[1] of a feminine noun ends in a double consonant, **o** or **e** is inserted in the genitive plural before the end-consonant for ease of pronunciation :

		Gen. Pl.
овца́,	sheep	ове́ц
доска́,	board	досо́к
ру́чка,	penholder, or small hand	ру́чек
ко́шка,	cat	ко́шек
игла́,	needle	и́гол
сосна́,	pine-tree	со́сен
ку́кла,	doll	ку́кол
земля́,	earth	земе́ль
па́лка,	stick	па́лок
сестра́,	sister	сестёр

When a feminine noun ends in **ня**, the genitive plural often

[1] Word without case-ending or other inflexion.

has an inserted **о** or **е** before the **н**; the soft sign **ь** is dropped
and the final **н** is hard :

Gen. Pl.

бáсня,	fable	бáсен
пéсня,	song	пéсен
кýхня,	kitchen	кýхон (but also кýхонь)
сóтня,	a hundred	сóтен
бáшня,	tower	бáшен

but: { бáрышня, young lady   бáрышень
{ дерéвня,   village   деревéнь

й and **ь** in penultimate syllable of nominative singular
are changed into **е** in genitive plural :

Gen. Pl.

свáдьба,	wedding	свáдеб
судьбá,	fate	судéб
нáнька,	nursemaid	нáнек
шéйка,	little neck	шéек
лéйка,	watering-can	лéек
копéйка,	copeck	копéек
чáйка,	sea-gull	чáек

§ 30. *Some Irregularities in the Declension of Feminine Nouns.*

(1) A number of masculine nouns have terminations of
feminine nouns. These are declined as feminine nouns,
although they retain their masculine character and
meaning :

дя́дя, uncle	ю́ноша, youth
судья́, judge	слугá, servant
Кóля[1] : diminutive of Николáй	
Сáша[1] : diminutive of Алексáндр ; etc.	

When such nouns are used with an adjective or pronoun
the adjective or pronoun takes the respective masculine
terminations : **ый, ий, óй** :

мой дя́дя, my uncle	стáрый слугá, old servant
наш судья́, our judge	

[1] Diminutives of names of persons (*masc.* and *fem.*) end in **я** (or **a** after
ж, ч, ш, щ).

(2) A large number of feminine nouns terminating in ия have the case-ending ии for dative and locative singular and ий for genitive plural :

	Dat. and Loc. Sing.	*Gen. Pl.*
ли́ния, line	ли́нии	ли́ний
импе́рия, empire	импе́рии	импе́рий
ли́лия, lily	ли́лии	ли́лий
мо́лния, lightning	мо́лнии	мо́лний
рели́гия, religion	рели́гии	рели́гий
А́нглия, England	А́нглии ⎱ No plural	
Росси́я, Russia	Росси́и ⎰	

(3) Feminine nouns ending in ья́ (я́ accented) have the case-ending е́й in genitive plural :

	Gen. Pl.
свинья́, swine	свине́й
скамья́, bench	скаме́й
статья́, item, article	стате́й
семья́, family	семе́й

But those feminine nouns which end in ья (я not accented) have ий as the case-ending of genitive plural :

	Gen. Pl.
лгу́нья, liar (female)	лгу́ний
го́стья, lady visitor	го́стий (to distinguish this form from госте́й, which is gen. pl. of гость)
болту́нья, chatterbox	болту́ний

(4) Some feminine nouns terminating in жа, ша, ча, ща have ей in genitive plural :

		Gen. Pl.
вожжа́,	horse's lead	вожже́й
при́тча,	parable	при́тчей
ханжа́,	hypocrite (*masc and fem.*)	ханже́й
ю́ноша,	youth (*masc.*)	ю́ношей
свеча́,	candle	свече́й

A few other feminine nouns (in **я**) also have **ей** as the case-ending of genitive plural :

Gen. Pl.

до́ля,	part	доле́й
заря́,	dawn	заре́й
дя́дя,	uncle	дя́дей
(*masc.*)		
ноздря́,	nostril	ноздре́й
западня́,	trap	западне́й
клешня́,	claw	клешне́й

§ 31. *Feminine Nouns terminating in* **ь**.

Feminine nouns ending in **ь** have a distinctive mode of declension. They are characterized by the case-ending **и** in genitive, dative, and locative singular. To this class belong a number of simple [original] nouns, such as ко́сть (bone), сме́рть (death), ве́сть (news, message), etc., as well as the vast class of derivative abstract nouns with the suffix **ость** (mainly derived from adjectives and corresponding to the English suffix *ness*).

Example :

Nom.	двер-ь (door)	двёр-и
Gen.	двёр-и	двер-е́й
Dat.	двёр-и	двер-я́м
Acc.	двер-ь	двёр-и
Instr.	двёр-ью	двер-я́ми [двер-ьми́]
Loc.	двёр-и	двер-я́х

Fleeting **о**. In feminine nouns ending in **ь**, the letter **о** before the final consonant of the stem is dropped only in a few nouns. In the singular the only cases affected are genitive, dative, locative, and in the plural all the cases :

Singular

Nom.	цéрков-ь (church)	любóв-ь (love)	лож-ь (falsehood)	рож-ь (rye)
Gen.	цéркв-и	любв-и́	лж-и	рж-и
Dat.	цéркв-и	любв-и́	лж-и	рж-и
Acc.	цéрков-ь	любóв-ь	лож-ь	рож-ь
Instr.	цéрков-ью	любóв-ью	лóж-ью	рóж-ью
Loc.	цéркв-и	любв-и́	лж-и	рж-и

Plural

Plural not used

Nom.	цéркв-и
Gen.	церкв-éй
Dat.	церкв-áм
Acc.	цéркв-и
Instr.	церкв-áми
Loc.	церкв-áх

The dative, instrumental, and locative cases are declined according to the hard declension

NOTE 1. When Любóвь denotes the name of a woman, the **o** is retained in all the cases.

NOTE 2. Feminine nouns of the abstract class with the suffix **ость** never drop the **o** in declension.

§ 31a. There is one masculine noun in this class, terminating in **ь** :

Nom.	пут-ь (road, way)	пут-и́
Gen.	пут-и́	пут-éй
Dat.	пут-и́	пут-я́м
Acc.	пут-ь	пут-и́
Instr.	пут-ём [1]	пут-я́ми
Loc.	пут-и́	пут-я́х

[1] In this case only there is a masculine case-ending.

§ 31*b.* A number of feminine nouns of the ь class throw their accent on to the case-ending in the locative case if the noun is preceded by the prepositions в (in) or на (on). The most frequently affected nouns of this class are :

		Locative
глушь,	thicket, wilderness	в глуши́
грудь,	breast	на груди́
грязь,	mud	в грязи́
дверь,	door	на двери́
кровь,	blood	в крови́
мель,	sandbank	на мели́
печь,	stove	{на}{в} печи́
пыль,	dust	в пыли́
Русь,	Russia	на Руси́
связь,	tie	в связи́
соль,	salt	в соли́
степь,	steppe	в степи́
тень,	shade	в тени́
цепь,	chain	на цепи́

§ 31*c.* Two feminine nouns ending in ь—мать, дочь—have the suffix **ep** inserted in all the cases of both singular and plural, with the exception of nominative and accusative singular :

	Singular		*Plural*	
Nom.	доч-ь	мат-ь	до́ч-ер-и	ма́т-ер-и
Gen.	до́ч-ер-и	ма́т-ер-и	доч-ер-е́й	мат-ер-е́й
Dat.	до́ч-ер-и	ма́т-ер-и	доч-ер-я́м	мат-ер-я́м
Acc.	доч-ь	мат-ь	доч-ер-е́й	мат-ер-е́й
Instr.	до́ч-ер-ью	ма́т-ер-ью	доч-ер-ьми́	мат-ер-ьми́
			[доч-ер-я́ми]	[мат-ер-я́ми]
Loc.	до́ч-ер-и	ма́т-ер-и	доч-ер-я́х	мат-ер-я́х

§ 32. *The Accent in the Declension of Feminine Nouns.*

(1) Most feminine nouns ending in **a**, **я**, in which the accent of the nominative singular does not fall on the case-ending, have a *fixed* accent which remains on the same syllable in all the cases of both singular and plural. In many feminine nouns the accent is not shifted in declension even when the accent is on the case-ending in nominative singular, particularly in derivative nouns with various inflexions, but also in many simple nouns.

Examples :

| княжна́, princess | госпожа́, mistress |
| клевета́, slander | толпа́, crowd |

(2) When the accent shifts it usually conforms to one of two modes :

(a) The accent remains on the case-endings in both singular and plural, with the exception of nominative plural, where it goes back to the vowel of the stem :

	Singular	*Plural*	*Singular*	*Plural*
Nom.	вдова́ (widow)	вдо́вы	свеча́ (candle)	све́чи
Gen.	вдовы́	вдов	свечи́	свеч
Dat.	вдове́	вдова́м	свече́	свеча́м
Acc.	вдову́	вдов	свечу́	све́чи
Instr.	вдово́ю	вдова́ми	свечо́ю	свеча́ми
Loc.	вдове́	вдова́х	свече́	свеча́х

To this group belong the nouns : волна́, wave ; звезда́,[1] star ; игра́, play ; игла́, needle ; овца́, sheep ; река́, river ; свинья́, pig ; сестра́,[1] sister ; слуга́, servant ; трава́, grass ; судья́, judge.

[1] Can also have the accent on the stem throughout the plural.

(b) The accent remains on the case-ending in both singular and plural, *with the exception of accusative singular, nominative and accusative plural* :

	Singular		*Plural*	
Nom.	борода́ (beard)	вода́ (water)	бо́роды	во́ды
Gen.	бороды́	воды́	боро́д	вод
Dat.	бороде́	воде́	борода́м	вода́м
Acc.	бо́роду	во́ду	бо́роды	во́ды
Instr.	бородо́ю	водо́ю	борода́ми	вода́ми
Loc.	бороде́	воде́	борода́х	вода́х

To this group belong : голова́, head ; гора́, mountain ; губа́, lip ; доска́, board ; зима́, winter ; нога́, leg ; рука́, hand ; спина́, back ; and many others.

NOTE. The nouns жена́ (wife), тюрьма́ (prison), стрела́ (arrow) have the accent on the case-endings of the singular, but on the first syllable throughout the plural :

	Singular		
Nom.	жена́	стрела́	тюрьма́
Gen.	жены́	стрелы́	тюрьмы́
Dat.	жене́	стреле́	тюрьме́
Acc.	жену́	стрелу́	тюрьму́
Instr.	женою́	стрелою́	тюрьмою́
Loc.	жене́	стреле́	тюрьме́

	Plural		
Nom.	жёны	стре́лы	тю́рьмы
Gen.	жён	стрел	тю́рем
Dat.	жёнам	стре́лам	тю́рьмам
Acc.	жён	стре́лы	тю́рьмы
Instr.	жёнами	стре́лами	тю́рьмами
Loc.	жёнах	стре́лах	тю́рьмах

(3) In a few feminine nouns terminating in ь, the accent remains, in all the cases of both singular and plural, on

c

the same syllable as in the nominative singular, particularly if they are polysyllabic :

нóвость, news   благодáрность, gratitude
кровáть, bedstead

But in the greater number of feminine nouns with the ь termination, the accent is on the same syllable as in the nominative singular in all the cases of the singular, and nominative plural ; in all the other cases of the plural (excepting the accusative of inanimate nouns) it falls on the case-endings :

Plural

вещь,	thing, object	вéщи, -éй, -áм, -áми, -áх
власть,	power, authority	влáсти, -éй, -ям, -ями, -ях
гость,	guest	гóсти, -éй, -ям, -ями, -ях
лóшадь,	horse	лóшади, -éй, -ям, -ями, -ях

§ 33. *Nouns :* (1) *used only in Singular ;* (2) *used only in Plural ;* (3) *of common gender.*

(1) *Used only in Singular*

картóфель (*m.*),	potatoes	крыжóвник,	gooseberries
капýста,	cabbage	малúна,	raspberries
моркóвь (*f.*),	carrot(s)	сморóдина,	currants
редúска,	radish(es)	молокó,	milk
рéдька,	black radish(es)	мáсло,	butter
рéпа,	turnip(s)	соль (*f.*),	salt
землянúка,	wild strawberries	пéрец,	pepper
зóлото,	gold	рожь (*f.*),	rye
серебрó,	silver	пшенúца,	wheat
желéзо,	iron	ячмéнь (*m.*),	barley
медь (*f.*),	copper, brass [1]	овёс,	oats
клубнúка,	strawberries	горóх,	pear
брусúка,	red bilberries	гречúха,	buckwheat

(2) *Used only in Plural*
(a) *Masculine*

близнец-ú [óв],	twins	обó-и [ев],	wallpaper
вес-ú [óв],	scales, weights	подштáнник-и [ов],	pants
дух-ú [óв],	scent	час-ú [óв],	clock, watch
коньк-ú [óв],	skates	штан-ú [óв],	trousers
поск-ú [óв],	socks	щипц-ú [óв],	pincers, tongs

[1] жёлтая медь.

(b) Feminine

брю́ки [брюк],	trousers	подтя́жки [подтя́жек],	braces
ви́лы [вил],	garden fork	по́хороны [похоро́н],	funeral
вра́ки [врак],	idle talk	пря́тки [пря́ток],	hide-and-seek
де́ньги [де́нег],	money	сли́вки [сли́вок],	cream
жму́рки [жму́рок],	blind-man's buff	су́мерки [су́мерек],	twilight
имени́ны [имени́н],	name's day	су́тки [су́ток],	a day and a night (24 hours)
кани́кулы [кани́кул],	vacations, holidays	гра́бли [гра́бель],	garden rake
ко́злы [ко́зел],	driver's seat	са́ни [сане́й],	sleigh
		се́ни [сене́й],	entrance-hall
макаро́ны [макаро́н],	macaroni		
но́жницы [но́жниц],	scissors	щи [щей],	cabbage soup
носи́лки [носи́лок],	stretcher		

(c) Neuter

воро́та [воро́т],	gate	черни́ла [черни́л],	ink
дрова́ [дров],	fire-wood	очки́ [очко́в],	spectacles
пери́ла [пери́л],	hand-rail, parapet		

NOTE. The termination of genitive plural of the words enumerated in (a), (b), (c) is given in brackets.

The terminations of dative, instrumental, and locative are :

-ам, -ами, -ах of hard nouns ;
-ям, -ями, -ях of soft nouns.

The accent is on the same syllable as in the genitive in all the other oblique cases. Inserted o or e of the genitive cases is dropped in the other cases.

(3). Of Common Gender

бродя́га,	vagabond	пла́кса,	whimperer
бедня́га,	poor creature, poor soul	пору́ка,	bail, surety
зайка,	stammerer	пьяница,	drunkard
кале́ка,	cripple	рази́ня,	gaping fool
ла́комка,	sweet-toothed person	ро́вня,	equal
левша́,	left-handed person	самоуби́йца,	suicide
малю́тка,	baby	самоу́чка,	self-taught person
неве́жда,	ignoramus	сирота́,	orphan
перя́ха,	untidy person	у́мница,	good boy or girl
обжо́ра,	glutton	ханжа́,	hypocrite, bigot

NOTE. These are declined as feminine nouns.

§ 33a. *The Diminutives.*

1. Nearly every Russian noun (and some adjectives) can have a diminutive form. The diminutive can express :

    (1) The diminutive value alone :

        дом, house, (dim.) до́мик

    (2) The diminutive, used in a sense of endearment :

        го́лос, voice ; голосо́чек, dear little voice

    (3) The diminutive, used in a sense of disdain :

        голоси́шко, poor sort of voice

    (1) The diminutive terminations of nouns are usually :
ик, ок, ек, ец for masculine nouns :

дом,	house	до́мик,	little house
го́лос,	voice	голосо́к,	small voice
ого́нь,	fire	огонёк,	little fire
хлеб,	bread	хле́бец,	small loaf

ко, цо for neuter nouns :

окно́,	window	око́шко,	little window
письмо́,	letter	письмецо́,	little letter

ка for feminine nouns :

нога́,	leg	но́жка,	little leg
кни́га,	book	кни́жка,	little book
рука́,	hand	ру́чка,	little hand

    NOTE. г, к are commuted into ж, ч.

    (2) The diminutive terminations for expressing endearment are :

ичек, очек for masculine nouns :

нож,	knife	но́жичек,	pretty little knife
го́лос,	voice	голосо́чек,	pretty little voice

ичка, очка, ечка, енька, ушка, юшка for feminine nouns :

сестра́,	sister	сестри́чка,	dear little sister
ма́ма,	mother	ма́менька,	dear mother
тётя,	aunt	тётушка,	dear auntie
ло́жка,	spoon	ло́жечка,	just a little spoon
дед,[1]	grandfather	де́душка,	dear grandfather
дя́дя,[1]	uncle	дя́дюшка,	dear uncle

ечко, ышко for neuter nouns :

кольцо́,	ring	коле́чко,	little ring
перо́,	feather	пёрышко,	little feather

(3) The diminutive terminations expressing disdain are :

ишка, ишко for masculine nouns :

мальчи́шка, little boy, urchin
городи́шко, little town (of no importance)

ёнка, онка for feminine nouns :

коро́ва,	cow	коровёнка,	poor sort of a cow
ла́вка,	shop	лавчо́нка,	poor sort of a shop
стару́ха,	old woman	старушо́нка,	insignificant old woman

ишко for neuter nouns :

де́ло, affair, matter   дели́шко, a trifling business [affair]

2. The most used diminutive terminations of adjectives are :

ова́тый, ева́тый, онькій, енькій :

бе́лый,	white·	белова́тый,	whitish
		бе́ленькій,	white little . . .
си́ній,	blue	синева́тый,	bluish
		си́ненькій,	blue little . . .
мя́гкій,	soft	мя́конькій,	soft little . . .

The terminations онькій, енькій give the diminutive idea to the qualified noun rather than to the adjective itself.

[1] Masculine.

§ 33b. *Derivation-Suffixes in Nouns.*

Besides the termination-suffixes of diminutives, enumerated in § 33a, there are other suffixes which are used for the formation of derivative nouns from roots or from other words. While it is impossible to give here a list of all the derivation-suffixes of nouns, or to treat in detail of their functions in all cases, a few of the most important suffixes are given below.

ец [ица] чик [чица] щик [щица] ник [ница] тель [тельница]	In nouns formed from adjectives and verbs, which signify trade, calling, profession, etc.

любимец [ица],[1] favourite, from любить, to love.
купец, merchant, from купить, to buy [купчиха].
разносчик [чица], hawker, from разносить, to carry round.
пильщик [щица], sawyer, from пилить, to saw.
огородник [ница], gardener, from огород [огородный], garden.
житель [тельница], inhabitant, from жить, to live.

ние [нье] тие [тье]	In verbal nouns (often with an abstract meaning) which signify action or state.

терпение, patience, from терпеть, to suffer.
учение [ученье], learning, study, from учить[ся], to learn.

(Derived from verbs whose past passive participle terminates in нный.)

понятие, conception, from понять, to understand.
житьё, living, from жить, to live.

(Derived from verbs whose past passive participle terminates in тый. (See § 86b, B.)

---

[1] [ица] for feminine nouns; occasionally: [иха].

ство
ствие
{ In nouns formed from nouns, adjectives, and verbs which signify : calling, trade, act or state.

ра́бство, slavery, from раб, slave.
де́йствие, action, act, from де́йствовать, to act.

(о)сть
(е)сть
{ In abstract nouns formed from adjectives which signify : (1) property, quality, state ; (2) act, object.

бе́дность, poverty, from бе́дный, poor.
ро́бость, timidity, from ро́бкий, timid.
ми́лость, grace, favour, from ми́лый, charming, pleasing.
мо́лодость, youth, from молодо́й, young.
све́жесть, freshness, from све́жий, fresh.

NOTE. For the function and meaning of *prefixes* in derivative nouns see § 63, note 4.

2. ADJECTIVES

§ 34. Russian adjectives have two forms :

(1) The attributive (long) form.
(2) The predicative (short) form.

Long form	Short form
но́вый дом, new house	дом нов, the house is new
но́вая кни́га, new book	кни́га нова́, the book is new
ста́рое вино́, old wine	вино́ ста́ро, the wine is old
ста́рые дома́, old houses	дома́ ста́ры, the houses are old

The attributive (long) form stands in the same relation to other words in the sentence as the noun which it qualifies, and, consequently, conforms with its noun as regards number, gender, and case :

в но́вый дом,　into the new house
от но́вого до́ма, from the new house
к но́вому до́му, towards the new house
с но́вым до́мом, with the new house
в но́вом до́ме,　in the new house

§ 35. *Declension of Attributive Adjectives.*

There are two classes of adjectives :

(1) the hard ;　(2) the soft.

Their nominative terminations are :

	Hard				Soft		
	Masc.	*Neut.*	*Fem.*		*Masc.*	*Neut.*	*Fem.*
Sing.	-ый -ой	-ое -óе	-ая -áя	*Sing.*	-ий	-ее	-яя
Plur.		-ые[-ы́е]				-іе	

Adjectives have six cases, as nouns. Their respective terminations·are :

		Masc.	*Neut.*	*Fem.*	*Pl. (all genders)*
Nom.	Hard.	-ый, -ой	-ое	-ая	-ые
	Soft.	-ий	-ее	-яя	-іе
Gen.	Hard.	-ого		-ой	-их
	Soft.	-его		-ей	-их
Dat.	Hard.	-ому		-ой	-ым
	Soft.	-ему		-ей	-им
Acc.	Hard.	{ as nom.[1] or gen. for masc. } as nom. for neuter		-ую	{ as nom.[1] or gen. for masc. and fem. } as nom. for neuter
	Soft.			-юю	
Instr.	Hard.	-ым		-ою [-ой]	-ыми
	Soft.	-им		-ею [-ей]	-ими
Loc.	Hard.	-ом		-ой	-их
	Soft.	-ем		-ей	·-их

NOTE. If the nominative terminations are ой, ая, ое, ы́е, the accent in declension will fall on the case-endings throughout.

[1] See § 18, note 1.

Examples :

Hard.	Masc. and Neut.	Fem.	Pl. (all genders)
Nom.	бѣл-ый (white) бѣл-ое	бѣл-ая	бѣл-ые
Gen.	бѣл-ого	бѣл-ой	бѣл-ыхъ
Dat.	бѣл-ому	бѣл-ой	бѣл-ымъ

Acc. M. { бѣл-ый or бѣл-ого } *N.* бѣл-ое   бѣл-ую   *as Nom. or Gen.* { бѣл-ые { for inanimate objects / бѣл-ыхъ { for animate objects }

| *Instr.* | бѣл-ымъ | бѣл-ою [-ой] | бѣл-ыми |
| *Loc.* | бѣл-омъ | бѣл-ой | бѣл-ыхъ |

Soft.	Masc. and Neut.	Fem.	Pl. (all genders)
Nom.	син-ій син-ее	син-яя	син-іе
Gen.	син-его	син-ей	син-ихъ
Dat.	син-ему	син-ей	син-имъ

Acc. M. { син-ій or син-его } *N.* син-ее   син-юю   *as Nom. or Gen.* { син-іе { for inanimate objects / син-ихъ { for animate objects }

| *Instr.* | син-имъ | син-ею [-ей] | син-ими |
| *Loc.* | син-емъ | син-ей | син-ихъ |

NOTE 1. After г, к, х, ж, ч, ш, щ, the vowel ы is supplanted by и in the case-endings :

тих-іе (soft, quiet)   свѣж-іе (fresh)
тих-ихъ   свѣж-ихъ
тих-имъ   свѣж-имъ

After ж, ч, ш, щ, a non-accented о is changed into е :

свѣж-его (fresh)   горяч-его (hot)
свѣж-ему   горяч-ему
свѣж-ею   горяч-ею
свѣж-ей   горяч-ей

NOTE 2. A number of nouns have terminations of adjectives. In declension they are treated as adjectives :

нищий, -ая,	beggar	пирожное,	sweet (pastry)
кормчий⎫	helmsman,	подлежащее,	subject ⎫
рулевой⎭	steersman	сказуемое,	predicate ⎬ gram.
лесничий,	forester	дополнение,	object ⎭
портной,	tailor	булочная,	baker's shop
рядовой,	soldier (private)	вселённая,	universe
подданный, -ая,	subject	горничная,	chamber-maid
часовой,	sentry	запятая,	comma
учёный,	savant	кладовая,	store-room
сумасшёдший,	insane person	мастерская,	workshop
-ая		мостовая,	paved street
жаркое,	roast beef	набережная,	quay
мороженое,	ice-cream	передняя,·	entrance-hall
насекомое,	insect	столовая,	dining-room

§ 36. Predicative (short) adjectives are distinguished by genders and numbers, but are not declined according to cases ; their terminations are :

	Masc.	Fem.	Neuter	Pl. (all genders).
Hard.·	—[1]	-а	-о	-ы
Soft.	-ь	-я	-е	· -и
	нов	нова́	ново	новы
	синь	синя́	сине	сини (see § 40)

§ 37. *Possessive Adjectives formed from Nouns.*

These are formed by adding **ов, ев, ёв, ин** (**ын** after **ц**) after the name of the person who possesses the object for which this form of adjective has been coined.

Examples :

Пётр	Петро́в дом, Peter's house
дя́дя	дя́дин сад, uncle's garden

For feminine and neuter the possessive adjectives end in :

Fem.	Neuter	Pl. (all genders)
-ова	-ово	-овы
-ева	,	-ево	-евы
-ёва	-ёво·	-ёвы
·-ина	-ино	-ины
-ына	-ыно	-ыны

---

[1] Stem ending in a consonant.

Possessive adjectives are declined as follows :

	Masc.	*Neuter*	*Fem.*	*Pl. (all genders)*
Nom.	Петро́в	Петро́в-о	Петро́в-а	Петро́в-ы
Gen.	Петро́в-а	Петро́в-а	Петро́в-ой	Петро́в-ых
Dat.	Петро́в-у	Петро́в-у	Петро́в-ой	Петро́в-ым
Acc.	*N. or G.*	Петро́в-о	Петро́в-у	*N. or G.*
Instr.	Петро́в-ым	Петро́в-ым	Петро́в-ою [-ой]	Петро́в-ыми
Loc.	Петро́в-ом	Петро́в-ом	Петро́в-ой	Петро́в-ых

Nom.	Ильи́н	Ильин-о́	Ильин-а́	Ильин-ы́
Gen.	Ильин-а́	Ильин-а́	Ильин-о́й	Ильин-ы́х
Dat.	Ильин-у́	Ильин-у́	Ильин-о́й	Ильин-ы́м
Acc.	*N. or G.*	Ильин-о́	Ильин-у́	*N. or G.*
Instr.	Ильин-ы́м	Ильин-ы́м	Ильин-о́ю [-о́й]	Ильин-ы́ми
Loc.	Ильин-о́м	Ильин-о́м	Ильин-о́й	Ильин-ы́х

NOTE. Nouns denoting proper names (mainly surnames) which have the terminations **ов, ев, ёв, ин**, etc., are declined as possessive adjectives, except in the locative case, which has the case-ending of **e** in masculine and neuter (feminine has the ending **ой** in the locative).

	Locative
Пу́шкин	Пу́шкин-е
Петро́в	Петро́в-е
Бородино́	Бородин-е́
Ники́тин	Ники́тин-е

This form of possessive adjective frequently gives place to the genitive case of the person to whom the object belongs :

    дом Петра́ instead of Петро́в дом
    сад дя́ди   ,,   дя́дин сад

§ 38. A number of generic adjectives, or those pertaining to species, are formed by adding the terminations **ий**, ья, ье, ьи to the stem of the noun from which they are formed :

бара́н, ram, бара́н-ий, бара́н-ья, бара́н-ье, бара́н-ьи
пти́ца, bird, пти́ч-ий, пти́ч-ья, пти́ч-ье, пти́ч-ьи
ры́ба, fish, ры́б-ий, ры́б-ья, ры́б-ье, ры́б-ьи

Adjectives of this class are declined as soft adjectives, with this difference, that the suffix ь is retained in the oblique cases before the case-endings.

Examples :

	Masc.	*Neuter*	*Fem.*	*Pl. (all genders)*
Nom.	пти́ч-ий	пти́ч-ье	пти́ч-ья	пти́ч-ьи
Gen.	пти́ч-ьего	пти́ч-ьего	пти́ч-ьей	пти́ч-ьих
Dat.	пти́ч-ьему	пти́ч-ьему	пти́ч-ьей	пти́ч-ьим
Acc.	пти́ч-ий	пти́ч-ье	пти́ч-ью	пти́ч-ьи
Instr.	пти́ч-ьим	пти́ч-ьим	пти́ч-ьею [-ьей]	пти́ч-ьими
Loc.	пти́ч-ьем	пти́ч-ьем	пти́ч-ьей	пти́ч-ьих

(See § 51 (3), Pronouns : чей, чья, чьё.)

§ 39. Nearly all qualitative (attributive) adjectives have a short (predicative) form.

The following classes of adjectives lack the short form :

(1) ' Species ' or generic adjectives, ending in чий, чья, чье. (See § 38.)

(2) Possessive adjectives, ending in ов, ев, ын, ин. (See § 37.)

(3) A number of adjectives ending in ский :

ру́сский, Russian   неме́цкий, German
англи́йский, English   etc.

o

(4) Material-adjectives :

серébряный,   made of silver
золотóй,   made of gold
мéдный,   made of copper
деревя́нный, made of wood
желéзный,   made of iron

NOTE 1. The qualitative adjective большóй has no short form of its own : that of велúкий is borrowed for the predicative form :

велúкий, great   велúк, great, big

NOTE 2. The adjectives рад (glad) and горáзд (capable, handy) have no long form.

§ 40. *Formation of the Predicative (short) form of Adjectives.*

The short form is obtained by dropping the termination of the long form $\begin{cases} \text{ый} \\ \text{ий} \end{cases}$, óй, in the masculine gender, and я and e in the feminine and neuter genders :

живóй (live)   жив
живáя   живá
живóе   жúво

сúний (blue)   синь ⎫ The short form of this
сúняя   синя́ ⎬ adjective is not in
сúнее   сúне ⎭ frequent use

Fleeting o *or* e. Occasionally o or e is inserted in the masculine short form for euphony where too many consonants remain on dropping the case-ending :

мéлкий ⎫
мéлкая ⎬ petty, small,   мéлок, мелкá

корóткий ⎫
корóткая ⎬ short,   корóток, короткá

лёгкий лёгкая } light,	лёгок,	легка
ловкий ловкая } smart,	ловок,	ловка
горький горькая } bitter,	горек,	горька
злой злая } evil, vicious,	зол,	зла
полный полная } full,	полон,	полна
кислый кислая } sour,	кисел,	кисла
тёмный тёмная } dark,	тёмен,	темна
умный умная } clever,	умён,	умна

§ 41. *Degrees of Comparison.*

When forming the comparative degree of an adjective from the positive degree, the following rules have to be observed :

(1) The terminations ый, ой, ий, ая, яя, ое, ее of the positive degree give place to the ending ée for all genders and numbers.

Positive	Comparative
белый, -ая, -ое, -ые	белее
синий, -яя, -ее, -ие	синее

NOTE. The comparative degree also has two forms : the long (attributive) and the short (predicative).

The short comparative form has a predicative meaning, that is to say, it supplies the predicate of the sentence in which it appears. The short comparative is not declined.

The long (attributive) form of the comparative degree has the terminations ейший, ейшая, ейшее, ейшие.[1]

[1] Or: айший, -ая, -ее, -ие, when stem ends in г, к, х.

This form is declined according to all cases of both singular
and plural, and has three genders :

прям   { -óй   прям-ée, прям-éйший, -ая, -ее
straight   { -áя
        { -óe

бéл   { -ый   бел-ée,   бел-éйший,   -ая, -ее
white   { -ая
      { -ое

сла́б   { -ый   слаб-ée, слаб-éйший, -ая, -ее
weak   { -ая
      { -ое

(2) If the stem of the adjective (adjective minus the case-
ending) ends in г, к, х, the short (predicative) form takes
e instead of ee, and the г, к, х are changed (commuted)
respectively into ж, ч, ш ; ск is changed into щ. (See
§ 13a.)

крéпк-ий, strong,   крéпч-е, крепч-а́йший, -ая, -ее
     -ая
     -ое

стро́г -ий, strict,   стро́ж-е, строж-а́йший, -ая, -ее
     -ая   exacting
     -ое

ти́х-ий, quiet,   ти́ш-е,   тиш-а́йший,   -ая, -ее
     -ая   soft
     -ое

лёгк-ий, light,   лёгч-е,   легч-а́йший,   -ая, -ее
     -ая   easy
     -ое

пло́ск-ий, flat,   пло́щ-е, площ-а́йший, -ая, -ее

Often ь is inserted, usually after an л :

мéлк-ий, petty,   мéльч-е, мельч-а́йший, -ая, -ее
     -ая . small,
     -ое   shallow,

There are, however, a few exceptions to the above rule :

бойк-ий, lively,   бойч-ée,[1] бойч ⎫
 -ая
 -ое
дик-ий, wild,   дич-ée,[1] дич ⎬ áйший, -ая, -ee [1]
 -ая
 -ое
лóвк-ий, smart,   ловч-ée,[1] ловч ⎭
 -ая
 -ое

(3) Adjective stems ending in д, т, frequently have these letters commuted into ж and ч ; ст into щ, in the short form only :

твёрд-ый, hard,   твёрж-е, тверд-éйший, -ая, -ee
 -ая
 -ое
худ-óй, bad, lean, хýж-е,   хýд-ший,   -ая, -ee
 -ая   худ-ée,   худ-éйший, -ая, -ee
 -ое
молод-óй, young,   молóж-е, млáд-ший,   -ая, -ee
 -áя
 -óе
чúст-ый, clean,   чúщ-е,   чист-éйший, -ая, -ee
 -ая
 -ое

Exceptions to this rule are :

богáт-ый, rich,   богáч-е, богат-éйший, -ая, -ee
 -ая   also
 -ое   богат-ée
гóрд-ый, haughty, горд-ée, горд-éйший, -ая, -ee
 -ая
 -ое

[1] Not frequently used ; бóлее бóйкий, бóлее лóвкий, etc., are more often used.

(4) A few adjectives with the stem ending in к form their comparative degree (both in the short and the long forms) a little irregularly : they drop the к for the short form, and commute the к into ч for the long form :

ре́дк-ий, infrequent, ре́ж-е, редч-а́йший, -ая, -ее
-ая
-ое

сла́дк-ий, sweet,   сла́щ-е, сладч-а́йший, -ая, -ее
-ая
-ое

коро́тк-ий, short, коро́ч-е, кратч-а́йший, -ая, -ее
-ая
-ое

то́нк-ий, thin, то́ньш-е, тонч-а́йший, -ая, -ее
-ая
-ое

у́зк-ий, narrow, у́ж-е (long form lacking) or
-ая   бо́лее у́зкий [1]
-ое

глубо́к-ий, deep, глу́б-же, глубоч-а́йший, -ая, -ее
-ая -ое

широ́к-ий, wide, шир-е, широч-а́йший, -ая, -ее
-ая -ое

дешёв-ый, cheap, дешёвл-е, дешев-е́йший, -ая, -ее
-ая -ое

(5) A few adjectives shorten the attributive form of their comparative :

высо́к-ий, high, вы́ш-е, вы́с-ший,   -ая, -ее
-ая -ое

[1] The adverbs : бо́лее (more) and ме́нее (less) are occasionally used in colloquial speech with the positive, instead of the long comparative.

низк-ий, low, -ая -ое	ниж-е,	низ-ший,	-ая, -ее
стáр-ый, old, -ая -ое	стáр-ше, (of persons only) старéе, (of objects and persons)	стáр-ший, стар-éйший,	-ая, -ее -ая, -ее

(6) A few adjectives take their comparative form from another adjective with a similar meaning :

велик-ий, great, -ая -ое	бóльше,	бóльший,	-ая, -ее
мáл-ый, small, -ая -ое	мéньше,	мéньший,	-ая, -ее
хорóш-ий, good, -ая -ее	лýчше,	лýчший,	-ая, -ее
далёк-ий, far distant,	дáльше,	дальнéйший,	-ая, -ее
-ая -ое			

If the short (predicative) form is used without any object of comparison, the particle по is added to it :

получше	means	a little better
побóльше	,,	a little more, or a little larger
помéньше	,,	a little less, or a little smaller
подáльше	,,	a little further
поближе	,,	a little nearer

§ 42. *The Superlative Degree.*

The superlative degree of Russian adjectives has no form of its own. It usually takes the long comparative form. (See § 41.)

Occasionally to the long comparative form is added the superlative particle наи :

наилу́чший, -ая, -ее, the best

наиме́ньший, -ая, -ее, the least (the smallest)

More often the pronoun са́мый (the very) is placed before the positive form of the adjective. This gives a less complicated form of superlative :

са́мый стро́гий, the most strict, exacting

са́мый can also precede the long comparative :

са́мый лу́чший, the very best. (See § 41 (5).)

Also in adverbial expressions :

са́мое бо́льшее, at the very most

са́мое ме́ньшее, at the very least

Frequently when forming a **predicative** superlative, the pronouns всего́, всех are placed after the short comparative :

лу́чше всего́, better than anything⎫
лу́чше всех, better than all ⎬ best of all

ме́ньше всего́, less than anything⎫
ме́ньше всех, less than all ⎬ least of all

The particle пре before the positive enhances the quality of the adjective :

предо́брый, -ая, -ое, most kind

прескве́рный, -ая, -ое, most rotten, bad

It is used in a predicative sense, and is not usually declined.

§ 43. *Formation of Adverbs from Adjectives.*

Adverbs formed from adjectives take the neuter predicative (short) form :

но́вый — но́во, new

хоро́ший — хорошо́, well, good

ужа́сный — ужа́сно, awful

по́здний — по́здно, late

кра́йний — кра́йне, extremely

Adverbs formed from adjectives ending in **ский** take **ски**, often preceded by the particle **по** :

> человéческий, human
> по-человéчески, humanly
> по-рýсски, in Russian
> по-англíйски, in English

§ 44. *The Accent in Adjectives.*

(1) Attributive adjectives in which the stress is *not* on the last syllable retain the accent of the nominative singular in all the cases of the singular and the plural.

(2) If the accent falls on the last syllable in the nominative singular, it goes to the case-endings in both singular and plural.

(3) Predicative (short) adjectives, with few exceptions, have the accent on the same syllable as in the long form for the masculine ; for the feminine, neuter, and plural the accent is shifted to the last syllable :

> велúкий   велúк, великá, великó, великú
>   big, great, large
> высóкий   высóк, высокá, высокó, высокú
>   high, tall
> тяжёлый   тяжёл, тяжелá, тяжелó, тяжелú
>   heavy

There are, however, exceptions to this rule, but the general tendency is for the feminine and the plural to shift the accent to the last syllable, particularly in dissyllabic adjectives.

(4) In the predicative (short) comparative the tendency is for the last syllable *but one* to take the accent—particularly in dissyllabic adjectives, but also in a few with three syllables :

> весёлый   веселéе,   gay, cheerful, joyful
> здорóвый   здоровéе,   sound, healthy
> зелёный   зеленéе,   green

o *

In adjectives of more than two syllables the accent in the comparative (short) form is usually on the same syllable as in the positive.

§ 45. *A list of Adjectives in frequent use, showing the Short (predicative) form in each case, also the Short Comparative (predicative) form.*

NOTE. The accent in adjectives remains on the same syllable throughout in the long (attributive) form. In the predicative form the accent is nearly always shifted to the last syllable in the feminine and the plural. · Where the accent varies in the short neuter and the plural, according to popular usage in different parts of the country, the alternative accent is indicated (ó [o]; ы́ [ы]).

In the short comparative form the accent is always on the last syllable but one, with the exception of polysyllabic adjectives. (See § 44.)

Positive (attributive)	Predicative	Short Comparative
бе́дный, -ая, -ое, -ые poor	бе́ден, бедна́, -ó [-o], -ы́ [-ы]	бедне́е
богáтый, -ая, -ое, -ые rich	богáт, -а, -о, -ы	богáче
небогáтый, -ая, -ое, -ые of moderate means	не богáт, -а, -о, -ы	no comparative form
бе́лый, -ая, -ое, -ые white	бел, -á, -ó [-o], -ы́ [-ы]	беле́е
чёрный, -ая, -ое, -ые black	чёрен, черна́, -ó, -ы́	черне́е
больнóй, -áя, -óе, -ы́е sick, ill	бóлен, больна́, -о, -ы́	больне́е
вдорóвый, -ая, -ое, -ые healthy	здорóв, -а, -о, -ы	здорове́е
бли́зкий, -ая, -ое, -ие near	бли́зок, близка́, -о, -и́	бли́же
далёкий, -ая, -ое, -ие far, distant	далёк, далекá, -ó, -и́	дáльше дáлее
дáльний, -яя, -ее, -ие distant	has no short forms	

Positive (attributive)	Predicative	Short Comparative
большо́й, -а́я, -о́е, -и́е big	велик, -а́, -о, -и́	бо́льше
вели́кий, -ая, -ое, -ие great		бо́лее
небольшо́й, -а́я, -о́е, -и́е not big	не вели́к, -а́, -о, -и́	no comparative form
ма́лый, -ая, -ое, -ые small	мал, мала́, -о́, -ы́	ме́ньше
ма́ленький, -ая, -ое, -ие small, tiny	has no short form	ме́нее
бу́дущий, -ая, -ее, -ие future	have no short forms	no comparative form
про́шлый, -ая, -ое, -ые past		
весёлый, -ая, -ое, -ые gay, joyful	ве́сел, весела́, -о, -ы	веселе́е
гру́стный, -ая, -ое, -ые sad, melancholy	гру́стен, грустна́, -о, -ы́	грустне́е
ску́чный, -ая, -ое, -ые weary, tedious	ску́чен, скучна́, -о, -ы	скучне́е
невесёлый, -ая, -ое, -ые sad, weary	не ве́сел, -а́, -о, -ы	no comparative form
ви́дный, -ая, -ое, -ые visible, apparent	ви́ден, видна́, -о, -ы	видне́е
вку́сный, -ая, -ое, -ые tasty	вку́сен, вкусна́, -о, -ы	вкусне́е
невку́сный, -ая, -ое, -ые tasteless	не вку́сен, -а́, -о, -ы	no comparative form
ве́рхний, -яя, -ее, -ие top	have no short or comparative forms	
ни́жний, -яя, -ее, -ие bottom		
высо́кий, -ая, -ое, -ие high	высо́к, -а́, -о́ [-о], -и́ [-и]	вы́ше
ни́зкий, -ая, -ое, -ие low	ни́зок, низка́, -о, -и	ни́же
глубо́кий, -ая, -ое, -ие deep	глубо́к, -а́, -о́, -и́	глу́бже
неглубо́кий, -ая, -ое -ие shallow	не глубо́к, -а́, -о́, -и́	no comparative form
глу́пый, -ая, -ое, -ые foolish, stupid	глуп, -а́, -о, -ы	глупе́е
у́мный, -ая, -ое, -ые wise	умён, умна́, -о́, -ы́	умне́е

Positive (attributive)	*Predicative*	*Short Comparative*
глухо́й, -а́я, -о́е, -и́е deaf	глух, -а́, -о, -и́	глу́ше
слепо́й, -а́я, -о́е, -ы́е blind	слеп, -а́, -о, -ы	слепе́е
голо́дный, -ая, -ое, -ые hungry	го́лоден, голодна́, -о, -ы	голодне́е
сы́тый, -ая, -ое, -ые fed	сыт, сыта́, -о, -ы	сыте́е
го́рький, -ая, -ое, -ие bitter	го́рек, горька́, -о, -и	{го́рче горче́е
сла́дкий, -ая, -ое, -ие sweet	сла́док, сладка́, -о, -и	сла́ще
горя́чий, -ая, -ее, -ие hot	горя́ч, -а́, -о́, -и́	бо́лее горя́чий -ая, -ее, -ие
тёплый, -ая, -ое, -ые warm	тёпел, тепла́, -о́, -ы́	тепле́е
холо́дный, -ая, -ое, -ые cold	хо́лоден, холодна́, -о, -ы	холодне́е
гро́мкий, -ая, -ое, -ие loud	гро́мок, громка́, -о, -и	гро́мче
ти́хий, -ая, -ое, -ие quiet	тих, тиха́, -о, -и	ти́ше
гря́зный, -ая, -ое, -ые dirty	гря́зен, грязна́, -о, -ы́	грязне́е
чи́стый, -ая, -ое, -ые clean, pure	чист, чиста́, -о, -ы	чи́ще
нечи́стый, -ая, -ое, -ые unclean, impure	не чист, -а́, -о, -ы	no comparative form
дешёвый, -ая, -ое, -ые cheap	дёшев, дешева́, -о, -ы́	деше́вле
дорого́й, -а́я, -о́е, -и́е dear	до́рог, дорога́, -о, -и	доро́же
недорого́й, -а́я, -о́е, -и́е inexpensive	не до́рог, -а́, -о, -и	no comparative form
дли́нный, -ая, -ое, -ые long (in distance)	дли́нен, длинна́, -о, -ы	длинне́е
до́лгий, -ая, -ое, -ие long (in sense of time)	до́лог, долга́, -о, -и	до́льше
коро́ткий, -ая, -ое, -ие short	коро́ток, коротка́, -о́, -и́	коро́че
кра́ткий, -ая, -ое, -ие short, brief, concise	кра́ток, кратка́, -о, -и	кра́тче
до́брый, -ая, -ое, -ые good, kind	добр, -а́, -о́, -ы́	добре́е

Positive (attributive)	Predicative	Short Comparative
хоро́ший, -ая, -ое, -ие good, of good quality	хоро́ш, -а́, -о́, -и́	лу́чше
худо́й, -а́я, -о́е, -ы́е bad	худ, худа́, -о, -ы	ху́же
плохо́й, -а́я, -о́е, -и́е bad	плох, -а́, -о, -и	пло́ше
злой, -а́я, -о́е, -ы́е bad, malicious	зол, зла, зло, злы	злѐе
зелёный, -ая, -ое, -ые green	зе́лен, -а́, -о, -ы	зеленѐе
жёлтый, -ая, -ое, -ые yellow	жёлт, желта́, -о, -ы	желтѐе
кра́сный, -ая, -ое, -ые red	кра́сеп, красна́, -о, -ы	краснѐе
си́ний, -ля, -ее, -ие blue	синь, си́ня, -е, -и (not in frequent use)	синѐе
живо́й, -а́я, -о́е, -ы́е live	жив, жива́, -о, -ы́	живѐе
мёртвый, -ая, -ое, -ые dead	мёртв, мертва́, -о, -ы́	no comparative form
краси́вый, -ая, -ое, -ые pretty	краси́в, -а, -о, -ы	⎰краси́вее ⎱кра́ше
некраси́вый, -ая, -ое, -ые ungainly	не краси́в, -а, -о, -ы	no comparative form in use
кре́пкий, -ая, -ое, -ие strong, hardy	кре́пок, крепка́, -о, -и	кре́пче
си́льный, -ая, -ое, -ые strong, powerful	силён, сильна́, -о, -ы́	сильнѐе
сла́бый, -ая, -ое, -ые weak	слаб, -а́, -о, -ы	слабѐе
лёгкий, -ая, -ое, -ие light, easy	лёгок, легка́, -о́, -и́	ле́гче
тяжёлый, -ая, -ое, -ые heavy	тяжёл, -а, -о́, -ы́	тяжелѐе
тру́дный, -ая, -ое, -ые hard (not easy)	тру́ден, трудна́, -о, -ы	труднѐе
ме́дленный, -ая, -ое, -ые slow	ме́дленен, ме́дленна, -о, -ы	ме́дленнее
ско́рый, -ая, -ое, -ые fast, quick	скор, -а́, -о, -ы	скорѐе
мо́крый, -ая, -ое, -ые wet	мокр, мокра́, -о, -ы	мокрѐе
сухо́й, -а́я, -о́е, -и́е dry	сух, суха́, су́хо, су́хи	су́ше

Positive (attributive)	*Predicative*	*Short Comparative*
молодо́й, -а́я, -о́е, -ы́е young	мо́лод, молода́, -о, -ы́	⎫ ⎬ моло́же ⎭
мла́дший, -ая, -ее, -ие, younger	no short form	
ста́рый, -ая, -ое, -ые old	стар, -а́, -о, -ы	старе́е
но́вый, -ая, -ое, -ые new	нов, -а́, -о, -ы	нове́е
ста́рший, -ая, -ее, -ие older, elder	no short form	ста́рше
мя́гкий, -ая, -ое, -ие soft	мя́гок, мягка́, -о, -и	мя́гче
твёрдый, -ая, -ое, -ые hard	твёрд, -а́, -о, -ы	твёрже
(1) ну́жный, -ая, -ое, -ые needful, necessary	ну́жен, нужна́, -о, -ы [и́]	нужне́е
непу́жный, -ая, -ое, -ые unnecessary, needless	не ну́жен, -а́, -о, -ы [и́]	no comparative form
(2) до́лжный, -ая, -ое, -ые owing, due, obliged	до́лжен, должна́, -о́, -ы́	no comparative form in use

(1) The short form of ну́жный, besides its predicative function, is extensively used in impersonal sentences in the neuter, followed by a verbal infinitive :

мне [нам] ну́жно . . .	I [we] have to . . .
мне [нам] ну́жно бы́ло . . .	I [we] had to . . .
мне [нам] ну́жно бу́дет . . .	I [we] shall have to . . .

The popular form for ну́жно is на́до, derived from на́добный [на́добно], necessary :

нам на́до . . .	we have to . . .
нам на́до бы́ло . . .	we had to . . .
нам на́до бу́дет . . .	we shall have to . . .

The logical subject always stands in the dative in impersonal sentences with ну́жно, на́до, as predicate, followed by an infinitive. But in such sentences as :

мне нужна́ кварти́ра	I need a flat
мне ну́жны бы́ли де́ньги	I needed money
мне нужна́ бу́дет ва́ша по́мощь	I shall need your help

the predicative form of ну́жный is used without a verbal infinitive.

(2) The predicative form of до́лжный is much used in personal sentences in the sense of (a) to have to, (b) to owe :

(a)
я до́лжен е́хать	I must go
я до́лжен был е́хать	I had to go
мы должны́ бу́дем остава́ться	we shall have to remain, stay
[нам на́до бу́дет остава́ться]	

(b)
я ему́ до́лжен пять рубле́й	I owe him five roubles
я ему́ был до́лжеп пять рубле́й	I owed him five roubles
я ему́ бу́ду до́лжеп пять рубле́й	I shall owe him five roubles

Note the reverse order in :

я до́лжен был	I had to
я был до́лжен	I owed
я до́лжен бу́ду	I shall have to
я бу́ду до́лжен	I shall owe

All the personal sentences in sub-division (a) can be turned into impersonal ones by the use of ну́жно [на́до] :

я до́лжен	= мне ну́жно
я до́лжен был	= мне́ ну́жно [на́до] бы́ло
я до́лжен бу́ду	= мне ну́жно бу́дет

должно́ [до́лжно] is used in the meaning : one must . . ., it ought to . . ., it must. . . .

э́то должно́ быть так	this must be so
э́то должно́ бы́ло случи́ться	this had to happen

должно́ быть used alone, adverbially, means : possibly, probably, it would seem.

Positive (attributive)	Predicative	Short Comparative
пра́вый, -ая, -ое, -ые right, just	прав, -а́, -о, -ы	праве́е (more to the right)
непра́вый, -ая, -ое, -ые unjust	пе прав, -а́, -о, -ы	no comparative form
ле́вый, -ая, -ое, -ые left	—	леве́е (more to the left)
по́лный, -ая, -ое, -ые full, complete	по́лон, полна́, -о, -ы́	полне́е
непо́лный, -ая, -ое, -ые incomplete	не по́лон, -а́, -о, -ы́	no comparative form
пусто́й, -а́я, -о́е, -ы́е empty	пуст, -а́, -о, -ы	пусте́е
прямо́й, -а́я, -о́е, -ы́е straight	прям, -а́, -о, -ы	пряме́е
криво́й, -а́я, -о́е, -ы́е crooked	крив, крива́, -о, -ы	криве́е

Positive (attributive)	Predicative	Short Comparative
свѣжий, -ая, -ее, -не fresh	свѣж, -а́, -о́, -й	свѣжѣе
несвѣжий, -ая, -ее, -не not fresh	не свѣж, -а́, -о́, -й	no comparative form
свѣтлый, -ая, -ое, -ые light	свѣтел, светла́, -о́, -ы́	свѣтлѣе
тѐмный, -ая, -ое, -ые dark	тѐмен, темна́, -о́, -ы́	темнѣе
тóнкий, -ая, -ое, -ие thin	тóнок, тонка́, -о, -и	тóньше
тóлстый, -ая, -ое, -ые thick	толст, -а́, -о, -ы	тóлще
ýзкий, -ая, -ое, -ие narrow	ýзок, узка́, -о, -и	ýже
широкий, -ая, -ое, -ие broad	широ́к, -а́, -о́, -й	ши́ре
цѐлый, -ая, -ое, -ые whole	цел, -а́, -о, -ы	no comparative form
чéстный, -ая, -ое, -ые honest	чéстен, -а́, -о, -ы́	честнѣе
нечéстный, -ая, -ое, -ые dishonest	не чéстен, -а́, -о, -ы́	no comparative form in use
я́сный, -ая, -ое, -ые clear	я́сен, ясна́, -о, -ы	яснѣе
нея́сный, -ая, -ое, -ые not clear, indistinct	не я́сен, -а́, -о, -ы	no comparative form

In adjectives with the negative particle не (which gives a reduced
meaning) the negative form can also be used predicatively, but the
particle не is then written separately :

небогáтый not rich	but	он не богáт	
немолодóй no longer young	,,	он не мóлод	
нестáрый not very old	,,	он не стар	
небольшóй дом a house of moderate size	,,	дом не велѝк	no comparative form
неинтерéсный uninteresting	,,	онá не интерéсна	
незнакóмый unknown	,,	он не знакóм мне	

Exception :

| нездорóвый
unhealthy, ailing | ,, | я нездорóв, -а, -о, -ы
I am unwell | |

§ 46. *A few Adjectives which have no Predicative or Comparative form :*

вечéрний ⎱ -яя, -ее, -ие,		of the evening
ýтренний ⎰		of the morning
дневнóй ⎱ -áя, -óе, -ы́е,		of the day
ночнóй ⎰		of the night
ежеднéвный ⎫		daily
еженедéльный ⎪		weekly
ежемéсячный ⎬ -ая, -ое, -ые,		monthly
ежегóдный ⎪		yearly
годи́чный ⎭		annual
сéверный ⎫		northern, northerly
ю́жный ⎪		southern, southerly
зáпадный ⎬ -ая, -ое, -ые,		western, westerly
востóчный ⎭		eastern, easterly
вчерáшний ⎫		of yesterday, yesterday's
сегóдняшний ⎪		of to-day, to-day's
зáвтрашний ⎪		of to-morrow, to-morrow's
тепéрешний ⎬ -яя, -ее, -ие,		of the present day
ны́нешний ⎪		of this time
всегдáшний ⎭		usual, habitual
вéрхний ⎱ -яя, -ее, -ие,		top one
ни́жний ⎰		bottom one
рáзный, -ая, -ое, -ые,		various, diverse
домáшний, -яя, -ее, -ие,		home-made, of the house, of the household
чужóй, -áя, -óе, -и́е,		a stranger (in this sense used as a noun)

§ 46a. *Participles as Adjectives.*

A number of participles, both active and passive, have by popular usage been turned into adjectives :

1. настоя́щий ⎫		present
прошéдший ⎪		past
бýдущий ⎬ -ая, -ее, -ие,		future
свéдущий ⎪		learned, skilled
имýщий ⎭		wealthy

Some adjectives, derived from participles, have changed their termination into **чий** :

2.

могу́чий		mighty
стоя́чий		standing, stagnant
кипу́чий	-ая, -ее, -ие,	boiling, boiling hot
ходя́чий		current
горя́чий		hot
плаку́чий		weeping

3. Derived from past passive participles :

варёный,	boiled
учёный (*noun*),	learned
жа́реный,	roasted
прида́ное (*noun*),	dowry
почте́нный,	esteemed
соверше́нный,	perfect
просвещённый,	enlightened
etc.	

3. PRONOUNS

§ 47. *Classes of Pronouns.*

1. **Personal pronouns:** я, I ; ты, thou ; он, he ; она́, she ; оно́, it ; мы, we ; вы, you ; они́, they.

2. **Possessive pronouns:** мой, -я́, -ё, -и́, my, mine ; тво-й, -я́, -ё, -и́, thy, thine ; сво-й, -я́, -ё, -и́, one's own ; его́, his ; её, her, hers ; наш, -а, -е, -и, our, ours ; ваш, -а, -е, -и, your, yours ; их, their, theirs.

3. **Demonstrative pronouns:** э́тот, э́та, э́то, э́ти, this, these ; тот, та, то, те, that, those ; так-о́й, -а́я, -о́е, -и́е, such ; таков-о́й, -а́я, -о́е, -ы́е, the mentioned ; сей, сия́, сие́, сии́, this, these ; о́ный, -ая, -ое, -ые, the named.

4. **Relative-Interrogative pronouns:**

котор-ый, -ая, -ое, -ые,	which
как-о́й, -а́я, -о́е, -и́е,	what sort of, which
чей, чья, чьё, чьи,	whose
каков, -а́, -о́, -ы́,	what sort of, how

NOTE. All the enumerated relative pronouns are also used as interrogative pronouns by adding the question mark.

5. **Definite pronouns:** сам, himself; самá, herself; самó, itself; сáми, themselves.

сáм-ый, -ая, -ое, -ые,	the very one (ones)
кáжд-ый, -ая, -ое, -ые,	each, every
вся́к-ий, -ая, -ое, -ие,	each, every one, any one
так-óй, -áя, -óе, -úе,	such a one
таков-óй, -áя, -óе, -ы́е,	such a one, that, the mentioned

6. **Indefinite pronouns:**

ктó-то,	someone, somebody
нéкто,	a certain one
кóе-кто	
ктó-нибýдь	someone or other
чтó-то,	something
нéчто,	a certain thing
кóе-что	
чтó-нибýдь	something or other
никтó,	no one
ничтó,	nothing
как-óй-то, -áя, -óе, -úе,	a certain
никак-óй, -áя, -óе, -úе,	not anyone
нéкотор-ый, -ая, -ое, -ые,	a certain, some
инó-й, -áя, -óе, -ы́е,	some other
друг-óй, -áя, -óе, -úе,	another

NOTE. To indefinite pronouns belong the adverbial pronouns :

скóлько,	how much, how many
стóлько,	so much, so many
нéсколько,	a few
мнóгое,	many a thing, many things
(used only in the singular)	
мнóгие,	many (many a man)

With the exception of мнóгое, they are used only in the plural and are declined as adjectives. (See § 35.)

скóлько, стóлько, нéсколько are occasionally used in the dative singular with the preposition по ; they are then treated as neuter nouns :

по скóльку ?　　how many to each ?
(поскóльку),[1]　(in so far as)
по стóльку,　　so many to each
(постóльку),[1]　(insomuch, to that extent)
по нéскольку,　a few to each

(The nouns which follow these are, however, in the genitive plural) :

я дал им по нéскольку рублéй,
I gave them a few roubles each

In the declension of these pronoun-adverbs the *accent* remains on the stem in нéсколько, мнóгое, мнóгие ; in скóлько, стóлько it is shifted to the case-endings :

скольки́х　　стольки́х
скольки́м　　стольки́м
скольки́ми　　стольки́ми

Declension of Pronouns

§ 48.　1. *Personal.*

Singular

Nom.	я	ты	он	онá	онó
Gen.	меня́	тебя́	егó	её	егó
Dat.	мне	тебé	емý	ей	емý
Acc.	меня́	тебя́	егó	её	егó
Instr.	мнóю [-ой]	тобóю [-óй]	им	éю [ей]	им
Loc.	мне	тебé	ём	ей	ём

Plural

Nom.	мы	вы	они́
Gen.	нас	вас	их
Dat.	нам	вам	им
Acc.	нас	вас	их
Instr.	нáми	вáми	и́ми
Loc.	нас	вас	их

[1] Used adverbially.

NOTE 1. Instrumental of мно́ю, тобо́ю, е́ю can be shortened into мной, тобо́й, ей. (See § 28, note 4.)

NOTE 2. The personal-reflexive pronoun себя́ (oneself) has no nominative case, and no plural. It can stand both for singular and plural.

Nom.	(none)
Gen.	себя́
Dat.	себе́
Acc.	себя́
Instr.	собо́ю [-о́й]
Loc.	себе́

NOTE 3. Accusative of он and оно́ is *always* его́.

NOTE 4. The oblique cases of the personal pronouns он, она́, оно́, они́ have an inserted н (for euphony) if they are used with a preposition :

у,	от,	него́,	неё,	них
перед,	с,	ним,	не́ю,	ни́ми
о,	на,	нём,	ней,	них
		etc.		

§ 49. 2. *Possessive.*

	Singular			*Plural*
Nom.	мо-й	мо-ё	мо-я́	мо-и́
Gen.	мо-его́		мо-е́й	мо-и́х
Dat.	мо-ему́		мо-ей	мо-и́м
Acc.	*N. or G.*	мо-ё	мо-ю́	*N. or G.*
Instr.	мо-и́м		мо-е́ю [-е́й]	мо-и́ми
Loc.	мо-ём		мо-е́й	мо-и́х

It will be noted that the case-endings of most possessive pronouns are similar to those of the oblique cases of он, она́, оно́, они́. (See § 48.)

твой, -я́, -ё, -и́
свой, -я́, -ё, -и́ } are similarly declined,

so are : наш, -а, -е, -и .
ваш, -а, -е, -и

	Singular			*Plural*
Nom.	наш наш-е	наш-а		наш-и
Gen.	наш-его	наш-ей		наш-их
Dat.	наш-ему	наш-ей		наш-им
Acc.	*N. or G.* наш-е	наш-у		*N. or G.*
Instr.	наш-им	наш-ею [-ей]		наш-ими
Loc.	наш-ем	наш-ей		наш-их

NOTE 1. сво-й, -я, -ё is only used when it directly refers to the subject of the sentence :

он пр́одал свой дом,	he sold his (own) house
он́а потер́яла сво́ю шл́япу,	she has lost her (own) hat
он́и зн́ают сво́их друз́ей,	they know their (own) friends

NOTE 2. But an ordinary possessive pronoun frequently takes the place of свой. One can say :

я пр́одал мой дом as well as я пр́одал свой дом.

мы б́ыли на н́ашем огор́оде (we were in our kitchen garden) as well as мы б́ыли на сво́ём огор́оде.

Often, to avoid ambiguity, the ordinary possessive is retained :

я возьм́у мо́ю кн́игу, а ты сво́ю ; or
я возьм́у сво́ю кн́игу, а ты тво́ю
(I shall take my book, and you yours)

§ 50.   3. *Demonstrative.*

	Singular			*Plural*
Nom.	т-от т-о	т-а		т-е
Gen.	т-ого	т-ой		т-ех
Dat.	т-ому́	т-ой		т-ем
Acc.	*N. or G.* т-о	т-у		*N. or G.*
Instr.	т-ем	т-ою [-ой]		т-еми
Loc.	т-ом	т-ой		т-ех

	Singular			*Plural*
Nom.	э́т-от	э́т-о	э́т-а	э́т-и
Gen.	э́т-ого		э́т-ой	э́т-их
Dat.	э́т-ому		э́т-ой	э́т-им
Acc.	*N. or G*	э́-то	э́т-у	*N. or G.*
Instr.	э́т-им		э́т-ою [-ой]	э́т-ими
Loc.	э́т-ом		э́т-ой	э́т-их

NOTE 1. так-о́й, таков-о́й, о́н-ый, -ая, -ое, -ые are declined as adjectives. (See § 35.)

NOTE 2. с-ей
с-ия́   are declined as он, она́, оно́, они́.
с-ие́   (See § 48.)
с-ий

The oblique cases are merely preceded by с.

Accusative of neuter is сие́ (popularly сё); of fem. : сию́.

This pronoun is not frequently used now, but it occurs in everyday speech in the expressions :

сию́ мину́ту, this minute
то и сё, this and that
сейча́с, in a minute
сего́дня, to-day

NOTE 3. тот, та, то, те mean 'that,' 'those,' but often denote 'the one,' 'the ones,' etc.

тот, кото́рый ... the one that ...

NOTE 4. тот, та, то, те, followed by the particle же, have the meaning of 'the same' (or 'the very same,' if followed by же са́мый) :

тот-же, the same
тот-же са́мый, the very same
так-о́й-же
 -а́я-же
 -о́е-же   mean : exactly as
 -и́е-же

§ 51. 4. *Relative and Interrogative.*

(1) котóр-ый, как-óй
    -ая,   -áя ⎱ are declined as adjectives. (See
    -ое,   -óе ⎰ § 35.)
    -ые,   -йе

	Singular		*Singular*			*Plural*
(2) *N.*	к-то	ч-то	(3) че-й	чь-ё	чь-я	чь-и
G.	к-огó	ч-егó		чь-егó	чь-ей	чь-их
D.	к-омý	ч-емý		чь-емý	чь-ей	чь-им
A.	к-огó	ч-то	*N. or G.*	чь-ё	чь-ю	*N. or G.*
I.	к-ем	ч-ем		чь-им	чь-éю	чь-йми
					[-ей]	
L.	к-ом	ч-ём		чь-ём	чь-ей	чь-их

NOTE 1. Relative кто, что are occasionally interchanged with котóр-ый, -ая, -ое, -ые (particularly in popular speech):
    человéк, котóрый был здесь вчерá
    человéк, что был здесь вчерá
    человéк, кто был здесь вчерá

NOTE 2. The particle же [ж] after кто ? что ? denotes accentuation : кто же ? who, then ? ; что же ? what, then ? ; кто же э́то ви́дел ? who, then, saw this ?
что is also used in the meaning of a conjunction. (See § 97.)

§ 52. 5. *Definite.*

(1) вся́кий, ка́ждый, -ая, -ое, -ие, -ые are declined as adjectives. (See § 35.)

	Singular			*Plural*
(2) *Nom.*	сам	сам-ó	сам-á	сáм-и
	himself	itself	herself	themselves
Gen.	сам-огó		сам-óй	сам-и́х
Dat.	сам-омý		сам-óй	сам-и́м
Acc.	сам-огó	сам-ó	сам-оё́	сам-и́х
Instr.	сам-и́м		сам-óю [-óй]	сам-и́ми
Loc.	сам-óм		сам-óй	сам-и́х

NOTE. сам is distinct from the definite adjective-pronoun са́мый. The latter means 'the very,' and has the same meaning as же ; the former means 'himself.'

	тот же тот са́мый } the same	
	тот же са́мый,	the very same
but :	он сам,	he himself
	она́ сама́,	she herself etc.

	Singular			*Plural*
(3) *Nom.*	вес-ь	вс-ё	вс-я	вс-е
Gen.		вс-его́	вс-ей	вс-ех
Dat.		вс-ему́	вс-ей	вс-ем
Acc.	*N. or G.*	вс-ё	вс-ю	*N. or G.*
Instr.		вс-ем	вс-е́ю [-ей]	вс-е́ми
Loc.		вс-ём	вс-ей	вс-ех

§ 53.   6. *Indefinite.*

Some negative and indefinite. pronouns are formed from interrogative-relative pronouns :

(1) By prefixing the particle **ни** :

что	— ничто́,	nothing
кто	— никто́,	no one
како́й	— никако́й,	not anyone

(See § 135 (6), as **ни** affects adverbs.)

(2) By prefixing the particle **не** :

кто	— не́кто,[1]	a certain man
что	— не́что,[1]	a certain thing
кото́рый	— не́который,	a certain person or object

(See § 135 (7).)

[1] Not declined.

(3) By adding the particle то :

кто-то,	someone	(not quite certain who or what,
что-то,	something	someone or something whose name, or what exactly, is immaterial)

какой-то ⎱ some person or thing (not quite certain
какая-то ⎰ who or what, giving the person or thing
какие-то a slightly contemptuous estimation)

(4) By adding the words нибудь, либо, or by prefixing кое [кой] :

кто-нибудь,	someone or other, anyone
что-нибудь,	something or other, anything
кое-кто,	someone ⎱ with a certain degree
кое-что,	something ⎰ of definiteness

кто-либо,	someone, anyone	(certainty imma-
что-либо,	something, anything	terial or problematical)

(See § 135, sub-section 3, in adverbial forms.)

4. Numerals

§ 54. *Classes of Numerals.*

There are two classes of numerals :

(*a*) **Cardinal** : один, one ; два, two ; etc.

(*b*) **Ordinal** : первый, first ; второй, second ; etc.

§ 54a. *List of Cardinal and Ordinal Numerals :*

	Cardinal		Ordinal
1	один, одна, одно	1st	перв-ый, -ая, -ое, -ые
2	два, две, два	2nd	втор-ой, -ая, -ое, -ые
3	три	3rd	трет-ий, -ья, -ье, -ьи
4	четыре	4th	четвёрт-ый, -ая, -ое, -ые
5	пять	5th	пят-ый, -ая, -ое, -ые
6	шесть	6th	шест-ой, -ая, -ое, -ые
7	семь	7th	седьм-ой, -ая, -ое, -ые
8	восемь	8th	восьм-ой, -ая, -ое, -ые

	Cardinal		*Ordinal*
9	девять	9th	девят-ый, -ая, -ое, -ые
10	десять	10th	десят-ый, -ая, -ое, -ые
11	одиннадцать	11th	одиннадцат-ый, -ая, -ое, -ые
12	двенадцать	12th	двенадцат-ый, -ая, -ое, -ые
13	тринадцать	13th	тринадцат-ый, -ая, -ое, -ые
14	четырнадцать	14th	четырнадцат-ый, -ая, -ое, -ые
15	пятнадцать	15th	пятнадцат-ый, -ая, -ое, -ые
16	шестнадцать	16th	шестнадцат-ый, -ая, -ое, -ые
17	семнадцать	17th	семнадцат-ый, -ая, -ое, -ые
18	восемнадцать	18th	восемнадцат-ый, -ая, -ое, -ые
19	девятнадцать	19th	девятнадцат-ый, -ая, -ое, -ые
20	двадцать	20th	двадцат-ый, -ая, -ое, -ые
21	двадцать один, одна, одно, etc.	21st	двадцать перв-ый, -ая, -ое etc.
30	тридцать etc.	30th	тридцат-ый, -ая, -ое, -ые etc.
40	сорок etc.	40th	сороков-ой, -ая, -ое, -ые etc.
50	пятьдесят etc.	50th	пятидесят-ый, -ая, -ое, -ые etc.
60	шестьдесят etc.	60th	шестидесят-ый, -ая, -ое, -ые etc.
70	семьдесят etc.	70th	семидесят-ый, -ая, -ое, -ые etc.
80	восемьдесят etc.	80th	восьмидесят-ый, -ая, -ое, -ые, etc.
90	девяносто etc.	90th	девяност-ый, -ая, -ое, -ые etc.
100	сто etc.	100th	сот-ый, -ая, -ое, -ые etc.
101	сто один, одна, одно, etc.	101st	сто перв-ый, -ая, -ое etc.
110	сто десять etc.	110th	сто десят-ый, -ая, -ое etc.
200	двести	200th	двухсот-ый, -ая, -ое
300	триста	300th	трёхсот-ый, -ая, -ое
400	четыреста	400th	четырёхсот-ый, -ая, -ое
500	пятьсот	500th	пятисот-ый, -ая, -ое
600	шестьсот	600th	шестисот-ый, -ая, -ое
700	семьсот	700th	семисот-ый, -ая, -ое

Cardinal	Ordinal
800 восемьсо́т	800th восьмисо́т-ый, -ая, -ое
900 девятьсо́т	900th девятисо́т-ый, -ая, -ое
1000 ты́сяча	1000th ты́сячн-ый, -ая, -ое
1453 { ты́сяча четы́реста пятьдеся́т три	1453rd[1] ты́сяча четы́реста пятьдеся́т трет-ий, -ья, -ье, -ьи

NOTE 1. Ordinal numerals take the termination тый or то́й, ая, ое if the cardinal ends in ть :

пять,	five,	пя́тый,	-ая, -ое
шесть,	six,	шесто́й,	-а́я, -о́е
де́вять,	nine,	девя́тый,	-ая, -ое
де́сять,	ten,	деся́тый,	-ая, -ое

NOTE 2. The numbers 11–19 are formed by adding надцать to the first part of the numeral, which denotes the number above 10 (на-дцать is a contraction of на де́сять) :

	Cardinal	Ordinal
eleven (1 + 10),	оди́ннадцат-ь	-ый
twelve (2 + 10),	двена́дцат-ь	-ый
thirteen (3 + 10),	трина́дцат-ь	-ый

§ 54b. Nouns used with the numbers 2, 3, 4 stand in the genitive singular :

два стола́,	two tables
три окна́,	three windows
четы́ре кни́ги,	four books

Nouns with numbers above 4 stand in the genitive plural :

пять столо́в,   пять о́кон,   пять кни́г

If a number above 4 precedes the noun челове́к the genitive plural used is челове́к (not люде́й) : пять

---

[1] In ordinals only the last number is declined : thus in this example only the word тре́тий is declined according to all the cases.

человѣк, шесть человѣк, сѣмьдесят, etc., человѣк, but мнóго людéй.[1]

With 21, 31, etc., the noun stands in either nominative or accusative :

> двадцать однá кнѝга (if subject of sentence)
> двадцать однý кнѝгу (if object)

With 22, 23, 24, 32, 33, 34, etc., the noun stands in genitive singular :

> двáдцать два фýнта
> двáдцать три кѝнги
> двáдцать четы́ре дня

but : двáдцать пять дней

óба (both) requires genitive singular :

> óба брáта, both brothers
>
> (See § 137, note to sub-section 7.)

§ 55. *Declension of Numerals.*

(1) Ordinal numerals are declined as adjectives in all genders and cases, and they conform in gender, case, and number to that of the noun which they qualify. (See § 35.)

пéрвый дом (first house)   второй день (second day)
пéрвого дóма   второго дня
пéрвому дóму   второму дню   etc.

NOTE. трéтий, -ья, -ье, -ьи is declined as an adjective of species.   (See § 38.)

(2) Cardinal numerals are declined in accordance with their terminations, respectively as masculine, feminine or neuter, some as nouns and some with predominantly adjectival terminations in the oblique cases.

---

[1] *Nom. pl.* лю́ди, people.

	Singular			*Plural*
Nom.	одúн одн-ó	одн-á		одн-ú (some)
Gen.	одн-огó	одн-óй		одн-úх
Dat.	одн-омý	одн-óй		одн-úм·
Acc.	*N. or G.* одн-ó	одн-ý		*N. or G.*
Instr.	одн-úм	одн-óю [-óй]		одн-úми
Loc.	одн-óм	одн-óй		одн-úх

Nom.	два две	три	четы́ре
Gen.	двух	трёх	четырёх
Dat.	двум	трём	четырём
Acc.	*N. or G.*	*N. or G.*	*N. or G.*
Instr.	двумя́	тремя́	четырьмя́
Loc.	двух	трёх	четырёх

(3) 5-30 and 50-80 are declined as feminine nouns ending in ь. (See § 31) :

Nom.	пять	шесть	семь	вóсемь
Gen.	пятú	шестú	семú	восьмú
Dat.	пятú	шестú	семú	восьмú
Acc.	пять	шесть	семь	вóсемь
Instr.	пятью́	шестью́	семью́	восемью́
Loc.	пятú	шестú	семú	восьмú

NOTE. In cardinal numbers consisting of two parts (denominations), each part is declined in accordance with its own mode of declension :

двáдцать одúн	двáдцать два	трúдцать три
двадцатú одногó	двадцатú двух	тридцатú трёх
двадцатú одномý	двадцатú двум	тридцатú трём
etc.	etc.	etc.

(4) In the numerals 50-80 both parts are likewise declined as feminine nouns ending in ь, although пятьдесят, шестьдесят, сéмьдесят, вóсемьдесят do not terminate in ь :

Nom.	пятьдеся́т	шестьдеся́т
Gen.	пяти́десяти	шести́десяти
Dat.	пяти́десяти	шести́десяти
Acc.	пятьдеся́т	шестьдеся́т
Instr.	пятью́десятью	шестью́десятью
Loc.	пяти́десяти	шести́десяти

etc.

(5) соро́к has a in all oblique cases, except accusative :

Nom.	со́рок
Gen.	сорока́
Dat.	сорока́
Acc.	со́рок
Instr.	сорока́
Loc.	сорока́

сто and девяно́сто change the o into an a in all oblique cases of singular, except accusative :

сто	девяно́сто
ста	девяно́ста
ста	девяно́ста

сто, when used with the numbers 2-9, is declined as a neuter noun in the plural (joined in one word) :

Nom.	две́сти	три́ста	четы́реста	пятьсо́т
Gen.	двухсо́т	трёхсо́т	четырёхсо́т	пятисо́т
Dat.	двумста́м	трёмста́м	четырёмста́м	пятиста́м
Acc.	две́сти	три́ста	четы́реста	пятьсо́т
Instr.	двумяста́ми	тремяста́ми	четырьмяста́ми	пятьюста́ми
Loc.	двухста́х	трёхста́х	четырёхста́х	пятиста́х

(6) ты́сяча is declined as a feminine noun.
миллио́н is declined as a masculine noun.

	Masc. Neut.	Fem.
(7) Nom.	о́ба	о́бе
Gen.	обо́их	обе́их
Dat.	обо́им	обе́им
Acc.	N. or G.	N. or G.
Instr.	обо́ими	обе́ими
Loc.	обо́их	обе́их

NOTE. One oblique case only of óба is used in the singular—the genitive—in the expression :

обóего пóла, of both sexes

§ 55a. NOTE 1. Numerals, both ordinal and cardinal, precede the noun which they qualify :

пéрвый урóк, first lesson
два часá, two hours etc.

Ordinals occasionally follow the noun, but only in cases where special emphasis is desired.

If cardinals follow the noun, an approximate number is implied :

два дня, two days
дня два, about two days
три гóда, three years
гóда три, about three years

NOTE 2. When 2, 3, 4 qualify a noun which is preceded by an adjective, the adjective can stand either in the genitive plural or, occasionally, in the nominative plural (but not in the genitive singular, although the noun is in the genitive singular) :

два крéпких столá, two strong tables
два стáршие брáта, two eldest brothers

(The latter form is not frequently used.)

NOTE 3. In giving the year of some event, only the last member of the number is declined :

in the year 1923 в тысяча девятьсóт трéтьем годý

This rule applies to all ordinal numerals, where the last member only is declined.

Dates (in the meaning of : on a certain date) are usually given in the genitive :

on the 10th May 1923 десятого мáя тысяча девятьсóт двáдцать трéтьего гóда

But in the expression ' to-day is the 10th of May ' the nominative is used : сегодня десятое мая.

NOTE. The form of question when asking ' what is to-day's date ? ' is : какое сегодня число ? The answer implies : число (*neuter*).

§ 55b. *Collective (group) Numerals.*

In Russian there are collective (group) numerals up to ten, besides the cardinals. They are :

> двое, трое, четверо, пятеро, шестеро, семеро,
> восьмеро, девятеро, десятеро

They denote a collective completed group. Their declensions are :

Nom. двое	трое	четверо	пятеро шестеро
Gen. двоих	троих	четверых	семеро восьмеро
Dat. двоим	троим	четверым	девятеро десятеро
Acc. N. or G.	N. or G.	N. or G.	are declined as
Instr. двоими	троими	четверыми	четверо
Loc. двоих	троих	четверых	

NOTE 1. Collective numerals are used mainly with masculine nouns designating persons (also with the neuter noun, дети, children) :

> двое мужиков, two peasants
> трое детей,   three children

двое, трое, четверо are also employed with nouns (all genders) which are used only in the plural. (See § 33, sub-section (2).)

> двое ворот, two gates
> двое суток, two days and two nights

but :   пять ворот (not пятеро ворот)
> пять суток (not пятеро суток)

In all oblique cases the simple series of numerals is used :
> двух суток (not двоих суток)

D

When used with such articles as носки́ (socks), сапоги́ (boots), it means pairs :

дво́е носко́в, two *pairs* of socks

дво́е сапо́г,   two *pairs* of boots

Note 2.   While collective numerals can be used without a noun as a predicate complement :

нас бы́ло тро́е, there were three of us,

the simple series of cardinal numerals must always be accompanied by a noun :

нас бы́ло пять челове́к, де́сять челове́к   etc.

there were five, ten of us   etc.

§ 55c. *Fractional Numerals.*

The most in use are полови́на (half) and полтора́ [1] (one and a half). Полови́на is declined as a feminine noun in **a**; in полтора́ [1] the oblique cases have an inserted y after пол (except accusative), and the case-endings are **a** throughout :

Masculine and Neuter.

Nom.	полтора́ рубля́	полтора́ста
	(1½ roubles)	(150)
Gen.	полу́тора рубле́й	полу́тораста
Dat.	полу́тора рубля́м	полу́тораста
Acc.	полтора́ рубля́	полтора́ста
Instr.	полу́тора рубля́ми	полу́тораста
Loc.	полу́тора рубля́х	полу́тораста

Feminine.   *Masculine.*

Nom.	полторы́ страни́цы	полчаса́
	(1½ pages)	(half an hour)
Gen.	полу́торы страни́ц	получа́са
Dat.	полу́торе страни́цам	получа́су
Acc.	полторы́ страни́цы	полчаса́
Instr.	полу́торою страни́цами	получа́сом
Loc.	полу́торе страни́цах	получа́се

[1] полторы́, when used with feminine nouns.

	Masculine	*Feminine*
Nom.	по́лдень	по́лночь
	(noon)	(midnight)
Gen.	полу́дня	полу́ночи
Dat.	полу́дню	полу́ночи
Acc.	по́лдень	по́лночь
Instr.	полу́днем	полу́ночью
Loc.	{ полу́дне but по полу́дни = p.m. }	полу́ночи

Note. полбуты́лки (half a bottle) is declined as полторы́; полфу́нта (half a pound) is declined as полчаса́. As по́лдень, по́лночь are declined полдня́ (half a day), полно́чи (half a night).

5. Verbs

§ 56. *Active and Neuter Verbs.*

Russian verbs are divided into **active** and **neuter**, corresponding to the English **transitive** and **intransitive** verbs. Some Russian neuter verbs can be turned into active verbs by the use of a prefix :

жить, to live, but * нажи́ть,[1] to gain, to acquire
быть, to be, „ * забы́ть,[1] to forget

§ 56a. *Reflexive Verbs.*

Verbs, both transitive and intransitive, can be made reflexive by tacking on the reflexive pronoun-particle ся (the Slavonic form for себя́, oneself) after the inflexion ть of the infinitive. If the inflexion of the infinitive is ти́, ся is shortened into сь.

мыть, to wash мы́ться, to wash oneself
брить, to shave бри́ться, to shave oneself
одева́ть, to dress одева́ться, to dress oneself

Note. In the verbs ending in ся (or сь after a vowel), the ся or сь is retained in all the tenses and all the persons in conjugation.

[1] See note to § 60, p. 104.

A few verbs have a reflexive termination without being proper reflexive verbs or having any reflexive meaning :

ошибáться, to err   гордúться, to be proud
боя́ться,   to fear   нрáвиться, to please, to be liked
надéяться, to hope   смея́ться, to laugh

In modern Russian these verbs express no meaning without ся.

§ 56b. A number of verbs in the reflexive form are used only in impersonal sentences :

нрáвиться[1] —мне нрáвится,   it pleases me, I like
хотéться   —мне хóчется,   I should like, I want
спáться   —мне не спúтся,   I cannot sleep
нездорóвиться—мне нездорóвится,   I do not feel well
снúться   —мне снúтся [снúлось], I see [saw] in my
                                  dream (see § 122).

The termination ся is usually not accented. There are, however, a few exceptions when ся is accented in the past tense :

звался,   was called
брался⎫
взялся⎭ took up
начался́, began

Many verbs of the reflexive form in ся can be classed as verbs describing a more or less passive state, hence the tendency to use them for impersonal sentences in which the grammatical subject becomes an inverted object. The expressions in the above examples could all be transcribed (paraphrased) so as to turn the sentences into personal ones :

Impersonal Sentence	*Personal Sentence*	
мне нрáвится	я люблю́,	I like
мне хóчется	я хочу́,	I want
мне не спúтся	я не могу́ спать,	I cannot sleep
мне нездорóвится	я нездорóв,	I am unwell
мне снúтся [снúлось]	я ви́жу [ви́дел] сон,	I see [saw] a dream

[1] This verb can also be used in personal sentences.

But the psychological meaning (or purpose) of the impersonal sentence to express primarily a passive, vague, or not quite clearly defined state, would be defeated by turning an impersonal sentence into a personal one ; the latter would express too much individual and defined volition. This observation holds good in the case of nearly all Russian impersonal sentences. (See § 122.)

§ 56c. *Reciprocal Verbs.*

Some verbs of the reflexive form ending in ся, сь have a reciprocal meaning :

дра́ться	— мы дерёмся ⎱	we fight
би́ться	— мы бьёмся ⎰	
руга́ться	— они́ руга́ются,	they swear at each other
боро́ться	— они́ бо́рются,	they wrestle
целова́ться	— они́ целу́ются,	they kiss (one another)

Many of these reciprocal verbs are often used in a neuter sense, where no reciprocal meaning can be traced at all :

я борю́сь means : I struggle

я бью́сь   „   I fight (against hard circumstances)

NOTE. The particle ся is pronounced са ; тьcя is pronounced тca.

§ 56d. A few Russian verbs, both transitive and intransitive, can be used side by side with their reflexive forms, both verbs expressing almost the same meaning :

(a) стуча́ть,	to knock	стуча́ться,	to knock at the door
признава́ть,	to admit	признава́ться,	to confess
слу́шать,	to listen	слу́шаться,	to obey

In the above verbs the reflexive form accentuates the personal element of the performance.

   (*b*)   белéть   —   белéться,   to appear white
             чернéть   —   чернéться,   to appear black
             серéть   —   серéться,   to appear grey

In each of these examples the two verbs express the idea in equal degree. The reflexive form is, however, more frequently used.

But : (*c*)   *побелéть   means   to turn white
             *почернéть   ,,   to turn black
             *посерéть   ,,   to turn grey   etc.

These three verbs, and others of a similar meaning, are not used in a reflexive form.

§ 57. *Tenses of the Indicative Mood.*[1]

Russian verbs can have three tenses :

      1. The present.   2. The past.   3. The future.

The future tense can be either a compound one, formed with the help of the present form of the auxiliary verb быть (to be) and the infinitive of the principal verb in imperfective verbs, or it can be a simple future in perfective verbs which is expressed by the present form of the verb itself, but has a future meaning (see § 58) :

    писáть   (*imp.*)   я бýду писáть, I shall be writing
  *написáть (*perf.*)   я напишý,   I shall write

§ 58. *Aspects.*

Russian verbs have two main aspects :

      (1) **Imperfective** (verbs denoting an incomplete action or state).

      (2) **Perfective** (verbs denoting a completed action or state).

Verbs of imperfective aspect describe an action, or a state, which is still going on at whatever time (tense) we refer to it (and which is not completed at that time). Imperfective verbs have three tenses : present, past, and future.

---

[1] For the conditional and the subjunctive moods see §§ 106, 132.

Verbs of perfective aspect describe an action, or just the moment of its commencement, which is already completed, or will be completed, at whatever time (tense) we refer to the action or state. Verbs of this class have only two tenses : past and future (simple).[1]

To the imperfective class also belong verbs which describe an action or a state which took place more than once in the past. These verbs are usually referred to as **iterative**. They are only used in the past tense :

пи́сывал,   used to write

гова́ривал, used to say

ха́живал,   used to go, etc.   (See § 62.)

§ 59. Every verb is capable of expressing many ideas of action or state.

1. (*a*) Repetition, or (*b*) continuity, of action or state :

чита́ть,   to read

писа́ть,   to write

спать,   to sleep

2. Beginning of action or state :

*нача́ть,   to begin

*запе́ть,   to start singing

3. Completion (termination) of action or state :

*сде́лать, to make (to have made)

*спеть,   to sing something (a single song)

4. Performance of action on a single occasion :

*ду́нуть, to blow once

*тро́нуть, to touch once

5. Momentary character of action :

*сверкну́ть, to flash

The first two ideas : repetition and continuity (No. 1), are conveyed by the aspect of the verb which denotes incomplete (unfinished) action or state, namely, by the **imperfective aspect**.

---

[1] The present *form* of their conjugation serves as the future tense.

The other ideas (Nos. 2, 3, 4, 5) are conveyed by the aspect of the verb which denotes completed action or state; namely, by the **perfective aspect**.

It follows that when the moment of inception, or termination, of the action or state is not uppermost in our mind, the aspect to be used is the imperfective, which gives merely the general idea of the action or state. The perfective aspect is used when the question of the beginning, or completion, of an action or state comes into play. The perfective is also used when the action is performed on a single occasion, or is only of a momentary character.

> он прие́хал [пришёл] вчера́, he arrived [came] yesterday (and remained)—**perfective**;
>
> он приезжа́л [приходи́л], he came (but did not stay and went back; or, he came more than once)—**imperfective**; etc.

§ 60. *Formation of Perfective Verbs.*

The student is advised to learn to recognize the structure of the infinitive of verbs. This will help him to discriminate between the aspects. He will learn by observation that the infinitive of derivative verbs usually consists of a stem (infinitive without the termination ть, ти) which comprises root, and often a suffix, and some prepositional prefix. Gradually he will also learn to distinguish the meaning of the prepositional prefixes and the changes which they effect in the meaning of the verb itself.

(*Note.—All perfective verbs in this book are marked *.*)

Perfective Verbs.

(1) Many simple (primary) imperfective verbs can be turned into perfectives by the use of a prepositional prefix:

е́хать,	to go on a journey
*по-е́хать,	to start on a journey
*при-е́хать,	to arrive
*пере-е́хать,	to travel across
*у-е́хать,	to go away etc.

Here the prefixes, besides giving the verbs a perfective meaning, also impart an idea of direction.

The function of certain prepositional prefixes is merely to lend to the imperfective verb the character of a perfective, and thus to give its present form a future meaning, without altering it fundamentally. To such prefixes belong по, на, с, у. But these and many other prepositional prefixes, besides turning the imperfective verb into a perfective, can also give it a modified meaning and direction, in accordance with the basic meaning of the directing prefix. The student will learn from experience and observation the exact changes in the meaning of the verb which are effected by various prepositional prefixes:

дѣлать,	to do, to make	(*imperfective*)
*с-дѣлать,	to do, to make	
*пере-дѣлать,	to alter	
*при-дѣлать,	to attach, to fix	
*на-дѣлать,	to make in a quantity	(*perfective*)
*за-дѣлать,	to stop up, block up	
*под-дѣлать,	to forge	

(See detailed statement about prefixes in § 63.)

(2) Although the greater number of primary verbs are of the imperfective aspect, there are a few primary verbs which are of the perfective aspect:

		The corresponding imperfective verbs are:
*бро́сить,	to throw	броса́ть
*ко́нчить,	to finish	конча́ть
*стать,	to become	станови́ться
*пасть [пад-ть],	to fall	па́дать
*пусти́ть,	to let (go)	пуска́ть
*лечь [лег-ть],	to lie down	ложи́ться
*сесть [сед-ть],	to sit down	сади́ться
*взять,[1]	to take	брать
*хвати́ть,	to snatch, to seize	хвата́ть

[1] This is a derivative verb. (See § 64, 7.)

D *

(3) Many perfective verbs are formed from imperfective verbs by changing the accented suffixes **á**, **я́**, **вá** of the latter into **и**, **е**, **ну**, or by shifting the accent :

пленя́ть,	to captivate	*плени́ть
пускáть,	to let (go)	*пусти́ть
прощáть,	to forgive	*прости́ть
давáть,	to give	*дать
покупáть,	to buy	*купи́ть
пáдать,	to fall	*пасть [*у-]
стоя́ть,	to stand	*стать
девáть,	to put	*деть
надевáть,	to put on	*надéть
избегáть,	to avoid	*избéгнуть
дуть,	to blow	*ду́нуть
кричáть,	to shout, to cry	*кри́кнуть
кидáть,	to throw	*ки́нуть
глядéть,	to glance	*гля́нуть
дви́гать,	to move	*дви́нуть
трóгать,	to touch	*трóнуть

NOTE 1. The perfective verbs ending in **нуть** signify that the action is only performed once. (See § 79 (*b*).)

NOTE 2. A number of verbs ending in **нуть** have an inchoative character (which is quite distinct from the meaning of one performance only). These are of the imperfective aspect and can be turned into perfectives by a prefix. (See § 79 (*a*).)

Perfective

тону́ть,	to be drowning	*утону́ть,	to be drowned
ги́бнуть,	to be perishing	*ноги́бнуть,	to perish
гáснуть,	to be extinguished	*погáснуть,	to become extinguished
мёрзнуть,	to be freezing	*замёрзнуть,	to get frozen
сóхнуть,	to turn dry	*засóхнуть,	to become dry
тяну́ть,	to draw, to drag	*дотяну́ть,	to draw to the end etc.

NOTE 3. Some imperfective verbs have their perfective counterpart in verbs of a different root :

ловить,	to catch	*поймать	
говорить,	to speak	*сказать,	to say
брать,	to take	*взять	
класть,	to put	*положить	
бить,	to beat	*ударить,	to strike
	(besides	*побить,	to give a beating)

§ 60a. A few verbs have both an imperfective and a perfective meaning (double aspect) :

велеть,	to bid	я велю,	I bid, I shall bid
казнить,	to execute	он казнит,	he executes, he will execute
ранить,	to wound	он ранит,	he wounds, he will wound

§ 60b. A few verbs have no imperfective aspect and are used in the perfective only :

*опомниться,	to come to oneself again, to recover
*очнуться,	to come back to consciousness
*погодить,	to wait
*поймать,	to catch
*сжалиться,	to take (have) pity

§ 60c. A number of verbs have no perfective aspect, and are only used in the imperfective. They are mainly neuter verbs which describe a general state :

зависеть (от + gen.),	to depend on
недомогать,	to be ailing
нуждаться (в + loc.),	to be in need (of)
обладать (instr.),	to be in possession of
обонять,	to smell
опасаться (gen.),	to fear, to be apprehensive (of)
отсутствовать,	to be absent
повиноваться (dat.),	to obey
подражать (dat.),	to imitate

предвѝдеть,	to foresee
припадлежа́ть (*dat.*),	to belong
прису́тствовать,	to be present
пресле́довать (*acc.*),	to persecute
сожале́ть (о + *loc.*),	to regret
содержа́ть,	to keep, maintain
состоя́ть $\begin{cases}(\text{из} + gen.) \\ (\text{при} + loc.)\end{cases}$	to consist of; to be (in the capacity of)
сто́ить,	to cost
уча́ствовать (в + *loc.*),	to participate
etc.	

§ 61. *Definite and Indefinite Verbs.*

In Russian nearly all verbs can imply both a definite (applied) meaning and an indefinite (general) meaning:

я учу́ can mean 'I teach now' and 'I teach habitually.'

However, the distinction between these two meanings is often expressed by two different verbs, or by the same verb in a different form (mostly in verbs conveying the idea of movement):

лета́ть,	to fly habitually
лете́ть,	to fly now on a definite occasion and in a definite direction
пти́ца лета́ет,	a bird flies (habitually)
челове́к хо́дит,	a man goes (,,), walks
ры́ба пла́вает,	a fish swims (,,)
пти́ца лети́т,	the bird flies (over the roof)
челове́к идёт,	the man goes (down the street)
ры́ба плывёт,	the fish swims (towards the boat)

Note 1. The definite verbs of this class are mostly simple (primary) verbs; the indefinite are derivatives (usually with the insertion of a suffix).

Note 2. Verbs in the indefinite class are always of the imperfective aspect, and their aspect is not altered even when a prepositional prefix is added for direction.

Definite verbs, on the other hand, become perfective by the addition of a prepositional prefix. (See § 63.)

Imperfective	*Perfective*
прилетáть, to come flying	*прилетéть
приходи́ть, to come (here)	*придти́
переноси́ть, to carry across ; to suffer	*перенести́

§ 61a. The most frequently used verbs, of both the indefinite and definite class, are :

Indefinite		*Definite*
видáть,	to see	ви́деть
слыхáть,	to hear	слы́шать
бéгать,	to run	бежáть
гоня́ть,	to drive	гнать
сажáть,	to plant	сади́ть
носи́ть,	to carry ; to wear	нести́
ходи́ть,	to go, to walk	итти́ [идти́]
води́ть,	to lead	вести́
вози́ть,	to cart	везти́
летáть,	to fly	летéть
плáвать,	to swim	плыть
éздить,	to travel	éхать

NOTE 1. The respective shade of meaning of the indefinite and definite forms of a Russian verb can be approximately conveyed in English as :

I do ⎫ (*indefinite*)   I am doing ⎫ (*definite*)
I read ⎭   I am reading ⎭

NOTE 2. видáть, слыхáть are never used ·in the present tense. They are used in the past only in an iterative sense :

не видáл,	не слыхáл
видáл,	слыхáл (See § 62.)

NOTE 3. The indefinite verbs бѣгать, сажáть, плáвать, ѣздить are not used for the formation of new imperfectives with a directional prefix; their iterative forms бѣгáть, сáживать, плывáть, езжáть take their place in such cases. (See §§ 63-64.)

§ 62. *Iterative Verbs.* (*See* § 58.)

The **imperfective-iterative** verbs are usually formed from imperfective verbs by changing the vowel of the stem in the infinitive (before ть) into ыва, ива, ва, or an accented á or я́.

быть,	to be	{бывáть,	
		{бывáл [бывáло], used to be [used to]	
дѣлать,	to do	{дѣлывать,	
		{дѣлывал,	used to do
гулять,	to stroll;	{гýливать,	
	to be idle	{гýливал	{used to stroll;
			{used to be idle
ходить,	to go	{хáживать,	
		{хáживал,	used to go
сидѣть,	to sit	{сúживать,	
		{сúживал,	used to sit
знать,	to know	{знавáть,	
		{знавáл, .	used to know
ѣхать,	to travel	{езжáть,	
		{езжáл,	used to travel
есть, [ѣд-ть]	to eat	{ѣдáть,	
		{ѣдáл,	used to eat
печь, [пек-ть]	to bake	{пекáть,	
		{пекáл,	used to bake
топúть,	to heat	{тáпливать,	
		{тáпливал,	used to heat

NOTE 1. з, д of the imperfective are commuted into ж in the iterative ; с is commuted into ш ; т is commuted into ч or щ.

Often an л is inserted for euphony if the stem of the imperfective ends in a labial consonant.

о of the root is changed into а.

NOTE 2. Iterative verbs can be turned into imperfectives by prefixing a prepositional prefix, often with the meaning of the newly formed verb slightly altered. (See §§ 63-64.)

§ 63. *Prepositional Prefixes which frequently modify or alter the original meaning of an Imperfective Verb to which they are attached, besides turning it into a Perfective one.* (*See § 60.*)

The meaning and direction which prepositional prefixes impart to verbs to which they are attached are set out below. Nearly all the newly formed perfective verbs can be turned again into imperfectives, with the identical modified meaning, by tacking on the same prepositional prefix to the iterative (or indefinite) form of each verb (see §§ 61-62). These modified imperfectives are given in the right-hand column.

NOTE 1. The perfective verbs are shown by an asterisk (*).

NOTE 2. The first and second person singular and third person plural are given after each infinitive. The form of the second person singular indicates the class of conjugation to which the verb belongs, and also shows whether the accent is fixed or not. For further guidance see § 70 for the formation of the present tense, and § 72 for the accent.

For the formation of the past tense see § 83 ; for the accent in the past tense see § 84 ; for the formation of the imperative see § 82.

в- [во-] = *motion inside :*

ит-ти́, to go	*вой-ти́, to enter	вход-и́ть
[ид-ти́]	вой-ду́, -дёшь, -ду́т	вхож-у́, вход-ишь
		вхо́д-ят
éх-ать, to travel,	*въе́х-ать, to drive in,	въезжá-ть
to drive	to enter, by driving	
	въе́д-у, въе́д-ешь	-ю, -ешь
	въе́д-ут	-ют
беж-áть, to run	*вбеж-áть, to run in	вбегá-ть
бег-у́, беж-и́шь	вбег-у́, вбеж-и́шь	-ю, -ешь
бег-у́т	вбег-у́т	-ют

вз- [взо-, воз-] = *motion upwards :*

ит-ти́	*взой-ти́, to rise (sun),	всход-и́ть
	to go up	
	взойд-у́, взойд-ёшь	всхож-у́, всхо́д-ишь
	взойд-у́т	всхо́д-ят

NOTE.   з changes into с before a voiceless consonant : встать (to get up) instead of взстать (с is then absorbed).

вы- = *motion from inside :*

ит-ти́	*вы́й-ти,[1] to get out, to	выход-и́ть
	go out	
	вы́д-у (й is dropped)	выхож-у́
	вы́д-ешь, вы́д-ут	выхо́д-ишь, выхо́д-ят
éх-ать	*вы́ех-ать, to drive out	выезжá-ть
	вы́ед-у, вы́ед-ешь	-ю, -ешь
	вы́ед-ут	-ют
беж-áть	*вы́беж-ать, to run out	выбегá-ть
	вы́бег-у, вы́беж-ишь	-ю, -ешь
	вы́бег-ут	-ют

до- = *completion (to a finish) :*

ит-ти́	*дой-ти́, to go as far	доход-и́ть
	дойд-у́, дойд-ёшь	дохож-у́, дохо́д-ишь
	дойд-у́т	дохо́д-ят
éх-ать	*доéх-ать, to drive as far	доезжá-ть
	*доéд-у, доéд-ешь	-ю, -ешь
	доéд-ут	-ют
беж-áть	*добеж-áть, to run as far	добегá-ть
	добег-у́, добеж-и́шь	-ю, -ешь
	добег-у́т	-ют

[1] вы always takes the stress-accent in perfective verbs, but not in imperfectives.

за- *has mostly a meaning of starting, also of turning in :*

ит-ти́	*зай-ти́, to look in ; to set (sun)	заход-и́ть
	зайд-у́, зайд-ёшь	захож-у́, захо́д-ишь
	зайд-у́т	захо́д-ят
ех-ать	*зае́х-ать, to look in (turn in) while driving	заезжа́-ть
	зае́д-у, зае́д-ешь	-ю, -ешь
	зае́д-ут	-ют
беж-а́ть	*забеж-а́ть, to run in	забега́-ть
	забег-у́, забеж-и́шь	-ю, -ешь
	забег-у́т	-ют

на- = 1. *do in quantities* (mostly with transitive verbs) ;
    = 2. *have enough* (mostly with reflexive verbs) ;
    = 3. *get close to an object* (almost step on it) ;
    = 4. *put on, or on top :*

1. бр-ать, to take	*набр-а́ть, to get a quantity	набира́-ть
бер-у́, бер-ёшь	набер-у́, набер-ешь	-ю, -ешь
бер-у́т	набер-у́т	-ют
2. пи-ть, to drink	*напи́-ться, to drink enough; to get drunk	напива́-ться
пь-ю, пь-ёшь	напь-ю́сь, напь-ёшься	-юсь, -ешься
пь-ют	напь-ю́тся	-ются
3. ит-ти́	*най-ти́, to come upon ; to find	наход-и́ть
пайд-у́, пайд-ёшь	нахож-у́, нахо́д-ишь
найд-у́т	нахо́д-ят
4. кры-ть, to cover	*накры́-ть, to cover up ; to cover over	накрыва́-ть
кро́-ю, кро́-ешь	накро́-ю, накро́-ешь	-ю, -ешь
кро́-ют	пакро́-ют	-ют

о- [об-, обо-] = *motion about, around :*

ит-ти́	*обой-ти́, to go round	обход-и́ть
	обойд-у́, обойд-ёшь	обхож-у́, обхо́д-ишь
	обойд-у́т	обхо́д-ят

от- [ото-] = *motion away from :*

ит-ти́	*отой-ти́, to go, move away	отход-и́ть
	-д-у́, -д-ёшь	отхож-у́, отхо́д-ишь
	-д-у́т	отхо́д-ят

пере- = 1. *motion across ;*
    = 2. *repetition ;*
    = 3. *doing over again :*

1. éх-ать	*переéх-ать, to drive across, over	переезжá-ть
	переéд-у, переéд-ешь	-ю, -ешь
	переéд-ут	-ют
2. читá-ть	*перечитá-ть, to read over again, anew	перечйтыва-ть
-ю, -ешь	-ю, -ешь	-ю, -ешь
-ют	-ют	-ют
3. дéла-ть, to do	*передéла-ть, to alter	передéлыва-ть
-ю, -ешь	-ю, -ешь	-ю, -ешь
-ют	-ют	-ют

по- 1. *denotes completion of action ;*
   2. *denotes action or state of short duration :*

1. ес-ть, to eat	*поéс-ть, to have a meal	поедá-ть, to be devouring
ем, ешь, ест	поéм, поéшь, поéст	-ю, -ешь
ед-ŭм, ед-йте	поед-ŭм, поед-йте	-ют
ед-я́т	поед-я́т	
2. говор-ŭть, to talk, to speak	*поговор-ŭть, to have a chat	поговáрива-ть, to go on talking
-ю́, -ŭшь	-ю́, -ŭшь	-ю, -ешь
-я́т	-я́т	-ют

под- 1. *denotes motion under, up to ;*
    2. *gives the meaning of doing slightly ;*
    3. *denotes subterfuge ;*
    4. *gives idea of preliminary action :*

1. éх-ать	*подъéх-ать, to drive up	подъезжá-ть
	подъéд-у, подъéд-ешь	-ю, -ешь
	подъéд-ут	-ют
2. крáс-ить, to paint	*подкрáс-ить, to touch up, to paint a little	подкрáшива-ть
крáш-у	подкрáш-у	-ю
крáс-ишь	подкрáс-ишь	-ешь
крáс-ят	подкрáс-ят	-ют
3. смотр-éть, to look	*подсмотр-éть, to espy	подсмáтрива-ть
смотр-ю́	подсмотр-ю́	-ю
смóтр-ишь	подсмóтр-ишь	-ешь
смóтр-ят	подсмóтр-ят	-ют

дѣла-ть, to do	*поддѣла-ть, to forge	поддѣлыва-ть
-ю, -ешь	-ю, -ешь	-ю, -ешь
-ют	-ют	-ют
4. готóв-ить, to prepare	*подготóв-ить, to coach, to prepare	подготовля́-ть
готóвл-ю	подготóвл-ю	-ю
готóв-ишь	подготóв-ишь	-ешь
готóв-ят	подготóв-ят	-ют

при- *denotes :* 1. *arrival ;* 2. *fixing, attaching :* .

1. ит-ти́	*прий-ти́, to come	приход-и́ть
	прид-у́, прид-ёшь	прихож-у́, прихóд-ишь
	прид-у́т (й is dropped)	прихóд-ят
ѣхать	*приѣх-ать, to arrive	приезжá-ть
	приѣд-у, приѣд-ешь	-ю, -ешь
	приѣд-ут	-ют
2. дѣла-ть	*придѣла-ть, to fix, attach	придѣлыва-ть
-ю, -ешь	-ю, -ешь	-ю, -ешь
-ют	-ют	-ют

про- *denotes :* 1. *action through ;* 2. *motion through ;*
3. *covering a certain unit of time or space :*

1. би-ть, to beat	*проби́-ть, to beat through	пробивáт-ть
бь-ю, бь-ёшь	пробь-ю́, пробь-ёшь	-ю, -ешь
бь-ют	пробь-ю́т	-ют
2.⎫ ит-ти́	*прой-ти́, to go through ;	проход-и́ть
3.⎭	to go a certain distance	

раз- *denotes :* 1. *division ;* 2. *dispersion ;*
3. *highest point of action or state :*

1. би-ть, to beat	*разби́-ть, to beat asunder, to break up, to smash	разбивá-ть
	разобь-ю́, разобь-ёшь	-ю, -ешь
	разобь-ю́т	-ют
2. ит-ти́, to go	*разой-ти́сь, to disperse, to separate	расход-и́ться
	разойд-у́сь	расхож-у́сь
	разойд-ёшься	расхóд-ишься
	разойд-у́тся	расхóд-ятся
3. тá-ять, to melt (snow, ice)	*растá-ять, to melt away	растáива-ть
-ю, -ешь, -ют	-ю, -ешь, -ют	-ю, -ешь, -ют

c- *denotes :* 1. *moving away (often sideways) ;*
             2. *coming together* (in reflexive verbs) *;*
             3. *completion of action :*

1. двйга-ть, to move	*сдвйп-уть, to shift	сдвигá-ть
-ю, -ешь, -ют	-у, -ешь, -ут	-ю, -ешь, -ют
2. ит-тй	*сой-тйсь, to come together	сход-йться
	сойд-ýсь, сойд-ёшься	схож-ýсь, схóд-ишься
	сойд-ýтся	схóд-ятся

NOTE.   сходйть means : just to go once.

3. жеч-ь, to burn	*сжечь, to burn up	сжигá-ть
[жег-ть]	сожг-ý, сожж-ёшь	-ю, -ешь
	сожг-ýт	-ют

y- *means mostly : away into distance ; disappearance :*

ит-тй	*уйтй, to go away	уходйть
бежáть	*убежáть, to run away	убегáть
éхать	*уéхать, to go away, on a journey	уезжáть

NOTE 1.   The prepositional prefixes вз [воз], раз, change into вс [вос], рас if they are tacked on to verbs beginning with a voiceless consonant :

       всходйть, to come up, to rise
    *растáять, to melt away

NOTE 2.   Besides the prepositional prefixes enumerated above there are a few others, such as: из, низ, без, пред, denoting roughly : out, down, without, before. The student is advised to verify the exact modified meaning of any compound verb by consulting the dictionary, even if he is clear about the meaning of the parent verb and of the directional meaning of the prepositional prefix.

NOTE 3.   If a prepositional prefix ending in a consonant is attached to a verb beginning with the soft vowels я, ю, е, a ъ (hard sign) is inserted for euphony. The soft и is usually turned into ы.

NOTE 4. A modified directional meaning is imparted by prepositional prefixes when they are attached to nouns derived from verbs :

вход,	entry
ухо́д,	departure
восхо́д,	rise (sunrise)
захо́д,	setting (of the sun)
прихо́д,	arrival ; income
расхо́д,	expenditure
дохо́д,	income
прохо́д,	passage
нахо́дка,	find
обхо́д,	roundabout way
отхо́д,	departure (of train)
отъе́зд,	departure (of a person)
перехо́д,	transition
перево́д,	translation
схо́дка,	meeting
сход,	meeting, descent
etc.	

§ 64. Below is a list of a few main groups of verbs in frequent use which receive a modified, and often different, meaning when prefixed by a prepositional prefix. In the list are set out :

(1) The original (parent) verb.

(2) The derivative perfective, through the addition of the prepositional prefix, with its modified meaning.

(3) The modified perfective turned imperfective again through the addition of an iterative suffix. (See §§ 61-62.)

It will be seen that not in all cases does the same prepositional prefix convey to the derivative verbs the identical meaning and direction.

NOTE.   In the conjugation patterns the 1st and 2nd person singular and 3rd person plural are given.

1. (a) говори́ть — -каза́ть group.

говор-и́ть	*сказ-а́ть	ска́зыва-ть
to speak	to tell	to say

Conjugation pattern.

-ю, -и́шь, -я́т	скаж-у́	-ю
	ска́ж-ешь	-ешь
	ска́ж-ут	-ют

Imperative.

-й, -йте	скажи́ [-те]	-й [-йте]

Past.   -л, -ла, -ло, -ли

Accent of past tense is on the same syllable as in the infinitive.

*вы́каз-ать, to show	выка́зыва-ть
*доказ-а́ть, to prove	дока́зыва-ть (*dat.*)
*заказ-а́ть, to order	зака́зыва-ть (у + *gen.*)
*наказ-а́ть, to punish	нака́зыва-ть
*оказ-а́ть, to render	ока́зыва-ть (*dat.*)
*оказ-а́ться, to turn out	ока́зыва-ться (*instr.*)
*отказ-а́ть, to refuse	отка́зыва-ть (*dat.*)
*отказ-а́ться (*neuter*), to refuse	отка́зыва-ться (от + *gen.*)
*переcказ-а́ть, to repeat	переcка́зыва-ть
*подсказ-а́ть, to prompt	подска́зыва-ть (*dat.*)
*показ-а́ть, to show	пока́зыва-ть (*dat.*)
*приказ-а́ть, to give an order	прика́зыва-ть (*dat.*)
*расска-за́ть, to relate, to tell	расска́зыва-ть (*dat.*)
*указ-а́ть, to indicate	ука́зыва-ть (*dat.*)

(b) говори́ть — гова́ривать group.

*вы́говор-ить, to reserve for oneself; to utter	выгова́рива-ть (себе́ + *acc.*)
	-ю, -ешь, -ют
*договор-и́ть, to finish talking	догова́рива-ть
*договор-и́ться, to come to an agreement	догова́рива-ться (о + *loc.*)
*заговор-и́ть, to begin to speak	загова́рива-ть
*наговор-и́ть, to slander	наговá́рива-ть

*отговор-и́ть, to dissuade	отгова́рива-ть
*переговор-и́ть, to talk over	перегова́рива-ть (о, об + *loc.*)
*поговор-и́ть, to have a talk	(no new imperfective form)
*подговор-и́ть, to incite, to induce	подгова́рива-ть
*приговор-и́ть, to condemn, to sentence	пригова́рива-ть
*уговор-и́ть, to persuade, to induce	угова́рива ть

NOTE. All the perfective forms in this group are conjugated as говор-и́ть — сказ-а́ть. All the imperfective forms are conjugated as говáр-ива-ть — скáзыва-ть. The imperfectives have a fixed accent.

2. да-вá-ть — да-ть group (to give) (*dat.* + *acc.*).

да-вá-ть   *дать

Conjugation pattern.

да-ю́	дам	дад-и́м
да-ёшь	дашь	дад-и́те
да-ю́т	даст	дад-у́т

Imperative. давáй, -те   дá-й, -те

*вы́да-ть, to issue, to give out	выд-ав-áть
*задá-ть, to set (a task or question, etc.)	зад-ав-áть
*отдá-ть, to return ; to give away	отд-ав-áть
*передá-ть, to hand over, to pass on, to tell	перед-ав-áть
*подá-ть, to hand, to serve	под-ав-áть
*придá-ть, to add, to attach	прид-ав-áть
*продá-ть, to sell	прод-ав-áть
*раздá-ть, to distribute	разд-ав-áть
*сдá-ть, to hand in	сд-ав-áть

NOTE 1. All the perfective forms in this group are conjugated as да-ть ; all the imperfective forms are conjugated as да-вá-ть. The suffix ва of the imperfective is dropped in the conjugation of the present tense. The accent is shifted to the personal terminations.

Note 2. The accent in the past of the perfectives is shifted to the last syllable in the feminine, but goes back to the prefix in the masculine, neuter, and plural :

задал,	-á, -о, -и	придал, -á, -о, -и
óтдал,	-á, -о, -и	прóдал, -á, -о, -и
пéредал,	-á, -о, -и	рóздал, -á, -о, -и [1]
пóдал,	-á, -о, -и	

3. бр-ать — взя-ть group (to take).

бр-ать	*взя-ть	*Iterative*
Conjugation pattern.		бирá-ть
бер-ý	возьм-ý	бирá-ю
бер-ёшь	возьм-ёшь	бирá-ешь
бер-ýт	возьм-ýт	бирá-ют
Imperative. бери, -те	возьми, -те	(not frequently used, except for forming imperfective forms)

*выбр-ать, to select	выбирá-ть
*забр-áть, to take away	забирá-ть
*набр-áть, to gather	набирá-ть
*отобр-áть,[2] to take away	отбирá-ть
*подобр-áть,[2] to pick up	подбирá-ть
*прибр-áть, to tidy up	прибирá-ть
*разобр-áть,[2] to sort out, to take to pieces	разбирá-ть
*собр-áть, to collect, to gather	собирá-ть
*убр-áть, to clear away	убирá-ть

Note. All perfective forms are conjugated as брать ; all imperfective as бирáть. The accent in the past of the perfectives is shifted to the last syllable in the feminine : убрáл, убралá, убрáло, убрáли.

4. -ста-вá-ть — ста-ть group (to become).

Note. -ставáть has no independent meaning of its own.

Conjugation pattern.

-ставáть	*стать
-ста-ю, -ста-ёшь, -ста-ют	стáн-у, стáн-ешь, стáн-ут
Imperative. -ставáй, -те	стáнь, -те
Past. -л, -ла, -ло, -ли	

Accent of past tense is on the same syllable as in the infinitive.

[1] Masculine, neuter, and plural change a of prefix into ó.

[2] The euphonic o of the prefix is dropped in the present form : отберý, подберý, etc.

*встá-ть, to get up	встá-вá-ть
*достá-ть, to get, to obtain	достá-вá-ть
*застá-ть, to find (a person), to meet with	застá-вá-ть
*настá-ть, to approach, to come (seasons, time)	настá-вá-ть
*остá-ться, to remain, to stay	остá-вá-ться
*отстá-ть, to get behind	отстá-вá-ть (*absolute*, or от + *gen.*)
*перестá-ть, to cease	перестá-вá-ть
*пристá-ть, to attach oneself	пристá-вá-ть (к + *dat.*)
*расстá-ться, to part	расстá-вá-ться (с + *instr.*)
*устá-ть, to get tired	устá-вá-ть

NOTE. All the perfective forms in this group are conjugated as стать; all the imperfectives as -ставáть. The suffix вa of the imperfective is dropped in the present tense, and the accent goes over to the personal terminations. In the past tense the suffix вa is not dropped.

5. бывá-ть — бы-ть group (to be).

Conjugation pattern.

бывáть	быть
бывá-ю, бывá-ешь, бывá-ют	бýд-у, бýд-ешь, бýд-ут
Imperative. бывáй, -те	бýдь, -те

*доб-ы́ть, to obtain, to procure	добывá-ть
*заб-ы́ть, to forget	забывá-ть
*поб-ы́ть, to stay a short time	побывá-ть
*приб-ы́ть, to arrive	прибывá-ть
*проб-ы́ть, to stay some definite time	пробывá-ть
*сб-ы́ть, to dispose of	сбывá-ть

NOTE. All the perfectives in this group are conjugated as быть; all the imperfectives as бывáть. The accent in the past of the perfectives is shifted to the last syllable in the feminine, but goes to the prefix in the masculine, neuter, and plural in:

добы́ть,   дóбыл,   -á, -о, -и
побы́ть,   пóбыл,   -á, -о, -и
прибы́ть, прúбыл, -á, -о, -и
пробы́ть, прóбыл, -á, -о, -и

6. дева́-ть — де-ть group (to put).

Conjugation pattern.

дева́ть	*деть
дева́-ю, дева́-ешь, дева́-ют	де́н-у, де́н-ешь, де́н-ут
Imper. дева́й, -те	де́нь, -те
Past. дева́л, -а, -о, -и	де́л, -а, -о, -и

*де́-ться, to put (get) oneself to take refuge	дева́-ться
*наде́-ть, to put on	надева́-ть
*оде́-ться, to dress oneself	одева́-ться
*разде́-ться, to undress oneself	раздева́-ться
*переоде́-ться, to change (clothes)	переодева́-ться

NOTE 1. The reflexive particle ся or сь is tacked on immediately after the personal termination in conjugation.

NOTE 2. The suffix ва in the imperfective verbs of groups 5 and 6 is *not* dropped in the conjugation of the present tense.

NOTE 3. All the perfectives in this group are conjugated as деть ; all the imperfectives as дева́ть.

7. -има́ть — -ять group (to take).

In verbs of this group the suffixes им and я are derived from a Slavonic root which had a nasal element of м. Prepositional prefixes take a euphonic н for the formation of derivatives, with the exception of взять (see § 73*f*), in the infinitive. -има́ть and -ять have no independent meaning in modern Russian.

*взя-ть (see Group 3)	взима́-ть, to collect (taxes, etc.)
Past. взял, взяла́, -о, -и	

*доня́-ть, to vex, to plague	донима́-ть
дойм-у́, дойм-ёшь, дойм-у́т	-ю, -ешь, -ют
Imper. дойми́, -те	-й, -йте
Past. до́нял, доняла́, до́няло, до́няли	

*заня́-ть, to occupy ; to borrow	занима́-ть
займ-у́, займ-ёшь, займ-у́т	-ю, -ешь, -ют
Imper. займи́, -те	-й, -йте
Past. за́нял, заняла́, за́няло, за́няли	

*наня́-ть, to hire   нанима́-ть
  найм-у́, найм-ёшь, найм-у́т   -ю, -ешь, -ют
Imper. найми́, -те   -й, -йте
Past. на́нял, наняла́, на́няло, на́няли

*обня́-ть, to embrace   обнима́-ть
  обним-у́, обни́м-ешь, обни́м-ут   -ю, -ешь, -ют
Imper. обними́, -те   -й, -йте
Past. о́бнял, обняла́, о́бняло, о́бняли

*отня́-ть, to take away   отнима́-ть (*acc.* + у, or
                                           от + *gen.*)
  отним-у́, отни́м-ешь, отни́м-ут   -ю, -ешь, -ют
Imper. отними́, -те   -й, -йте
Past. о́тнял, отняла́, о́тняло, о́тняли

*переня́-ть, to intercept ; to imitate   перенима́-ть (*acc.* + у
                                           + *gen.*)
  перейм-у́, перейм-ёшь, перейм-у́т   -ю, -ешь, -ют
Imper. перейми́, -те   -й, -йте
Past. пе́ренял, переняла́, пе́реняло, -ли

*подня́-ть, to raise, to lift   поднима́-ть
  подним-у́, подни́м-ешь, подни́м-ут   -ю, -ешь, -ют
Imper. подними́, -те   -й, -йте
Past. по́днял, подняла́, по́дняло, -ли

*поня́ть, to grasp, to understand   понима́-ть
  пойм-у́, пойм-ёшь, пойм-у́т   -ю, -ешь, -ют
Imper. пойми́, -те   -й, -йте
Past. по́нял, поняла́, по́няло, -ли

*приня́-ть, to receive, to accept   принима́-ть
*приня́-ться, to set oneself to   принима́-ться (за + *acc.*)
  прим-у́ (сь), при́м-ешь (ся)   -ю, -ешь (сь, ся)
  при́м-ут (ся)   -ют (ся)
Imper. прими́, -те   -й, -йте (сь)
Past. при́нял, приняла́, при́няло, -ли [ся, ась, ось, ись]

*сня-ть, to take off   снима́-ть (*acc.* + с + *gen.*)
  сним-у́, сни́м-ешь, сни́м-ут   -ю, -ешь, -ют
Imper. сними́, -те   -й, -йте
Past. спял, сняла́, сня́ло, -ли

*сня-ться, to take one's photograph   снима́-ться
    сним-у́сь, сним-ешься, сним-утс   -юсь, -ешься, -ются
Imper. сним-и́сь, сним-и́тесь   -йся, -йтесь
Past. сня́лся, сня́лась, сня́лись

*уня́-ть, to restrain, to calm   унима́-ть (*acc.*)
    уйм-у́, уйм-ёшь, уйм-у́т   -ю, -ешь, -ют
Imper. уйми́, -те   -й, -йте
Past. уня́л, уняла́, уняло́, -ли́

NOTE. In the imperfective forms the euphonic н of the infinitive is retained in conjugation throughout. In the perfective forms the н is retained only if the prepositional prefix ends in a consonant (от, об, под, с). If the prepositional prefix ends in a vowel the н is dropped in conjugation. The я of the perfective infinitive (-ять) is replaced in conjugation by йм after a prefix ending in a vowel, and by им after a prefix ending in a consonant.

The accent. In the perfective verbs of this group the accent is on the personal terminations in the present form if the prefixes end in a vowel (до, за, на, пере, по, у), with the exception of при. But if the prefix ends in a consonant (об, от, под, с) the accent is on the personal termination in the first person of the present form but goes back by one syllable in all the other persons. The same applies to приня́ть. In the past tense the accent is shifted to the last syllable in the feminine ; in the masculine, neuter, and plural it goes back to the prefix.

8. ходи́ть — итти́ group. (See § 63.)

9. е́здить — сзжа́ть-е́хать group. (See § 63.)

9*a.* бежа́ть — бега́ть group. (See § 63.)

10. нос-и́ть — нес-ти́ group (to carry, to wear).

Conjugation pattern.
нош-у́, но́с-ишь, но́с-ят   нес-у́, нес-ёшь, нес-у́т
Imper. нос-и́, -и́те   нес-и́, -и́те
Past. носи́л, -а, -о, -и   нёс, несла́, -о́, -и́

нес-тй, to carry	*внес-тй, to carry in	внос-йть (в + acc.)
	*вы́нес-ти, to carry out ; to endure	вынос-йть (из + gen.)
	*донес-тй, to carry as far : to report	донос-йть (до + gen., acc = dat.)
	*занес-тй, to take in ; to enter (in book-keeping)	занос-йть
	*отнес-тй, to take to a certain place	относ-йть
	*перенес-тй, to carry across ; to bear, to endure	перепос-йть
	*понес-тй, to carry away	понос-йть, to run down somebody, to slander
	*пронес-тй, to carry past	пронос-йть
	*принес-тй, to fetch	принос-йть
	*разнес-тй, to carry in all directions	разнос-йть
	*унес-тй, to carry away	унос-йть

NOTE. All the perfectives in this group are conjugated as нестй ; all the imperfectives as носйть.

11. воз-йть — вез-тй group (to cart).

Conjugation pattern.

вож-у́, во́з-ишь, во́з-ят	вез-у́, вез-ёшь, вез-у́т
Imper. воз-й, -йте	вез-й, -йте
Past. возйл, -а, -о, -и	вёз, везла́, -о́, -й

везтй	*ввез-тй, to cart in ; to import	ввоз-йть (в + acc.)
	*вы́вез-ти, to cart out	вывоз-йть (из + gen.)
	*довез-тй, to cart as far	довоз-йть (до + gen.)
	*завез-тй, to cart in ; to cart beyond	завоз-йть
	*навез-тй, to cart in quantities	навоз-йть
	*отвез-тй, to cart off	отвоз-йть
	*повез-тй, to cart off, away	(no corresponding imperfective; повоз-йть means to go on carting for a little time)
	*перевез-тй, to cart across	перевоз-йть (через + acc.)
	*развез-тй, to cart in all directions	развоз-йть
	*свез-тй, to cart off, to cart together	своз-йть
	*увез-тй, to cart away	увоз-йть

NOTE. All the perfectives in this group are conjugated as везтй ; all the imperfectives as возйть.

12. вод-и́ть — вес-ти́ group (to lead).

Conjugation pattern.

вож-у́, во́д-ишь, во́д-ят	вед-у́, вед-ёшь, вед-у́т
Imper. вод-и́, -и́те	вед-и́, -и́те
Past. води́л, -а, -о, -и	вёл, вела́, -о́, -и́

вес-ти́		
	*ввес-ти́, to lead in	ввод-и́ть (в + *acc.*)
	*вы́вес-ти, to lead out	вывод-и́ть (из + *gen.*)
	*довес-ти, to lead as far; to bring (to the notice)	довод-и́ть (до + *gen.*)
	*завес-ти́, to install; to lead beyond	завод-и́ть
	*павес-ти́, to lead on; to direct	навод-и́ть
	*отвес-ти́, to lead away	отвод-и́ть
	*повес-ти́, to lead off	(no corresponding imperfective)
	*перевес-ти́, to transfer; to translate	перевод-и́ть
	*провес-ти́, to lead past, to conduct (to dupe someone, to pass the time)	провод-и́ть
Note.	*провод-и́ть means: to escort, to see off (see § 66)	провож-а́ть
	*развес-ти́, to distribute; to separate; to cultivate	развод-и́ть
	*свес-ти́, to lead on one occasion; to bring together; to settle (account)	свод-и́ть
	*увес-ти́, to lead away	увод-и́ть

Note. All the perfectives in this group are conjugated as вести́ ; all the imperfectives as води́ть.

13. па́дать — [у] пасть [пад-ть] group (to fall).

Conjugation pattern.

	*упа́сть
па́д-аю, -ешь, -ют	упад-у́, -ёшь, -у́т
Imper. па́да-й, -йте	-и́, -и́те
Past. па́дал, -а, -о, -и	пал, -а, -о, -и

*попа́сть (в + *acc.*), to fall into ; to hit	попада́ть
*пропа́сть, to be lost	пропада́ть
*распа́сться, to fall to pieces, to fall to ruin (*absolute,* or на + *acc.*)	распада́ться

*совпа́сть (с + *instr.*), to coincide with	совпада́ть
*спасть (с + *gen.*), to fall off	спада́ть
*упа́сть, to fall (off)	(no new imperfective form)

NOTE. All the perfectives in this group are conjugated as упа́сть. All the imperfectives as па́дать.

14. **кла́дыва-ть — клас-ть [клад-ть]; -лага́-ть — -ло́ж-йть group (to put).**

Conjugation pattern.

кла́дыва-ю, -ешь, -ют кла́д-у́, -ёшь, -у́т
-лага́-ю, -ешь, -ют -ло́ж-у́, -ишь, -ат
Imper. -й, -йте -́й, -йте
Past: -л, -ла, -ло, -ли клал, -а, -о, -и -ложи́л, -а, -о, -и

*вложи́ть (в + *acc.*), to put in, to pay in	вкла́дывать
*вы́ложить (из + *gen.*), to put out (lay out), to unpack	выкла́дывать
*доложи́ть, to add (*acc.*), to report (*dat.*)	докла́дывать
*заложи́ть, to pledge, to mortgage (в + *loc.*); to harness (horse) (в + *acc.*)	закла́дывать
*изложи́ть, to expound, to state	излага́ть
*наложи́ть, to put on, to impose	{ накла́дывать, to put on налага́ть, to impose
*отложи́ть, to put aside, to postpone (на + *acc.*)	откла́дывать
*подложи́ть, to put under	подкла́дывать
*положи́ть, to put	полага́ть, to suppose
*положи́ться (на + *acc.*), to depend upon	полага́ться
*переложи́ть (из + *gen.* + в + *acc.*), to put to another place ; to change horses	перекла́дывать
*предложи́ть (*dat.*), to offer	предлага́ть
*приложи́ть, to attach ; to enclose (при + *loc.*); to apply, to affix (*acc.* + к + *dat.*)	прикла́дывать прилага́ть
*разложи́ть, to analyse ; to resolve (на + *acc.*) ; to lay out, to unpack	{ разлага́ть раскла́дывать
*разложи́ться, to become decomposed	разлага́ться
*сложи́ть, to put together	скла́дывать
*уложи́ть, to put away, to pack up (trunk, etc.) (*acc.* + в + *acc.*)	укла́дывать

NOTE 1. All the perfectives are conjugated as -ложи́ть ; all the imperfectives either as кла́дывать or as -лага́ть.

Note 2. New imperfectives are formed from the iterative кла́дывать when the new verb has a concrete, literal meaning. If the verb has a metaphorical meaning it is formed from the iterative -лага́ть.

§ 65. *Formation of Perfective Verbs from Imperfectives in frequent use by prefixing a prepositional prefix without altering their fundamental meaning.*

The prefixes so used are : по, с, (раз), на, у (see § 60). The appropriate prefix used for the perfective is given in brackets :

благодар-и́ть [*по-], to thank
 -ю́, -и́шь, -я́т
буд-и́ть [*раз-], to wake, to call
 буж-у́, бу́д-ишь, бу́д-ят
бежа́ть [*по-], to run (see § 63)
вари́ть [*с-], to cook
 вар-ю́, ва́р-ишь, ва́р-ят
ве́р-ить [*по-], to believe, to trust
 -ю, -ишь, -ят
ви́д-еть [*у-], to see
 ви́ж-у, ви́д-ишь, ви́д-ят
везти́ [*по-], to cart (see § 64)
вести́ [*по-], to lead (see § 64)
говори́ть [*по-], to speak (see § 64)
гор-е́ть [*с-], to burn
 -ю́, -и́шь, -я́т
гото́в-ить [*при-], to prepare
 гото́в-лю, -ишь, -ят
де́ла-ть [*с-], to do
 -ю, -ешь, -ют
де́латься [*с-], to become (*instr.*)
ду́ма-ть [*по-], to think
 -ю, -ешь, -ют
дыш-а́ть [*по-], to breathe (*absolute and instr.*)
 дыш-у́, ды́ш-ишь, ды́ш-ат
гуля́-ть [*по-], to stroll, to take a walk
 -ю, -ешь, -ют

е́здить [*с-],[1] to travel
е́хать [*по-], to travel (see § 63)
есть [*по-], to eat (see § 63)
жда-ть [*подо-], to wait (*absolute and gen.*)
 жд-у, жд-ёшь, жд-ут
жела́-ть [*по-], to wish (*gen.*)
 -ю, -ешь, -ют
жечь [*с-], to burn (see § 73)
за́втрака-ть [*по-], to have breakfast
 -ю, -ешь, -ют
зв-ать [*по-], to call
 зов-у́, зов-ёшь, зов-у́т
знако́м-иться [*по-], to get, to become, acquainted (с + *instr.*)
 -люсь, -ишься, -ятся
зна-ть [*у-], to know
 -ю, ешь, -ют
звон-и́ть [*по-], to ring, to ring up (*dat.*)
 звон-ю́, звон-и́шь, звон-я́т
игра́-ть [*по-], to play
 -ю, -ешь, -ют
иск-а́ть [*по-], to seek, to look for (*gen.*)
 ищ-у́, и́щ-ешь, и́щ-ут
итти́ [*по-], to go (see § 63) [2]

[1] to travel on one occasion (see § 63).
[2] иду́, идёшь, иду́т.

каз-а́ться [*по-], to appear, to seem (*instr.*)
   каж-у́сь, ка́ж-ешься, ка́ж-утся

крич-а́ть [*за-], to shout, to cry
   -у́, -и́шь, -а́т

кур-и́ть [*по-], to smoke
   кур-ю́, ку́р-ишь, ку́р-ят

ку́ша-ть [*по-], to eat
   -ю, -ешь, -ют

леж-а́ть [*по-], to lie; [*лечь, to lie down] (see § 73).
   леж-у́, леж-и́шь, леж-а́т

люб-и́ть [*по-], to love, to be fond of
   люб-лю́, лю́б-ишь, лю́б-ят

молч-а́ть [*по-], to be silent
   молч-у́, молч-и́шь, молч-а́т
   also *замолча́ть, to stop talking, to shut up

мёрзн-уть [*по-], to freeze
   -у, -ешь, -ут
*замёрзн-уть, to become frozen

моч-ь [*с-], to be able to, to be in a position to
   мог-у́, мо́ж-ешь, мо́г-ут

нест-и́ [*по-, *с-], to carry (see § 64).

носи́ть [*по-], to wear (see § 64)

нра́в-иться [*по-], to please, to be pleasing (*dat.*)
   -люсь, -ишься, -ятся

обе́да-ть [*по-], to dine, to have dinner
   -ю, -ешь, -ют

пе-ть [*с-], to sing
   по-ю́, по-ёшь, по-ю́т

печ-ь [*с-, *ис-], to bake
   пек-у́, печ-ёшь, пек-у́т

пис-а́ть [*на-], to write
   пиш-у́, пи́ш-ешь, пи́ш-ут

пи-ть [*по-, *вы-], to drink
   пь-ю, пь-ёшь, пь-ют

пла́к-ать [*по-], to cry, to weep
   пла́ч-у, пла́ч-ешь, пла́ч-ут
*запла́к-ать, to start crying

E

плат-и́ть [*за-], to pay
   плач-у́, пла́т-ишь, пла́т-ят, pronounced as пло́тишь, пло́тят

по́мн-ить [*вс-], to remember
   -ю, -ишь, -ят

прос-и́ть [*по-], to ask, to request (*absolute* and *gen.*)
   прош-у́, про́с-ишь, про́с-ят

рабо́та-ть [*по-], to work
   -ю, -ешь, -ют

рв-ать [*по-], to tear
   рв-у, рв-ёшь, рв-ут

ре́з-ать [*по-], to cut
   ре́ж-у, ре́ж-ешь, ре́ж-ут

сид-е́ть [*по-], to sit
   сиж-у́, сид-и́шь, сид-я́т

сл-ать [*по-], to send, to dispatch
   шл-ю, шл-ёшь, шл-ют

слу́ша-ть [*по-], to listen
   -ю, -ешь, -ют

слы́ш-ать [*у-], to hear
   -у, -ишь, -ат

смотр-е́ть [*по-], to look
   смотр-ю́, смо́тр-ишь, смо́тр-ят

сме-я́ться [*по-], to laugh
   сме-ю́сь, сме-ёшься, сме-ю́тся

сп-ать [*по-], to sleep
   сп-лю́, сп-ишь, сп-ят

ста́в-ить [*по-], to put, to put up, to place
   -лю, -ишь, -ят

сто-я́ть [*по-], to stand
   сто-ю́, сто-и́шь, сто-я́т

сто́-ить, to cost. (No perfective in use.)
   сто́-ю, сто́-ишь, сто́-ят

сты-ть [сты́н-уть], [*о-], to turn cold (food, etc.)
   -ну, -нешь, -нут

теря́-ть [*по-], *to* lose
   -ю, -ешь, -ют

тон-у́ть [*у-, *по-], to drown, to sink
   тон-у́, то́н-ешь, то́н-ут

топ-и́ть [*вы-], to heat (stove)
   [*у-], to drown
   [*рас-], to melt
топ-лю́, то́п-ишь, то́п-ят
*затоп-и́ть, to light (stove)
уме́-ть [*с-], to be able to, to have
   the ability
   -ю, -ешь, -ют
у́жина-ть [*по-], to sup
   -ю, -ешь, -ют
учи́-ть[ся], [*по-], to teach (to
   study, with ся)
   уч-у́[сь], у́ч-ишь[ся], у́ч-ат[ся]

хот-е́ть [*за-], to wish, to want
   хоч-у́, хо́ч-ешь, хо́чет; хоти́м,
   хоти́те, хотя́т
цел-ов-а́ть[ся] [*по-], to kiss (one
   another) (с + instr.)
   цел-у́-ю[сь], цел-у́-ешь[ся], цел-
   у́-ют[ся]
чита́-ть [по-], to read
   -ю, -ешь, -ют
ши-ть [*с-], to sew
   шь-ю, шь-ёшь, шь-ют

NOTE. In all the verbs in the above list the prepositional prefix imparts to the perfective form just the idea of completion, or of commencement, of the action or state ; occasionally it also shows that the action or state goes on for a short time only (mostly with the prefix *по). In no case does the prepositional prefix lend to the perfective verb any altered or materially modified meaning. Consequently there is normally no need to find a new imperfective form for such verbs, with the same prepositional prefix, for expressing an idea of duration or repetition. Exceptions are presented by the verbs горе́ть, жечь, слать. New imperfective forms can be formed for these : сгора́ть, сжига́ть, посыла́ть.

§ 66. A few verbs in current use take their perfective form by changing the iterative suffix а́, й of the imperfective form into и or у (ну), or by dropping the iterative suffixes ыв, ив, и, ы :

возвраща́-ться, to return

*возвра-ти́ться
   -щу́сь, -ти́шься, -тя́тся

встреча́-ть[ся] (с + instr.), to meet

*встре́-тить[ся]
   -чу[сь], -тишь[ся], -тят[ся]

вынима́-ть, to take out

*вы́н-уть
   -у, -ешь, -ут

замеча́-ть, to notice

*заме́-тить
   -чу, -тишь, -тят

зараба́тыва-ть, to earn

*зарабо́та-ть
   -ю, -ешь, -ют

засыпа́-ть, to fall asleep   *засн-у́ть [1]
         -у́, -ёшь, -у́т

конча́-ть, to finish   *ко́нч-ить
         -у, -ишь, -ат

нагиба́-ться, to stoop   *нагн-у́ться [2]
         -у́сь, -ёшься, -у́тся

начина́-ть, to begin   *нач-а́ть
         -ну́, -нёшь, -ну́т

оставля́-ть, to leave   *оста́в-ить
         -лю, -ишь, -ят

отворя́-ть, to open   *отвор-и́ть
         -ю́, -ишь, -ят

отвеча́-ть, to answer   *отве́-тить
         -чу, -тишь, -тят

отдыха́-ть, to rest   *отдохн-у́ть
         -у́, -ёшь, -у́т

па́да-ть, to fall   *(у) па́сть [пад-ть]
         упад-у́, -ёшь, -у́т

повторя́-ть, to repeat   *повтор-ить
         -ю́, -и́шь, -я́т

позволя́-ть (*dat.*), to permit, to allow   *позво́л-ить
         -ю, -ишь, -ят

поздравля́-ть, to congratulate   *поздра́в-ить
         -лю, -ишь, -ят

пока́зыва-ть   *показа́ть
         (See § 64 for other verbs of the -каза́ть group.)

покупа́-ть, to buy   *куп-и́ть
         -лю́, -ишь, -ят

получа́-ть, to receive   *получ-и́ть
         -у́, -ишь, -ат

помога́-ть (*dat.* + в + *loc.*), to assist   *помо́чь
         помогу́, помо́жешь, помо́гут

поправля́-ть, to repair, to correct   *попра́в-ить
         -лю, -ишь, -ят

посеща́-ть, to visit   *посе-ти́ть
         -щу́, -ти́шь, -тя́т

посыла́-ть   *посла́ть
         (See note to § 65.)

починя́-ть, to repair   *почин-и́ть
         -ю́, -ишь, -ят [-и́шь, -я́т]

[1] See note to просну́ться, next page.
[2] б is dropped before н for euphony.

предлагá-ть (*dat.*), to offer	*предложи́ть предложу́, предло́жишь, предло́жат
прибавля́-ть, to add	*приба́в-ить -лю, -ишь, -ят
провожá-ть, to escort, to see off (see § 64, group 12)	*проводи́ть провожу́, прово́дишь, прово́дят
просыпá-ться, to wake up	*просн-у́ться [1] -у́сь, -ёшься, -у́тся
решá-ть, to decide; to solve	*реш-и́ть -у́, -и́шь, -áт
решá-ться (на + *acc.*), to make up one's mind	*реш-и́ться -у́сь, -и́шься, -áтся
сажá-ть [сади́ть], to seat, to plant	*посад-и́ть саж-у́, сáд-ишь, сáд-ят
сообщá-ть, to communicate	*сообщ-и́ть -у́, -и́шь, -áт
спрáшива-ть, to ask, to enquire	*спрос-и́ть спрош-у́, спрóс-ишь, спрóс-ят
соглашá-ться (с + *instr.*; also на + *acc.*), to agree	*соглас-и́ться соглаш-у́сь, соглас-и́шься, соглас-я́тся
успевá-ть, to succeed; to be in time	*успé-ть -ю, -ешь, -ет
устрáива-ть, to arrange, to fix up	*устрó-ить -ю, -ишь, -ят

NOTE 1. All the **imperfective** verbs in this list retain the **a** of the stem (before the ть) in conjugation. The terminations are -ю, -ешь, -ют. The accent remains on the same syllable as in the infinitive throughout.

NOTE 2. Nearly all the above imperfective verbs were originally derived from their perfective variety by the insertion of an iterative suffix and by the commutation of the consonants: д into ж, с into ш, т into ч and щ, or by the insertion of a euphonic л after labial consonants. (See § 62, note 1, and § 63.)

[1] п is dropped before н for euphony.

§ 67. *Reflexive and Reciprocal Verbs.*

бри́-ться [*по-], to shave oneself	бре́-юсь, бре́-ешься, бре́-ются *Imper.* бре́-йся, бре́-йтесь
возвраща́ться (с, из + *gen.*) *возврати́ться to return	(see § 66)
встреча́ться (с + *instr.*) *встре́титься to meet	(see § 66)
[по]закрыв-а́ться (*instr.*)	-а́юсь, -а́ешься, -а́ются *Imper.* -а́йся, -а́йтесь
*[по]закр-ы́ться, to cover oneself over	-о́юсь, -о́ешься, -о́ются *Imper.* -о́йся, -о́йтесь
купа́-ться *вы́купа-ться to bathe	-юсь, -ешься, -ются *Imper.* -йся, -йтесь
лож-и́ться [*лечь], to lie down	-у́сь, -и́шься, -а́тся *Imper.* -и́сь, -и́тесь
мы́-ться [*по-, *у-], to wash oneself	мо́-юсь, мо́-ешься, мо́-ются *Imper.* мо́-йся, мо́-йтесь
одева́-ться, to dress oneself раздева́-ться, to undress oneself переодева́-ться, to change clothes	-юсь, -ешься, -ются *Imper.* -йся, -йтесь
*оде́-ться, to dress oneself *разде́-ться, to undress oneself *переоде́-ться, to change clothes	-нусь, -нешься, -нутся *Imper.* -нься, -ньтесь
поднима́-ться, to get up ; to rise	-юсь, -ешься, -ются *Imper.* -йся, -йтесь
*подн-я́ться, to raise oneself	подним-у́сь, подни́м-ешься, подни́м-утся *Imper.* подним-и́сь, подним-и́тесь
спуска́-ться, to descend	-юсь, -ешься, -ются *Imper.* -йся, -йтесь
*спуст-и́ться, to descend	спущ-у́сь, спу́ст-ишься, спу́ст-ятся *Imper.* спуст-и́сь, спуст-и́тесь
цел-ова́ться [*по-] (с + *instr.*), to kiss	-у́юсь, -у́ешься, -у́ются *Imper.* -у́йся, -у́йтесь

§ 68. *Neuter Verbs, ending in* ся.

жа́л-оваться [*по-], to complain	-уюсь, -уешься, -уются *Imper.* -уйся, -уйтесь
бо-я́ться [*по-], to fear (*gen.*)	-ю́сь, -и́шься, -я́тся *Imper.* -йся, -йтесь
браться *взяться, to take up, to 　undertake (за + *acc.*)	} (see § 64)
год-и́ться [*при-], to be of use	гож-у́сь, год-и́шься, год-я́тся *Imper.* год-и́сь, год-и́тесь (not in 　frequent use)
извиня́-ться *извин-и́ться (пе́ред + *instr.*) 　to apologize	-ю́сь, -ешься, -ются -ю́сь, -и́шься, -я́тся *Imper.* -йся, -йтесь 　-и́сь, -и́тесь
кла́ня-ться	-ю́сь, -ешься, -ются *Imper.* йся, -йтесь
*поклон-и́ться 　to greet, to send greetings	-ю́сь, -и́шься, -ятся *Imper.* -и́сь, -и́тесь
наде́-яться [*по-], to hope (на 　+ *acc.*)	-юсь, -ешься, -ются *Imper.* -йся, -йтесь
поправля́-ться	-юсь, -ешься, -ются *Imper.* -йся, -йтесь
*попра́в-иться 　to recover, to improve	-люсь, -ишься, -ятся *Imper.* -ься, -ьтесь
приход-и́ться *прий-ти́сь, to come about, to be 　obliged to (*dat.* in impersonal 　sentences)	} (see § 63)
просту́жива-ться	-юсь, -ешься, -ются *Imper.* -йся, -йтесь
*просту-ди́ться 　to catch a chill, cold	-жу́сь, -дишься, -дятся *Imper.* -ди́сь, -ди́тесь
сад-и́ться	саж-у́сь, сад-и́шься, сад-я́тся *Imper.* сад-и́сь, сад-и́тесь
*сес-ть 　to sit down	ся́д-у, ся́д-ешь, ся́д-ут *Imper.* сядь, ся́дьте
серд-и́ться [*рас-], to be, become 　angry (на + *acc.*)	серж-у́сь, се́рд-ишься, се́рд-ятся *Imper.* серд-и́сь, серд-и́тесь

случа́-ться	-юсь, -ешься, -ются
*случ-и́ться	-у́сь, -и́шься, -а́тся
to happen	*Imper.* случи́сь [1]
собира́-ться	-юсь, -ешься, -ются
	Imper. -йся, -йтесь
*собр-а́ться	собер-у́сь, собер-ёшься,
to get ready	собер-у́тся
	Imper. собер-и́сь, собер-и́тесь
удивля́-ться (*dat.*)	-юсь, -ешься, -ются
	Imper. -йся, -йтесь
*удив-и́ться	удив-лю́сь, удив-и́шься, удив-я́тся
	Imper. удив-и́сь, удив-и́тесь
уч-и́ться [*по-, *на-], to learn, to study (*dat.*)	уч-у́сь, у́ч-ишься, у́ч-атся
	Imper. уч-и́сь, уч-и́тесь

§ 69. *Reflexive Verbs used in a passive sense.* (See § 131.)

		Past	
встреча́-ться, to be met with	-ется, ются	{ -лся / -лась / -лось }	-лись
да-ва́-ться, to be given ; to be staged (play or opera)	да-ётся, да-ю́тся	,,	,,
де́ла-ться, to become ; to be done	-ется, -ются	,,	,,
изда-ва́-ться, to be published	изда-ётся, изда-ю́тся	,,	,,
конча́-ться, to end	-ется, -ются	,,	,,
называ́-ться, to be called	-ется, -ются	,,	,,
находи́-ться, to be found	нахо́д-ится, нахо́д-ятся	,,	,,
начина́-ться, to begin	-ется, -ются	,,	,,
объясня́-ться, to be explained	-ется, -ются	,,	,,
печа́та-ться, to be printed	-ется, -ются	,,	,,
пис-а́ться, to be written	пиш-ется, пиш-утся	,,	,,
поднима́-ться, to be raised	-ется, -ются	,,	,,
позволя́-ться, to be allowed	-ется, -ются	,,	,,
чита́-ться, to be read	-ется, -ются	,,	,,
стро́-иться, to be built	стро́-ится, стро́-ятся	{ -ился / -илась / -илось }	-ились

Note 1. Verbs of the above class are mainly used in the third person singular or plural.

[1] Singular only used in a conditional sense (see § 106). Imperfective imperative not in use.

NOTE 2.   To convey the **perfective** meaning, either in the past or in the future, the short passive participle of the perfective verb (without ся) is used with был, была, было, были, or бу́дет :

печа́таться : кни́га печа́тается
the book is printed (being printed)

кни́га была́ напеча́тана
the book was printed

кни́га бу́дет напеча́тана
the book will be printed

издава́ться : кни́га издаётся
the book is published

кни́га была́ и́здана
the book was published

кни́га бу́дет и́здана
the book will be published

NOTE 3.   Many transitive verbs can be used in the reflexive form in a passive sense.

§ 70. *Conjugation of Verbs.*

Russian verbs are divided into two main groups for purposes of conjugation :

1. Verbs of the first conjugation.
2. Verbs of the second conjugation.

1. Verbs of the first conjugation have the following personal terminations :

			де́лать	чита́ть	писа́ть
Sing.	*1st pers.*	-у, -ю	я де́ла-ю	я чита́-ю	я пиш-у́
	2nd „	-ешь	ты де́ла-ешь	ты чита́-ешь	ты пи́ш-ешь
	3rd „	-ет	он, -а́, -о́ де́ла-ет	он, -а́, -о́ чита́-ет	он пи́ш-ет
Plur.	*1st* „	-ем	мы де́ла-ем	мы чита́-ем	мы пи́ш-ем
	2nd „	-ете	вы де́ла-ете	вы чита́-ете	вы пи́ш-ете
	3rd „	-ут, -ют	они́ де́ла-ют	они́ чита́-ют	они́ пи́ш-ут

2. Verbs of the second conjugation have these personal terminations :

		сидѣ́ть	носи́ть	горѣ́ть
Sing. 1st *pers.*	-у, -ю	я сиж-у́	я нош-у́	я гор-ю́
2nd ,,	-ишь	ты сид-и́шь	ты но́с-ишь	ты гор-и́шь
3rd ,,	-ит	он, -а́, -о́ сид-и́т	он, -а́, -о́ но́с-ит	он гор-и́т
Plur. 1st ,,	-им	мы сид-и́м	мы но́с-им	мы гор-и́м
2nd ,,	-ите	вы сид-и́те	вы но́с-ите	вы гор-и́те
3rd ,,	-ат, -ят	они́ сид-я́т	они́ но́с-ят	они́ гор-я́т

NOTE 1. The conjugation-group to which a verb belongs is determined by the termination of the second person singular : if this is ешь or ёшь, the verb is of the first conjugation, and all the other persons, except the third plural, will have е as the conjugation vowel ; the third person plural will have the termination ут or ют. But if the termination of the second person singular is ишь, the verb is of the second conjugation ; then и will be the conjugation vowel and the third person plural will have the termination ат or ят.

NOTE 2. After ж, ч, ш, щ, the vowels я, ю are replaced by а, у.

NOTE 3. The accented е of the personal termination is changed into ё, which is retained after ж, ч, ш, щ, but is pronounced as о.

§ 71. *Types of Conjugation.*

While it is possible to determine the conjugation-group of a verb from the second person singular, it is not always possible to decide that from the infinitive. In order to give the student some guidance as to the best way of deciding from the infinitive to what group a Russian verb belongs, a certain attempt at classification will be made which should enable the beginner to find his way in what will at first seem to him as the maze of the Russian verb. The verbs most often used can be committed to memory

E *

by constant conjugation *aloud*. After a time practice and observation will simplify the task.

All Russian verbs, according to the terminations of their infinitive, can be divided into 7 categories : 5 of the first conjugation and 2 of the second conjugation.

1. To the first conjugation belong :

    (*a*) all verbs with a consonantal stem, the infinitive of which ends in тъ, ти ; to these also belong verbs ending in чь (which is a commutation of г-тъ, к-тъ), and

    (*b*) the greater number of verbs with the infinitival ending of атъ, ятъ, отъ, утъ, ытъ. To this subdivision belong a small number of primary verbs ending in итъ (see § 75, group *c*) and a few in етъ.

2. To the second conjugation belong all verbs with the infinitival ending of итъ (except the few primary verbs mentioned above), and some ending in етъ (or атъ after ж, ч, ш, щ).

A full statement of the conjugation of verbs according to their categories is set out in §§ 73-81.

§ 72. *Preliminary General Statement about the Accent in the Conjugation of Russian Verbs.*

1. THE ACCENT IN THE PRESENT TENSE (or future in Perfectives)

The student will note three types of accent in the present tense of verbs :

Type 1. The accent remains on the stem (on the same syllable as in the infinitive) in all the persons of the present :

    вя́н-утъ, to wither ; вя́н-у, вя́н-ешь, вя́н-ут

Type 2. The accent is on the personal termination in the first person of the present, but goes back to the stem in all the other persons :

тон-у́ть, to be drowning ; тон-у́, то́н-ешь, то́н-ут

Type 3. The accent is on the personal termination in all the persons of the present :

бр-ать, to take ; бер-у́, бер-ёшь, бер-у́т

NOTE. The accent of the imperative is on the same syllable as in the first person of the present tense :

вя́н-у — вянь ; тон-у́ — тони́ ; бер-у́ — бери́

2. THE ACCENT IN THE PAST TENSE

The accent in the past tense corresponds largely to the accent in the infinitive. Three types of accent are usually prevalent in the past tense :

Type 1. The accent remains on the stem :

мыть, to wash ; мыл, мы́ла, мы́ло, мы́ли

Type 2. The accent goes to the termination in the feminine only ; in masculine, neuter, and plural it remains on the stem :

жить, to live ; жил, жила́, жи́ло, жи́ли

Type 3. The accent is always on the termination :

нес-ти́, to carry ; нёс, несла́, несло́, несли́

The appropriate types of accent will be stated for each category of verbs.

A. VERBS OF THE FIRST CONJUGATION (Categories I-V)

§ 73. I. *To the first category* belong all primary or root-verbs in which either the root or the stem ends in a consonant (with the exception of verbs in sub-divisions (*f*), (*g*), (*h*), the stem of which ends in a vowel) :

(*a*) грес-ти́ [греб-ти́], to row,   греб-у́,   греб-ёшь,   греб-у́т
     скрес-ти́ [скреб-ти́], to scratch,   скреб-у́,   скреб-ёшь,   скреб-у́т

> NOTE. **б** of the root (stem) is replaced by **с** in the infinitive.

(*b*) вез-ти́, to cart,   вез-у́,   вез-ёшь,   вез-у́т
     грыз-ть, to gnaw,   грыз-у́,   грыз-ёшь,   грыз-у́т
     полз-ти́, to crawl,   полз-у́,   полз-ёшь,   полз-у́т
     лез-ть, to crawl, to climb,   лéз-у,   лéз-ешь,   лéз-ут
     нес-ти́, to carry,   нес-у́,   нес-ёшь,   нес-у́т
     тряс-ти́, to shake,   тряс-у́,   тряс-ёшь,   тряс-у́т
     пас-ти́, to shepherd,   пас-у́,   пас-ёшь,   пас-у́т

(*c*) тер-éть, to rub,   тр-у,   тр-ёшь,   тр-ут
    *запер-éть, to lock up,   запр-у́,   запр-ёшь,   запр-у́т
    *умер-éть, to die,   умр-у́,   умр-ёшь,   умр-у́т

> NOTE. The **е** of the stem is dropped in conjugation of the present tense (form).

(*d*) печь [пек-ть], to bake,   пек-у́,   печ-ёшь,   пек-у́т
     течь [тек-ть], to run, to flow,   тек-у́,   теч-ёшь,   тек-у́т
     сечь [сек-ть], to whip ; to chop,   сек-у́,   сеч-ёшь,   сек-у́т
     толо́чь [толо́к-ть], to mix,   толк-у́,   толч-ёшь,   толк-у́т
     влечь [влек-ть], to drag,   влек-у́,   влеч-ёшь,   влек-у́т
     стричь [стриг-ть], to cut, to shear,   стриг-у́,   стриж-ёшь,   стриг-у́т
     жечь [жег-ть], to burn,   жг-у,   жж-ёшь,   жг-ут
     берéчь [берéг-ть], to guard, to   берег-у́,   береж-ёшь,   берег-у́т
       look after
    *запря́чь [запря́г-ть], to harness,   запряг-у́, запряж-ёшь, запряг-у́т
    *лечь [лег-ть], to lie down,   ляг-у,   ляж-ешь,   ляг-ут
     мочь [мог-ть], to be able to,   мог-у́,   мо́ж-ешь,   мо́г-ут

> NOTE. In all the verbs of this sub-section the **г-ть** and **к-ть** of the infinitive are commuted into **чь**. In conjugation of the present tense (form), the **г** and **к** are commuted into **ж** and **ч** before soft (jotated) vowels.

(*e*) вес-ти́ [вед-ти́], to lead,	вед-у́,	вед-ёшь,	вед-у́т
брес-ти́ [бред-ти́], to saunter,	бред-у́,	бред-ёшь,	бред-у́т
*сес-ть [сед-ть], to sit down,	ся́д-у,	ся́д-ешь,	ся́д-ут
клас-ть[клад-ть], to put, to put down,	клад-у́,	клад-ёшь,	клад-у́т
крас-ть [крад-ть], to steal,	крад-у́,	крад-ёшь,	крад-у́т
*пас-ть [пад-ть], to fall,	пад-у́,	пад-ёшь,	пад-у́т
пряс-ть [пряд-ть], to spin,	пряд-у́,	пряд-ёшь,	пряд-у́т
плес-ти́ [плет-ти́], to plait,	плет-у́,	плет-ёшь,	плет-у́т
мес-ти́ [мет-ти́], to sweep	мет-у́,	мет-ёшь,	мет-у́т
рас-ти́ [раст-ти́], to grow,	раст-у́,	раст-ёшь,	раст-у́т
цвес-ти́ [цвет-ти́], to blossom,	цвет-у́,	цвет-ёшь,	цвет-у́т
*прочёс-ть [прочёт-ть], to read through	прочт-у́,	прочт-ёшь,	прочт-у́т

NOTE.   The д and т of the root (stem) of the verbs of this sub-section are commuted into с in the infinitive.

(*f*) жа-ть,[1] to press, to squeeze,	жм-у,	жм-ёшь,	жм-ут
жа-ть,[2] to reap, to harvest,	жн-у,	жн-ёшь,	жн-ут
*нача́-ть, to begin,	начн-у́,	начн-ёшь,	начн-у́т

(See remark to жать [2].)

*взя-ть, to take,	возьм-у́,	возьм-ёшь,	возьм-у́т

(я is derived from a Slavonic nasal sound with the element of м ; see remark to жать [1].)

мя-ть, to crumple,	мн-у,	мн-ёшь,	мн-ут

(See remark to жать [2].)

(*g*) плы-ть, to swim,	плыв-у́,	плыв-ёшь,	плыв-у́т
слы-ть, to be known as,	слыв-у́,	слыв-ёшь,	слыв-у́т
жи-ть, to live,	жив-у́,	жив-ёшь,	жив-у́т

(в is inserted for euphony.)

(*h*) пе-ть, to sing,	по-ю́,	по-ёшь,	по-ю́т

§ 74. *The Accent.*

In nearly all the verbs in Category I (see § 73), the accent is on the personal termination in the present tense (future in perfective verbs).   The only exceptions are :

лезть : лéз-у, лéз-ешь	
*сесть : ся́д-у, ся́д-ешь	} Type 1
*лечь : ля́г-у, ля́ж-ешь	
мочь : мог-у́, мóж-ешь	Type 2

[1] The a is derived from a Slavonic nasal sound with the element of м.
[2] The a is derived from a Slavonic nasal sound with the element of н.

In the **past tense** of verbs of the first category, all the three types of accent (see § 72) can be found. It may be useful to note that in nearly all cases where the accent remains on the stem in the present tense (or form), it will fall on the same syllable in the past tense as in the present (Type 1) (see §§ 83-84):

лезть : лéз-у, лéз-ещь ; лез, лéзла, лéзло, лéзли

*сесть : сЯд-у, сЯд-ешь ; сел, сéла, сéло, сéли

Exception :

*лечь : лЯг-у, лЯж-ешь ; лёг ; лег-лá, лег-лó, лег-лú (Type 3).

If the accent falls on the personal termination in the present tense (or future of perfectives), it will in most cases also be on the termination in the past tense (Type 3) :

нес-тú : нес-ý, нес-ёшь ; нёс, нес-лá, нес-лó, нес-лú

In a few cases, however, the accent remains on the stem in the past tense, even if it falls on the personal terminations in the present tense (Type 1) :

мять : мну, мнёшь ; мял, мЯла, мЯло, мЯли

жать : $\begin{Bmatrix} \text{жму, жмёшь} \\ \text{жну, жнёшь} \end{Bmatrix}$; жал, жáло, жáла, жáли

The same also applies to красть, класть, прясть, пасть, сечь, стричь, грызть. In all these verbs the accent in the past is on the stem throughout (Type 1).

$$\left.\begin{array}{l} \text{кра-л} \\ \text{кла-л} \\ \text{пря-л} \\ \text{па-л} \\ \text{сек}^{[1]} \\ \text{стриг} \\ \text{грыз} \end{array}\right\} \text{-ла, -ло, -ли}$$

[1] Also: секлá, -ó, -ú.

In the verbs взять and жить the accent remains on the stem in masculine, neuter, and plural of the past tense. In the feminine it is shifted to the last syllable :

взял, взяла́, взя́ло ; взя́ли
жил, жила́, жи́ло ; жи́ли

In умере́ть and нача́ть the accent goes to the prefix in masculine, neuter, and plural, and is shifted to the last syllable in the feminine :

у́мер, умерла́, у́мерло, у́мерли
на́чал, начала́, на́чало, на́чали (Туре 2)

§ 75. II. *To the second category* belong verbs of the first conjugation of which the infinitive has the terminations оть, ыть, six monosyllabic verbs in ить (sub-division (c)), and the large class of verbs ending in ать, ять ; also еть and уть. These verbs have the distinctive feature of having the ending ю in the first person singular present, and ют in the third person plural. The past tense has the terminations л, ла, ло, ли, which replace the termination ть of the infinitive.

The verbs of sub-division (d) retain the vowel before ть in conjugation, except дава́ть, узнава́ть, встава́ть, which drop the suffix ва in the present tense.

(a)	поло́-ть, to weed,	пол-ю́,	по́л-ешь,	по́л-ют
	коло́-ть, to chop,	кол-ю́,	ко́л-ешь,	ко́л-ют
	моло́-ть, to mill, to grind,	мел-ю́,	ме́л-ешь,	ме́л-ют
	поро́-ть, to tear, to whip,	пор-ю́,	по́р-ешь,	по́р-ют
(b)	мы-ть, to wash,	мо́-ю,	мо́-ешь,	мо́-ют
	ры-ть, to dig,	ро́-ю,	ро́-ешь,	ро́-ют
	кры-ть, to cover,	кро́-ю,	кро́-ешь,	кро́-ют
	вы-ть, to howl,	во́-ю,	во́-ешь,	во́-ют
	ны-ть, to ache, to grieve,	но́-ю,	но́-ешь,	но́-ют
(c)	бри-ть, to shave,	бре́-ю,	бре́-ешь,	бре́-ют
	би-ть, to beat,	бь-ю,	бь-ёшь,	бь-ют
	ши-ть, to sew,	шь-ю,	шь-ёшь,	шь-ют
	ли-ть, to pour,	ль-ю,	ль-ёшь,	ль-ют
	ви-ть, to wind,	вь-ю,	вь-ёшь,	вь-ют
	пи-ть, to drink,	пь-ю,	пь-ёшь,	пь-ют

(d) зна-ть, to know,   зна́-ю,   зна́-ешь, зна́-ют
    дава́-ть,[1] to give,   да-ю́,   да-ёшь,   да-ю́т
    узнава́-ть,[1] to recognize,   узна-ю́, узна-ёшь, узна-ю́т
    встава́-ть,[1] to get up,   вста-ю́, вста-ёшь, вста-ю́т
    чита́-ть, to read,   чита́-ю, чита́-ешь, чита́-ют
    де́ла-ть, to do,   де́ла-ю, де́ла-ешь, де́ла-ют
    гуля́-ть, to stroll,   гуля́-ю, гуля́-ешь, гуля́-ют
    уме́-ть, to be able, to know, уме́-ю,   уме́-ешь, уме́-ют
    ду-ть, to blow,   ду́-ю,   ду́-ешь,   ду́-ют

NOTE. In all the verbs of this sub-division the end-vowel of the stem is retained in conjugation (with the exception of : дава́ть, узнава́ть, встава́ть).

§ 76. The accent of the present tense in the verbs of this category can be of all the three types (see § 72), as follows :

In the verbs of sub-division (a) the accent is of Type 2 (shifting accent) :

поло́-ть, пол-ю́, по́л-ешь

In the verbs of sub-division (c) the accent belongs to Type 3 (always on the personal termination), except :

бри-ть, бре́-ю, бре́-ешь

In the verbs of sub-divisions (b), (d) the accent belongs to Type 1 (it always remains on the same syllable in conjugation as in the infinitive) :

зна-ть, зна́-ю, зна́-ешь

Exceptions : дава́ть, узнава́ть, встава́ть, which drop the suffix ва, and the accent goes to the personal termination.

The accent of the past tense in all the verbs of Category II is on the same syllable as in the infinitive :

поло́-ть : поло́л, -а, -о, -и
дава́ть : дава́л, -а, -о, -и
гуля́ть : гуля́л, -а, -о, -и

---

[1] The suffix ва is dropped in the present tense of these verbs. (See § 64, groups 2, 4.)

Exceptions are : лить, вить, пить, which shift the accent to the feminine termination in the past :

$$\begin{aligned}
&\text{лила́,} &&\text{but ли́ло, ли́ли} \\
&\text{вила́,} &&\text{,, ви́ло, ви́ли} \\
&\text{пила́} &&\text{,, пи́ло, пи́ли}
\end{aligned}$$

§ 77. III. *To the third category* belong a few simple (primary) verbs ending in ать. They drop the entire termination of ать in the conjugation of the present tense. In the past ать is changed into ал, ала, ало, али.

The accent in the present falls on the personal terminations. In the past it is on the same syllable as in the infinitive, excepting the feminine, where it is on the last syllable :

Exceptions :	соса́ть — соса́ла
	ржать — ржа́ла
occasionally also : ·	ткать — тка́ла
	лгать — лга́ла

The verbs of this group are :   *Past. Fem.*

сос-а́ть, to suck,	сос-у́,	сос-ёшь,	сос-у́т	
тк-ать, to weave,	тк-у,	тк-ёшь,	тк-ут	
лг-ать, to lie,	лг-у,	лж-ёшь,	лг-ут	
вр-ать, to fib,	вр-у,	вр-ёшь,	вр-ут	врала́
жр-ать, to devour,	жр-у,	жр-ёшь,	жр-ут	жрала́
бр-ать, to take,	бер-у́,	бер-ёшь,	бер-у́т	брала́
др-ать, to tear,	дер-у́,	дер-ёшь,	дер-у́т	драла́
рж-ать, to neigh,	рж-у, ·	рж-ёшь,	рж-ут	
зв-ать, to call,	зов-у́,	зов-ёшь,	зов-у́т	звала́
рв-ать, to tear,	рв-у,	рв-ёшь,	рв-ут	рвала́
жд-ать, to wait,	жд-у,	жд-ёшь,	жд-ут	ждала́

Note 1. брать, драть take a euphonic е, звать takes a euphonic о in the conjugation of the present tense. In лгать the г is commuted into ж before a soft vowel in the conjugation of the present tense.

Note 2. All the verbs in Category III have у in the first person singular and ут in the third person plural of the present tense.

§ 78. IV. *To the fourth category* belong :

(*a*) A number of verbs of the first conjugation, ending in ать with a preceding

с	з	д	т	ст	г	к	ск	сл

which change into

ш	ж	ж	ч	щ	ж	ч	щ	шл

and

б	п	м

which change into

бл	пл	мл

(See § 13*a*.)

The accent is a variable one in the present tense, belonging to all the three types. (See § 72.)

The commutation of consonants, or the insertion of the euphonic л, which takes place in the first person singular, is extended to all the persons of the present tense, both singular and plural.

In the past the accent remains on the same syllable as in the infinitive in all verbs of this sub-division.

колеб-а́ть, to shake,	коле́бл-ю,	коле́бл-ешь,	-ют
треп-а́ть, to scutch (flax), to pull about,	трепл-ю́,	тре́пл-ешь,	-ют
щип-а́ть, to pluck,	щипл-ю́,	щи́пл-ешь,	-ют
сы́п-ать, to strew, to scatter,	сы́пл-ю,	сы́пл-ешь,	-ют
дрем-а́ть, to slumber,	дремл-ю́,	дре́мл-ешь,	-ют
пря́т-ать, to hide,	пря́ч-у,	пря́ч-ешь,	-ут
свист-а́ть,[1] to whistle,	свищ-у́,	сви́щ-ешь,	-ут
ре́з-ать, to cut,	ре́ж-у,	ре́ж-ешь,	-ут
ма́з-ать, to smear, to paste,	ма́ж-у,	ма́ж-ешь,	-ут
вяз-а́ть, to tie, to bind,	вяж-у́,	вя́ж-ешь,	-ут
пис-а́ть, to write,	пиш-у́,	пи́ш-ешь,	-ут
дви́г-ать, to move,	дви́ж-у,	дви́ж-ешь,	-ут
пла́к-ать, to cry,	пла́ч-у,	пла́ч-ешь,	-ут
скак-а́ть, to gallop,	скач-у́,	ска́ч-ешь,	-ут
иск-а́ть, to seek,	ищ-у́,	и́щ-ешь,	-ут
сл-ать, to send, ètc.	шл-ю,	шл-ёшь,	-ют
стл-ать, to spread,	стел-ю́,	сте́л-ешь,	сте́л-ют

[1] свист-е́ть belongs to Category VII (*a*) of the second conjugation.

(b) Verbs ending in **овать, евать** which drop the termination **ать** in the conjugation of the present tense ; the suffixes **ов, ев** are changed into **у, ю** respectively :

ков-а́ть, to forge,	ку-ю́,	ку-ёшь,	ку-ю́т
сов-а́ть, to thrust,	су-ю́,	су-ёшь,	су-ю́т
плев-а́ть, to spit,	плю-ю́,	плю-ёшь,	плю-ю́т
ночев-а́ть, to lodge at night,	ночу́-ю,	почу́-ешь,	ночу́-ют
воев-а́ть, to wage war,	вою́-ю,	вою́-ешь,	вою́-ют
сове́тов-ать, to advise,	сове́ту-ю,	сове́ту-ешь,	сове́ту-ют
диктов-а́ть, to dictate,	дикту́-ю,	дикту́-ешь,	дикту́-ют
торгов-а́ть, to trade,	торгу́-ю,	торгу́-ешь,	торгу́-ют
рисов-а́ть, to draw,	рису́-ю,	рису́-ешь,	рису́-ют
атаков-а́ть, to attack,	атаку́-ю,	атаку́-ешь,	атаку́-ют
танцов-а́ть, to dance,	танцу́-ю,	танцу́-ешь,	танцу́-ют

In the past tense the termination **ать** is changed into **ал, ала, ало, али**, with the accent on the same syllable as in the infinitive. The suffixes **ов, ев** are retained in the past tense.

The **accent** of the **present tense** of these verbs is on the same syllable as in the infinitive in derivative verbs. In primary (simple) verbs it is on the personal termination :

кова́ть,   ку-ю́,   ку-ёшь
плева́ть,   плю-ю́,   плю-ёшь

Note. The verbs, здоро́-ваться (to salute), сомне-ва́ться (to doubt), do not belong to this class :

(здоро́-ваюсь, -ваешься, -ваются)
(сомне-ва́юсь, -ва́ешься, -ва́ются)

(c) To this sub-division belong a few verbs in **ять** (**яться**) with a preceding vowel. The **accent** remains on the same syllable in the conjugation of the **present** and **past tenses** :

ла́-ять, to bark,	ла́-ю,	ла́-ешь,	ла́-ют ;	ла́ял, -а, -о, -и
та́-ять, to melt,	та́-ю,	та́-ешь,	та́-ют ;	та́ял, -а, -о, -и
се́-ять, to sow,	се́-ю,	се́-ешь,	се́-ют ;	се́ял, -а, -о, -и
сме-я́ться, to laugh,	сме-ю́сь,	сме-ёшься,	сме-ю́тся ;	
		смея́лся, -лась, -лось, -лись		

Note. All the verbs in Category IV have **ю** in the termination of the first person singular and **ют** in the third person plural (except where the stem ends in ж, ч, ш, щ). The vowel before ть of the infinitive is dropped in conjugation.

§ 79. V. *To the fifth category* belong :

(*a*) Verbs in нуть which have an inchoative meaning, and also with the meaning of going over from one state into another. They are mainly formed from adjectives :

сле́п-нуть, to go blind,	сле́пн-у,	сле́пн-ешь,	-ут
глóх-нуть, to go deaf,	глóхн-у,	глóхн-ешь,	-ут
сóх-нуть, to go dry,	сóхн-у,	сóхн-ешь,	-ут

The **accent** in the **present** and the **past** remains on the same syllable as in the infinitive.

In the past of verbs of this class the entire ending нуть is dropped :

*о-сле́п-нуть, to have gone blind,	осле́п,	осле́пла,	осле́пли
*о-глóх-нуть, to have gone deaf,	оглóх,	оглóхла,	оглóхли
сóх-нуть,	сох,	сóхла, -о,	-и
*за-сóх-нуть, to have gone dry,	засóх,	засóхла,	засóхли

Note. In the imperfective forms of these verbs the suffix ну is occasionally retained in the past tense :

сле́пнул, глóхнул

(*b*) A number of verbs ending in нуть, which describe either a quick action or one in a series of similar actions (mainly implying movement) :

хлеб-áть, to take liquid food			
*хлеб-ну́ть, to sip once,	хлебн-у́,	хлебн-ёшь,	-у́т
ляг-áть, to kick			
*ляг-ну́ть, to kick once,	лягн-у́,	лягн-ёшь,	-у́т
крич-áть, to shout, to cry			
*крúк-нуть, to shout out once,	крúкн-у,	крúкн-ешь,	-ут
кид-áть, to throw			
*кú-нуть, to throw once,	кúн-у,	кúн-ешь,	-ут

To this group belong verbs ending in **нуть** which convey impressions of sound :

> свист-а́ть, to whistle
> *свист-нуть, свист-ну, свист-нешь
> хлоп-ать, to clap
> *хлоп-нуть, хлоп-ну, хлоп-нешь

All verbs of sub-division (*b*) with the suffix **ну** are of the perfective aspect. In the conjugation of the future and past tenses the accent remains on the same syllable as in the infinitive. The suffix **ну** is not dropped in the past tense :

> хлопнул, хлопнула, хлопнули, etc.

B. Verbs of the Second Conjugation

§ **80.** VI. *To this category* belong all derivative verbs in **ить.**

The past tense ends in **ил, ила, ило, или.**

The **accent of the present tense** in verbs in this category follows all the three types. (See § 72.)

The **accent in the past tense** follows the infinitive and first person singular of the present :

сол-и́ть, to salt,	сол-ю́,	со́л-ишь	Accent is of Type 2;	
цен-и́ть, to value,	цен-ю́,	цен-и́шь		
ход-и́ть, to walk,	хож-у́,	хо́д-ишь		3rd person plural ends in ят (or ат after ч).
люб-и́ть, to love,	любл-ю́,	лю́б-ишь	ценить can also follow Type 3.	
вар-и́ть, to boil, to cook,	вар-ю́,	ва́р-ишь		
уч-и́ть, to teach,	уч-у́,	у́ч-ишь		
ра́н-ить, to wound,	ра́н-ю,	ра́н-ишь	Accent is of Type 1.	
сто́-ить, to cost,	сто́-ю,	сто́-ишь		
стро́-ить, to build,	стро́-ю,	стро́-ишь		

NOTE. д, з, before **ить** change into **ж** in the first person singular present ; **т** changes into **ч** ; labials **б, в, п, м** have an inserted **л**, for euphony, in the first person present singular only. (See § 13*a*.)

§ 81.   VII. *To this category* belong both primary and derivative verbs of the second conjugation ending in **еть**
(formerly **ѣть**) or **атъ** after **ж, ч, ш, щ.**   The past tense
ends in **ел,** or **ал.**   Verbs of this category are mainly
intransitive.   Some of these verbs describe sounds or
imitation of sounds.

(*a*) вел-е́ть, to bid,	вел-ю́,	вел-и́шь,	-я́т
гор-е́ть, to burn,	гор-ю́,	гор-и́шь,	-я́т
скрип-е́ть, to scratch,	скрип-лю́,	скрип-и́шь,	-я́т
шум-е́ть, to make noise,	шум-лю́,	шум-и́шь,	-я́т
сид-е́ть, to sit,	сиж-у́,	сид-и́шь,	-я́т
лет-е́ть, to fly,	леч-у́,	лет-и́шь,	-я́т

NOTE.   Commutation of consonants and insertion of
euphonic **л** the same as in § 80.

(*b*) леж-а́ть, to lie,	леж-у́,	леж-и́шь,	-а́т
слы́ш-ать, to hear,	слы́ш-у,	слы́ш-ишь,	-ат
сто-я́ть, to stand,	сто-ю́,	сто-и́шь,	-я́т
бо-я́ться, to fear,	бо-ю́сь,	бо-и́шься,	-я́тся

NOTE.   The vowel before **ть** of the infinitive in verbs
of sub-sections (*a*) and (*b*) is dropped in the conjugation
of the present tense.

The **accent** of the **present** is either on the stem or on the
personal termination.   In both cases it is a fixed one.
The **accent** of the **infinitive** and the **past tense** are usually
on the same syllable :

сид-е́ть,	сиж-у́,	сид-е́л
гор-е́ть,	гор-ю́,	гор-е́л
слы́ш-ать,	слы́ш-у,	слы́ш-ал

§ 82. *Formation of the Imperative Mood.*

The imperative mood is used only for two persons : second
person singular and second person plural.   It is best formed
from the third person plural of the present tense (or future
in perfective verbs) by dropping the personal terminations
ут, ют, ат, ят, and by replacing these by **и** for the
singular and **ите** for the plural.   For the accent it is useful
to follow the first person singular of the present tense.   If

the stem of the verb ends in a vowel, the **и**, **ите** are changed into **й**, **йте** :

пряс-ть, to spin $\begin{cases} \text{пряд-ý} \\ \text{пряд-ýт} \end{cases}$ пряд-й, пряд-йте
[пряд-ть]

дýма-ть, to think $\begin{cases} \text{дýма-ю} \\ \text{дýма-ют} \end{cases}$ дýма-й, дýма-йте

пис-áть, to write $\begin{cases} \text{пиш-ý} \\ \text{пиш-ут} \end{cases}$ пиш-й, пиш-йте

In stems of one syllable only, when the *termination* of the second person *is not accented*, the endings of the imperative **и**, **ите** change into **ь**, **ьте**. If the stem in the third person plural ends in **ь**, it is changed into **е** for the imperative :

вép-ить, to believe $\begin{cases} \text{вép-ю} \\ \text{вép-ят} \end{cases}$ вер-ь, вép-ьте

бы-ть,   to be $\begin{cases} \text{бýд-у} \\ \text{бýд-ут} \end{cases}$ буд-ь, бýд-ьте

ли-ть,   to pour $\begin{cases} \text{ль-ю} \\ \text{ль-ют} \end{cases}$ ле-й, лé-йте

би-ть,   to beat, $\begin{cases} \text{бь-ю} \\ \text{бь-ют} \end{cases}$ бе-й, бé-йте
          to strike

The following verbs have an irregular formation of the imperative :

есть,   to eat $\begin{cases} \text{е-м} \\ \text{ед-я́т} \end{cases}$ еш-ь, éш-ьте
[ед-ть]

лечь,   to lie $\begin{cases} \text{ля́г-у} \\ \text{ля́г-ут} \end{cases}$ ляг, ля́г-те
[лег-ть]

An accommodation imperative for expressing a wish is formed also for the third person (singular and plural) by attaching the verbal forms **пусть**, or **пускáй** (let), to the third person singular and plural of the present tense (or future of perfective verbs) :

пусть он читáет   let him read
пусть они читáют   let them read

NOTE. пусть and пускáй (let) are used with the indicative mood (third person of the present singular or plural, *not* with the infinitive as in English).

§ 83. *Formation of the Past Tense.*[1]

The past tense of Russian verbs is formed for all persons by changing ть of the infinitive into л, ла, ло, ли for masculine, feminine, neuter, and plural :

читáть : читá-л, -ла, -ло, -ли

я читáл (*masc.*)	мы читáли ⎫
я читáла (*fem.*)	вы читáли ⎬ (*plural*)
ты читáл (*masc.*)	они читáли ⎭
ты читáла (*fem.*)	
он читáл (*masc.*)	
онá читáла (*fem.*)	

NOTE 1. In reflexive or similar verbs ending in ться, the ся is tacked on after the л, but is altered into сь after vowels :

вернý-ться, to return

я ⎫
ты ⎬ вернý-лся   мы ⎫
он ⎭   вы ⎬ вернý-лись
              они ⎭

онá вернý-лась

NOTE 2. If the stem of the verb ends in one of the consonants с, з, г, к, х or б, the л is usually dropped, for euphony, in the masculine gender singular :

вез-ти́, to cart   вёз   (not вёзл)
                but : везлá
                    везли́

[1] For formation of Conditional Mood see Appendix I, p. 308.

нес-ти́,   to carry,   нёс   (not нёсл)
            but : несла́
            несли́

сечь,   to whip,   сек   (not секл)
[сек-ть]   but : секла́
            секли́

печь, ʹ   to bake,   пёк   (not пёкл)
[пек-ть]   but : пекла́
            пекли́

мочь,   to be able,   мог   (not могл)
[мог-ть]   but : могла́
            могли́

also тере́-ть,   to rub,   тёр   (not тёрл).
            but : тёрла
            тёрли

умере́-ть, to die,   у́мер   (not у́мерл)
            but : умерла́
            у́мерли

NOTE 3.   In stems ending in д, т, these consonants
are usually dropped before the л :

пасть,   to fall,   пал (not падл)
[пад-ть]   пала (,, па́дла)
           па́ло (,, па́дло)
           па́ли (,, па́дли)

вести́,   to lead,   вёл (,, вёдл)
[вед-ти́] вела́ (,, ведла́)
           вело́ (,, ведло́)
           вели́ (,, ведли́)

есть,   to eat,   ел (,, едл)
[ед-ть]   е́ла (,, е́дла)
           е́ли (,, е́дли)

иттй [ид-ти] (to go) forms the past tense from an obsolete verb, шед-ть, dropping the д :

шёл
шла
шло

рас-тй, to grow, рос
росла́
росли́

NOTE 4. A number of verbs ending in нуть, when they have an inchoative meaning (see § 79), drop the ending нуть in the past tense :

сóх-нуть, to go dry,   сох, сóх-ла, сóх-ло, сóх-ли
*оглóх-нуть, to have   оглóх, оглóх-ла, оглóх-ли
  gone deaf
*погáс-нуть, to become погáс, погáс-ла, погáс-ли
  extinguished
*исчéз-нуть, to vanish, исчéз, исчéз-ла, исчéз-ли

§ 84. *The Accent in the Past Tense (general summary).*

I. In nearly all verbs terminating in ать, ять, еть, ить, ыть, уть, нуть, the accent remains on the same vowel in conjugation as in the infinitive. (See § 72.)

NOTE. Exceptions to this rule are :

(1) A number of primary, mainly monosyllabic, verbs in which the feminine of the past has the accent on the last syllable :

быть — была́,   жить — жила́
брать — брала́,   дать — дала́

(2) A number of verbs with a prepositional prefix to which the accent is shifted in the past tense in masculine and neuter singular, and in the plural. In the feminine singular the accent is on the last syllable. To this class also belong compounds of the verb -ять. (See § 64, group 7.)

*понять, to understand,   пóнял, -ли, понялá
*продáть, to sell,   прóдал, -ли, продалá
*начáть, to begin,   нáчал, -ли, началá
*налúть, to pour in, to fill,   нáлил, -ли, налилá

II. In the past tense of verbs terminating in зть, сть, ереть, the accent is on the root vowel :

грыз-ть,	to gnaw,	грыз,	гры́зла,	гры́зли
крас-ть,	to steal,	крал,	крáла,	крáли
ес-ть,	to eat,	ел,	éла,	éли
тер-éть,	to rub,	тёр,	тёрла,	тёрли

III. In the past tense of verbs terminating in сти, зти, чь [г-ть, к-ть], the accent falls on the last syllable. (See § 72, 2, Type 3, of past.)

вестú,	to lead,	вёл,	велá,	велú
везтú,	to cart,	вёз,	везлá,	везлú
нестú,	to carry,	нёс,	неслá,	неслú
мочь,	to be able to,	мог,	моглá,	моглú
* поджéчь,	to set fire to,	поджёг,	подожглá,	подожглú

Exception : стричь, to clip, to cut

стриг, стрúгла, стрúгли

§ 85. *Accent of the Past Tense in Reflexive and similar verbs, ending in* ся.

In those verbs (mainly primary) where the feminine takes the accent on the last syllable in the past tense (see § 72, 2, Type 2, past), the accent will also be on the last syllable of masculine, neuter, and plural when the reflexive particles ся, сь are tacked on, although these forms would not have the accent on the last syllable if they had no ся or сь :

рвать, рвалá : рвалáсь
    to tear   рвался́   (but : рвáло, рвáли)
                   рвалóсь
                   рвалúсь

гнать, гнала́ :   гнала́сь
  to drive   гнался́   (but : гна́ло, гна́ли)
                     гнало́сь
                     гнали́сь

роди́ть, родила́ :   родила́сь
  to give birth to   роди́лся́   (but : роди́ло, роди́ли)
                     родило́сь
                     родили́сь

(but also : роди́лся, роди́лись)

§ 86. *Participles.*

Participles are not often used in the spoken language, but they are frequently used in the written language. They have the same terminations, and are declined, as adjectives.

§ 86a. I. *Formation of the Present and Past Active Participles.*

(*a*) The present of active participles is formed by replacing the т of the personal termination of the third person plural of the present tense with the terminations щий, щая, щее, щие :

чита́ю-т — чита́ю-щий, -щая, -щее, -щие
ру́бя-т — ру́бя-щий, -щая, -щее, -щие
сидя́-т — сидя́-щий, -щая, -щее, -щие

The accent of the present active participle is usually on the same syllable as in the third person plural of the present tense. In a few verbs the accent goes forward by one syllable :

кормить,   ко́рмя-т,   кормя́-щий, -щая, -щее, -щие
  to feed
платить,   пла́тя-т,   платя́-щий, -щая, -щее, -щие
  to pay   (pronounced
             пло́тят)
смотре́ть,   смо́тря-т,   смотря́-щий, -щая, -щее, -щие
  to look

(b) The past active participle is formed by replacing the
л of the past tense with вший, вшая, вшее, вшие, or by
adding ший, шая, шее, шие if the stem of the verb
ends in a consonant :

сиде́-ть,	сиде́-л	— сиде́-вший,	-вшая, -вшее, -вшие
писа́-ть,	писа́-л	— писа́-вший,	-вшая, -вшее, -вшие
чита́-ть,	чита́-л	— чита́-вший,	-вшая, -вшее, -вшие
*умер-е́ть,	у́мер,	— уме́р-ший,	-шая, -шее, -шие
*принес-ти́,	принёс	— принёс-ший,	-шая, -шее, -шие
*отвез-ти́,	отвёз	— отвёз-ший,	-шая, -шее, -шие

The **accent** in the past active participle is usually on the
syllable which precedes the terminations ший, шая, шее,
шие.

NOTE 1. Both the present and the past active
participles are occasionally used as attributive verbal
adjectives. They have no short (predicative) form.
They are declined as adjectives according to gender and
number in all their cases. (See § 46a.)

NOTE 2. In reflexive verbs the particle ся is tacked
on after the terminations :

-щий,	-щая,	-щее,	-щие
-вший,	-вшая,	-вшее,	-вшие
-ший,	-шая,	-шее,	-шие

NOTE 3. Both transitive and intransitive verbs can
have present and past active participles.

§ **86b.** II. *Formation of the Present and Past Passive
Participles.* (Formed from transitive verbs only.)

A. The present passive participle is formed from the
first person plural of the present tense by tacking on the

terminations ый, ая, ое, ые for the long (attributive) form, and а, о, ы for the short (predicative) form.

читáем	— читáем-ый,	-ая,	-ое,	-ые
	читáем,	-а,	-о,	-ы
гóним	— гонúм-ый,	-ая,	-ое,	-ые
	гонúм,	-а,	-о,	-ы
ведём	— ведóм-ый,	-ая,	-ое,	-ые
	ведóм,	-а,	-о,	-ы
несём	— несóм--ый,	-ая,	-ое,	-ые
	несóм,	-а,	-о,	-ы

NOTE 1. ё of the present tense is changed into о.

NOTE 2. Present passive participles have a short (predicative) form for all three genders, and for the plural.

NOTE 3. The accent in the present passive participle is usually on the same syllable as in the present tense if the conjugation vowel is е. If this is ё or и, these vowels take the accent in the present passive participle.

B. The past passive participle is formed by replacing the л of the past tense with нный, нная, нное, нные for the long (attributive) form, and н, на, но, ны for the short (predicative) form :

читá-л	— чúта-нный,	-нная,	-нное,	-нные
	чúта-н,	-на,	-но,	-ны
писá-л	— пúса-нный,	-нная,	-нное,	-нные
	пúса-н,	-на,	-но,	-ны

To this class belong all the verbs ending in ать and all derivative verbs in еть, ить.

NOTE 1. и of the stem in the past tense changes into е in the past passive participle.

NOTE 2. з, с, г, к of the stem in the past tense are commuted into ж, ш, ж, ч in the past passive participle.

же-чь — жёг, жжё-нный, -нная, -нное, -нные
[же-гт]

NOTE 3. After labials of the stem, a euphonic л is inserted in the past passive participle :

купи́-ть — куп-и́л, ку́п-ленный, -нная, -нное, -нные
                 ку́п-лен,   -лена, -пено, -лены

Verbs ending in уть, ыть, ереть, and a few primary in ить (all of the first conjugation class), replace the л by тый, тая, тое, тые (т, та, то, ты for the short form) in the formation of the past passive participle :

кры-ть — кры-л,	кры́-тый,	-тая,	-тое,	-тые
to cover	кры-т,	-та,	-то,	-ты
коло́-ть — коло́-л,	ко́ло-тый,	-тая,	-тое,	-тые
to chop, split	ко́ло-т	-та,	-то,	-ты
ши-ть — шил,	ши́-тый,	-тая,	-тое,	-тые
to sew	ши-т,	-та,	-то,	-ты

To this class belong брить лить, бить, вить, пить (see § 75), and also жить (see § 73).

§ 86c. *A list of Past Passive Participles of Verbs in frequent use.*

NOTE. Of the participles, the past passive participle is the most frequently used, both in the long and in the short (predicative) form. They are used in passive constructions in principal and subordinate clauses (see § 131). The past passive participle of the perfective aspect is that most often used. Of the long form the masculine only is given. The feminine and neuter have the terminations ая, ое.

Predicative

бить [*по-], to beat, to give a beating; [*у-], to kill	по-) у-} би́тый,	по-) у-} би́т, -а, -о, -ы
*взять, to take,	взя́тый,	взят, -а́, -о, -ы
брить [*по-], to shave	(побри́тый, (вы́бритый,	побри́т) вы́брит } -а, -о, -ы
*бро́сить, to throw,	бро́шенный,	бро́шен, -а, -о, -ы
вари́ть [*с-], to cook,	сва́ренный,	сва́рен, -а, -о, -ы
везти́ [*с-], to cart,	свезённый,	свезён, -а́, -о́, -ы́
нести́ [*у-], to carry,	унесённый,	унесён, -а́, -о́, -ы́
*вы́брать, to select,	вы́бранный,	вы́бран, -а, -о, -ы
*сказа́ть, to say,	ска́занный,	ска́зан, -а, -о, -ы
*заказа́ть, to order,	зака́занный,	зака́зан, -а, -о, -ы
греть [*со-], to warm,	согре́тый,	согре́т, -а, -о, -ы
де́лать [*с-], to make,	сде́ланный,	сде́лан, -а, -о, -ы
крыть {[*за-], to cover, {[*от-], to uncover	за-) от-} кры́тый,	за-) от-} крыт, -а, -о, -ы
*оде́ть, to dress,	оде́тый,	оде́т, -а, -о, -ы
*наде́ть, to put on,	наде́тый,	наде́т, -а, -о, -ы
*разде́ть, to undress,	разде́тый,	разде́т, -а, -о, -ы
*забы́ть, to forget,	забы́тый,	забы́т, -а, -о, -ы
*нача́ть, to begin	(начато́й) (на́чатый)	на́чат, -а, -о, -ы
обеща́ть, to promise,	обе́щанный,[1]	обе́щан, -а, -о, -ы
*обяза́ть, to oblige,	обя́занный,	обя́зан, -а, -о, -ы
*огорчи́ть, to grieve, to vex,	огорчённый,	огорчён, -а́, -о́, -ы́
*[о]ко́нчить, to finish,	[о]ко́нченный,	[о]ко́нчен, -а, -о, -ы
мыть [*по-, *у-], to wash	(по-) у-} мы́тый,	по-) у-} мыт, -а, -о, -ы
*отосла́ть, to send away,	ото́сланный,	ото́слан, -а, -о, -ы
*посла́ть, to send,	по́сланный,	по́слан, -а, -о, -ы
печь [*ис-], to bake,	испечённый,	испечён, -а́, -о́, -ы́
писа́ть [*на-], to write	напи́санный,	напи́сан, -а, -о, -ы
*заплати́ть, to pay,	запла́ченный (pronounced запло́ченный)	запла́чен, -а, -о, -ы
*заня́ть, to occupy; to borrow	за́нятый [о́й],	за́нят, -а́, -о, -ы
*подня́ть, to lift,	по́днятый,	по́днят, -а́, -о, -ы
*приня́ть, to receive,	при́нятый,	при́нят, -а́, -о, -ы
*поня́ть, to understand,	по́нятый,	по́нят, -а́, -о, -ы

[1] This participle has a perfective character.

Predicative

		Predicative
*снять, to take off	{ снятóй } { снятый }	снят, -á, -о, -ы
*приложить, to attach, to enclose	прилóженный,	прилóжен, -а, -о, -ы
рéзать [*с-], to cut,	срéзанный,	срéзан, -а, -о, -ы
*рáнить, to wound,	рáненный,	рáнен, -а, -о, -ы
*прочитáть, to read through,	прочúтанный,	прочúтан, -а, -о, -ы
*купúть, to buy,	кýпленный,	кýплен, -а, -о, -ы
*приготóвить, to prepare,	приготóвленный,	приготóвлен, -а, -о, -ы
*продáть, to sell,	прóданный,	прóдан, -á, -о, -ы
*лишúть, to deprive,	лишённый,	лишён, -á, -ó, -ú
*найтú, to find,	нáйденный,	нáйден, -á, -о, -ы
шить [*с-], to sew,	сшúтый,	сшит, -а, -о, -ы

§ 87. *The Accent in the Past Passive Participle.* (For the accent in the present passive participle see § 86*b*.)

(1) In nearly all the verbs which form their past passive participle with the **нн** suffix (**н** for predicative forms), the accent falls on the syllable immediately preceding the termination (see § 86*b*):

читáть — чúтанный
*купúть — кýпленный

If the suffix **нн** (**н**) is preceded by **e**, this **e** will take the accent only if the verbs from which the passive participles are formed have the termination of the infinitive in **сть, зть, сти, зти, чь**; also in a few verbs terminating in **ить** which belong to accent Type 3 (see § 72):

*запрячь,	to harness,	запряжённый
*прочéсть,	to read through,	прочтённый
*привезтú,	to bring by carting,	привезённый
*покорúть,	to subjugate,	покорённый
*отличúть,	to distinguish,	отличённый

(2) In verbs which form their past passive participle

F

with the т suffix the accent in the participle is on the same syllable as in the past tense :

*надýть,   надýл,   надýтый,   inflated
*заперéть,   зáпер,   зáпертый,   locked
*закрýть,   закрýл,   закрýтый,   covered

Exceptions to this rule present verbs terminating in оть and нуть. These throw the accent back by one syllable in the past passive participle :

колóть,   колóл,   кóлотый,   chopped
*обманýть,   обманýл,   обмáнутый,   deceived

§ 88. Gerunds (Verbal Adverbs).

(1) The present gerund is formed by changing the terminations ут, ют, ат, ят of the third person plural of the present tense into я (or а after ж, ч, ш, щ) :

читá-ют — читá-я
говор-я́т — говор-я́
жив-ýт   — жив-я́

(2) The past gerund is formed by replacing the л of the past tense with вши (or в only), or ши, in the same way as in the case of the past participle (see § 86a, I (b)) :

сидé-л   — сидé-вши   (or сидé-в)
сдéла-л   — сдéла-вши (or сдéла-в)
сказá-л —. сказá-вши (or сказá-в)
пёк   — пёк-ши
нёс   — нёс-ши

Note 1.   In reflexive verbs the particle ся (сь) is placed after вши, в, ши :

умы́-лся — умы́-вшись

Note 2.   In the present gerund the accent is either on the last syllable or on the last syllable but one (the accent mainly follows that of the third person plural of the present tense) :

	звать,	to call,	зов-у́т	— зов-я́
	класть, [клад-ть]	to lay,	клад-у́т	— клад-я́
	жить,	to live,	жив-у́т	— жив-я́
	жева́ть,	to chew,	жу-ю́т	— жу-я́
	смея́ться,	to laugh,	сме-ю́тся	— сме-я́сь
but :	лежа́ть,	to lie,	леж-а́т	— лёж-а
	сиде́ть,	to sit,	сид-я́т	— си́д-я
	молча́ть,	to be silent,	молч-а́т	— мо́лч-а

In the past gerund the accent is always on the syllable preceding the terminations вши, в, ши :

*написа́вши — написа́ть
*закры́вши   — закры́ть
*прочита́вши — прочита́ть

If the accent of the infinitive is *not* on the last syllable, the accent of the past gerund always follows that of the infinitive :

ду́мать   — ду́мавши
*сде́лать — сде́лавши

Note 3.   The gerunds are not declined and have no special terminations for genders or numbers.

Note 4.   The gerund of the auxiliary verb быть is :
Present : бу́дучи
Past :   быв

Note 5.   The cardinal function of the verbal adverb (gerund) is to present a verbal form describing a phase of the action or state while it is going on, or when referring to such a phase while it was going on in the past. For both these purposes the present verbal adverb (gerund) is sufficient.   One can say :

Я слу́шал его́ игру́ на роя́ле, прислу́шиваясь в то же вре́мя к тому́, что происхо́дит на дворе́.

I listened to his playing the piano, at the same time trying to hear what was going on outside.

The past verbal adverb is mostly used when referring to an action or state now finished :

написа́в письмо́, я пошёл спать
having written the letter, I went to sleep

Verbal adverbs in the past form are not often used for imperfective verbs. But there is also a tendency to use the present verbal adverb for a perfective verb :

подойдя́ ко мне, он ни́зко поклони́лся (instead of подоше́дши)
coming up to me, he made a low bow

придя́ домо́й, он сейча́с взя́лся за рабо́ту (instead of прише́дши)
coming home, he at once began to work

A number of verbal adverbs are now used as adverbs :

несмотря́ на, notwithstanding
смотря́ по, according to
мо́лча, in silence, etc.

6. ADVERBS

§ 89. An adverb is a word that modifies or qualifies an adjective, verb, or other adverb, expressing a relation of place, time, circumstance, manner, etc.

§ 90. *Group A.*

By their origin adverbs represent many groups. To the largest group belong those derived from adjectives. They can be formed from all qualitative adjectives, and also from some others.

(1) Adverbs derived from adjectives are usually in the neuter of the short (predicative) form. They qualify verbs. They can also have a comparative form. Many of these

adverbs can be used as a complete impersonal sentence
with an implied predicate (see § 122, note (d)):

хорошо́, well	лу́чше, better	гора́здо лу́чше, much better лу́чше всего́, better still, best of all
гро́мко, loudly	гро́мче, louder	гро́мче всего́, loudest of all
ско́ро, quickly, soon	скоре́е, sooner, quicker	гора́здо скоре́е, much sooner скоре́е всего́, soonest
легко́, lightly, easily	ле́гче, easier, lighter	гора́здо ле́гче, much easier ле́гче всего́, easiest of all
по́здно, late	поздне́е } по́зже } later	гора́здо поздне́е } [по́зже] } much later
ра́но, early	ра́ньше, earlier	гора́здо ра́ньше, much earlier

NOTE. Adverbs in the comparative form are often
qualified by the particle по and the adverb как мо́жно:

получше, как мо́жно лу́чше,	a little better in the best possible way
поскоре́е, как мо́жно скоре́е,	a little quicker quickest possible, as soon as possible
полегче, как мо́жно ле́гче,	a little lighter as lightly as possible
погро́мче, как мо́жно гро́мче,	a little louder as loudly as possible
попо́зже, попозднее, как мо́жно поздне́е,	a little later as late as possible
пора́ньше, как мо́жно ра́ньше,	a little earlier as early as possible

(2) Other adverbs from adjectives are:

(a) возмо́жно }
мо́жно } possible

ну́жно }
на́добно }
на́до } necessary

These have a verbal character, and are
used in all three tenses: present, past,
and future:

возмо́жно }
мо́жно } it is possible

(воз)мо́жно бы́ло, it was possible
(воз)мо́жно бу́дет, it will be possible

ну́жно ⎱
на́добно ⎬ it is necessary
на́до ⎰

ну́жно ⎱
на́добно ⎬ бы́ло, it was necessary
на́до ⎰

ну́жно ⎱
на́добно ⎬ бу́дет, it will be necessary
на́до ⎰

To this class belong a few adverbs formed from adjectives, which are used in impersonal sentences with a verbal meaning :

Present	*Past*	*Future*
тепло́, it is warm	бы́ло тепло́, it was warm	бу́дет тепло́, it will be warm
жа́рко, it is hot	бы́ло жа́рко	бу́дет жа́рко
хо́лодно, it is cold	бы́ло хо́лодно	бу́дет хо́лодно
ве́село, it is cheerful	бы́ло ве́село	бу́дет ве́село
ску́чно, it is dull	бы́ло ску́чно	бу́дет ску́чно
ра́но, it is early	бы́ло ра́но	бу́дет ра́но
по́здно, it is late	бы́ло по́здно	бу́дет по́здно
прия́тно, it is pleasant	бы́ло прия́тно	бу́дет прия́тно
неприя́тно, it is unpleasant	бы́ло неприя́тно	бу́дет неприя́тно
удо́бно, it is comfortable, convenient	бы́ло удо́бно	бу́дет удо́бно
неудо́бно, it is inconvenient, uncomfortable	бы́ло неудо́бно	бу́дет неудо́бно
хорошо́, it is good, it is all right	бы́ло хорошо́	бу́дет хорошо́
пло́хо ⎱ it is bad скве́рно ⎰	бы́ло пло́хо бы́ло скве́рно	бу́дет пло́хо бу́дет скве́рно

But ordinarily adverbs formed from adjectives go to qualify verbs, and have no other function :

я чита́ю гро́мко,   I read aloud
он пи́шет ме́дленно,   he writes slowly

Such adverbs are distinct in meaning from short neuter adjectives which stand as predicates for neuter nouns.

(*b*) должно́ быть ⎱ probably
вероя́тно ⎰

внеза́пно, suddenly
вообще́, generally
гора́здо, much (with comparative)

и́менно, namely
ина́че, otherwise
кра́йне, extremely
по кра́йней ме́ре, at least
по ме́ньшей ме́ре, at the least

лишь, only

очень, very

мгновенно, momentarily

наверно ⎫

наверное ⎭ for certain

наверную ⎫

наверняка ⎭ as a certainty

подобно, similar

давно, long ago, long since

недавно, recently

(c) вдалеке, far off

вкратце, briefly

вполне, entirely

впрочем, besides, as for the rest

набело, clean ; fair (copy)

наскоро, hurriedly, in haste

начисто, clean ; fair (copy) .

(d) досыта, to satiation

издалека, from afar

сдуру, from stupidity

слегка, lightly

снова, again, anew

спроста, in simplicity

сперва, firstly

(e) понемногу, little by little

повидимому, evidently

понапрасну, all for nothing

потихоньку, very quietly

(f) по-русски, in Russian

по-английски, in English

по-новому, in the new way, manner

по-старому, in the old manner, fashion

по-волчьи, in the manner of wolves

(but волком, as a wolf)

по-собачьи, in the manner of dogs

(but собакой, as a dog)

по-медвежьи, in the manner of bears

(but медведем, as a bear)

по-братски, in a brotherly manner

по-дружески, in a friendly manner

(but другом, as a friend)

§ 91. *Group B.*

Adverbs derived from : (a) *Nouns ;* (b) *Numerals ;*
(c) *Pronouns*

(*a*) Those derived from nouns are mainly formed from oblique cases, with or without a preposition. (Preposition and noun are merged in the adverb.)

вверх, upwards

вниз, downwards

вверху, at the top

наверху, on the top

внизу, at the bottom

вдаль, into the distance

вдали, in the distance

издали, from a distance

вне, outside (used as preposition)

внутри, inside (used as prep.)

извне, from outside

изнутри, from inside

возле, near (mainly used as prep.)

подле, beside (mainly used as prep.)

вперёд, forward

назад, backward

впереди, in front (used as prep.)
позади, behind (used as prep.)
направо, to the right
налѣво, to the left
справа, from the right
слѣва, from the left
спереди, at the front
сзади, at the back
около, about (used as prep.)
кругомъ, around
наравнѣ, on level with
вдоль, alongside (used as prep.)
кромѣ, besides, beside (used as prep.)
поперёкъ, across (used as prep.)
наружу, outside
снаружи, from outside
взамѣнъ, in exchange
вмѣсто, instead (used as prep.)
вмѣстѣ, together
[врозь]⎫
врознь ⎬ apart, separately
прежде, before
послѣ, afterwards, after (used as prep.)
наконецъ, at last
напримѣръ, for instance
не в примѣр, incomparably
слишкомъ, too much
черезчуръ, overmuch
отчасти, partly
насилу, with difficulty
кстати, by the way ; appropriately
некстати, inappropriately
вслухъ, aloud
наизусть, by heart
напрасно, in vain
нарочно, on purpose
натощакъ, on an empty stomach
настежь, wide open
поневолѣ, willy-nilly, against one's will
точь-в-точь, exactly
врядъ, hardly, scarcely
вряд-ли, doubtful if . . .
нельзя, impossible

до-нельзя, to the utmost
даромъ, as a gift, for nothing
дома, at home
домой, homewards
верхомъ, on horseback
бѣгомъ, at a run
шагомъ, at a walking pace
лѣсомъ, by way of the forest
полемъ, by way of the field
дорогой, along the road
весною, in the spring
лѣтомъ, in the summer
осенью, in the autumn
утромъ, in the morning
днёмъ, in the day-time
вечеромъ, in the evening
ночью, in the night
порой ⎫
временами ⎬ at times
по временам ⎭
вчера, yesterday
сегодня, to-day
завтра, to-morrow
послезавтра, the day after to-morrow
ежедневно, daily
еженедѣльно, weekly
ежемѣсячно, monthly
ежегодно, yearly
третьего дня⎫
позавчера ⎬ the day before yester-
позавчера ⎭ day
наконецъ, at last
сначала, at first
тотчасъ, the same minute, instantly
наканунѣ, on the eve
сейчасъ, immediately
сейчасъ-же, the very moment
вдругъ, suddenly
сию минуту, this moment
о сю пору, about this time
нынѣ, at present
отнынѣ, from now
донынѣ, till now

поездом, by train   весом, in weight, by weight
трамваем, by tram   длиною, of the length
автобусом, by bus   величиною, of the size
пароходом, by steamer   глубиною, of the depth
берегом, along the shore, bank   толщиною, of the thickness
морем, by sea   шириною, of the width

NOTE. The unit of weight or measurement after these adverbs usually stands in the accusative preceded by the preposition в :

длиною в два метра, of the length of two metres   в величину, in size
весом в два килограма, of the weight of two kilos   в глубину, in depth
в длину, in length   в толщину, in thickness
    в ширину, in width
    etc.

(b) Adverbs derived from Numerals.

однажды,[1] once   вчетверо, four times as much
дважды,[1] twice   впятеро, five times as much
трижды,[1] thrice   теперь, now
вдвоём, two together   однако, however
втроём, three together   во-первых, firstly
вдвое, twice as much   во-вторых, secondly
втрое, thrice as much   в-третьих, thirdly

(c) Adverbs derived from Pronouns and Pronoun-roots.

авось, perhaps, may be   зачем, why
вот, here   иногда, sometimes
вон, there   как, how
весьма, very   кое-как, somehow
везде, everywhere   как-нибудь, in some way or other
всегда, always   как-то, such as; somehow
вовсе, at all   как можно, as possible
вовсе не, not at all   как можно ? how is it possible ?
где, where   когда, when
кое-где, somewhere (in some places)   когда-нибудь, at some time or other
где-нибудь, somewhere or other
где-то, somewhere   когда-то, some time ago
здесь, here   куда, whither

[1] Not in frequent use except однажды in the meaning of: once (upon a time).

F *

куда́-нибудь, somewhere or other (anywhere)

куда́-то, somewhere

не́где, no room (place) where to . . .

нигде́, nowhere

не́когда, no time to . . .

никогда́, never

всю́ду
повсю́ду } everywhere

не́куда, nowhere to . . .

никуда́, nowhere

отку́да, where from

отсю́да, from here

отту́да, from there

туда́, there
сюда́, here } (motion)

тут, here
там, there } (rest)

тогда́, then

пока́, while

пока́мест, meanwhile

ско́лько, how much

поско́льку, in so far as

мно́го, much

немно́го, not much, a little

сто́лько, so much

посто́льку, insomuch, to that extent

так, so

так себе́, ' so-so,' ' middling '

таки́, though

всё-таки }
всё-же } all the same, nevertheless

всё (colloquial for всё вре́мя, see всегда́), all the time, always

всё равно́, it's all the same, it makes no difference

всего́, in all, altogether

опя́ть-таки́, again, and then, once again; again, you see . . .

то́лько, only

не́сколько, a few

ниско́лько, none at all, not in the least

совсе́м, altogether, quite, entirely

не совсе́м, not quite

ничего́, that's nothing

ничего́ себе́, not so bad

совсе́м не, not at all

само́-собо́ю, by itself

ужо́ли }
неужо́ли } is it possible, indeed

по-мо́ему, in my opinion, in my own way

по-сво́ему, in one's own way

по-на́шему, in our own way, in our opinion

§ 92. *Group C.*

To group *C* belong a few primary adverbs and those derived from verbs.

(a) *Primary Adverbs.*

е́ле }
едва́ } scarcely, hardly

едва́-ли, doubtful, hardly

едва́ не, almost

еще́, still, yet

еще́ не }
нет еще́ } not yet

еще́-бы, I should think so ; of course

не, not

нет, no

да, yes

уже́, already

уже́ не, no longer

уже́ нет, no longer, no more (when нет is a predicate)

(b) Adverbs derived from verbs.

зна́чит, so it means (used parenthetically)

ка́жется, so it seems (used parenthetically)

ви́дишь [вишь], you see (used parenthetically)

бы́ло, on the point of, very nearly, about to

бу́дет, enough, that will do

бу́дто, бу́дто-бы, as if

пуска́й, пусть, let; 'all right'; 'I don't care'

почти́, almost

знать, it seems, apparently (used parenthetically)

спаси́бо, thanks

мо́лча, in silence

спустя́, on the passing, elapsing (of time)

мо́жет быть, perhaps (used parenthetically)

ста́ло-быть, consequently (used parenthetically)

чуть, scarcely, hardly

чуть не, almost, scarcely not

чуть-чуть, just a little

чуть бы́ло не, very nearly

ничу́ть, not in the least

ведь, indeed, but; well then, now you must know

де́скать | mean: says he (she), say they. Are used to introduce,
де | in a narrative,
мол | words, and even thoughts, of another person

пожа́луй, perhaps; if you like

пожа́луйста, please, if you please

неча́янно ⎱ inadvertently, by acci-
невзнача́й ⎰ dent

то-есть, that is to say

ра́зве, then? perhaps? is it true that? perhaps only?

7. PREPOSITIONS

§ 93. *Meaning and Function of Prepositions.*

A close acquaintance with the meaning of Russian prepositions (and adverbs used as prepositions), and the cases of declinable parts of speech which they govern, is very important, as the student will have to acquire a thorough and practical knowledge of the various cases required after each preposition. He will have to make himself thoroughly familiar with the respective inflexions of each case before he can tackle Russian texts intelligently, and also in order to make his own Russian intelligible.

Many prepositions are used as prepositional prefixes to verbs, both for the purpose of forming perfective verbs from imperfective ones, and also to give to the verbs a modified directional, and often different, meaning in accordance with the basic meaning of the prepositional prefix. (See §§ 63-65.)

§ 94. *The function* of prepositions, and adverbs used as prepositions, is to indicate *concretely* the position and movement in space of objects, and *abstractly* their position in relation to time. The meaning of prepositions can be divined from the direction which is given to them by the verb:

итти́ в го́род ⎫
е́хать в го́род ⎭ (*acc.*), to go [travel] to town

жить в го́роде (*loc.*), to live in town

Prepositions govern various cases in accordance with the meaning and direction of the verb in the sentence (either apparent or implied). Consequently some prepositions can govern more than one case, as in the above example.

§ 95. Prepositions are divided into three main groups:

(1) Those of movement, answering to the question: отку́да? where from?

из го́рода, from town
от го́рода, away from town

с горы́, down hill
со ста́нции, from the railway station

(2) Those of movement, answering to the question: куда́? where to?

в го́род, into town
к го́роду, in the direction of the town
ко мне, towards me
за́ город, beyond the town, into the country

на́ гору, up the hill
на ста́нцию, to the railway station
по́д гору, down hill
че́рез мост, over the bridge
сквозь тума́н, through the mist

(3) Those of stable position, answering to the question: где? where?

в го́роде, in town
на горе́, on the hill
при мне, with me
за́ городом, outside the town
над го́родом, over the town
по́д городом, near the town
пе́ред го́родом, in front of the town

ме́жду го́родом ⎫ between the town
и село́м ⎭ and the village
по бе́регу, along the bank
по гора́м, on the hills
по ту сто́рону, over the other side
о́коло до́ма, around the house
во́зле до́ма, near the house
про́тив до́ма, in front of the house

Prepositions outside these three groups :

без, without	про, concerning
с [со], with	про} for (intended for)
о, about	для}
без меня, without me	за, for (in exchange for), on behalf of
с ним, with him	про меня, for me, concerning me
со мною, with me	о нём, about him

A detailed list of prepositions (and adverbs used as prepositions), and the cases which they govern is given below. (See § 96.)

The student will note that some directional prepositions of movement have their distinct reverse-counterparts, such as :

(a) в — из ; (b) к — от ; (c) на — с (со) ;
(d) за — из-за

(a) я éду в гóрод
   I go to town

я приéхал из гóрода
I came from town

я идý в шкóлу
   I go to school

я идý из шкóлы
I come from school

я идý в теáтр
   I go to the theatre

я идý из теáтра
I come from the theatre

я идý в óперу
   I go to the opera

я идý из óперы
I come from the opera

(b) я идý к шкóле
   I go towards the school

я идý от шкóлы
I come away from the school

(c) мы éдем на стáнцию
   we go to the station

мы éдем со стáнции
we come from the station

мы éдем на собрáние
   we go to the meeting

мы éдем с собрáния
we come from the meeting

мы éдем на пóчту
   we go to the post office

мы éдем с пóчты
we come from the post office

мы éдем на вéчер
   we go to a party (evening)

мы éдем с вéчера
we come from a party

мы éдем на рынок
   we go to the market

мы éдем с рынка
we come from the market

я вы́шел на у́лицу
I went into the street

он пришёл с у́лицы
he came from the street

я вы́шел на двор
I went into the yard (outside)

он пришёл со двора́
he came from the yard

(d) мы пое́дем за-грани́цу (motion)
we shall go abroad
он за-грани́цей (rest)
he is abroad

он прие́хал из-за грани́цы
he came [arrived] from abroad

мы пое́дем за́ город (motion)
we shall go beyond the town (for
an outing)
за́ городом (rest)

он прие́хал из-за́ города
he came [arrived] from beyond
the town

за́ реку (motion)
to the other side of the river
за реко́й (rest)
at the other side of the river

из-за реки́
from the other side of the river

(e) на — под ; под — из-под

(e) на́ гору, up hill
под стол (motion)
under the table
под столо́м (rest)

под гору, down hill
из-под стола́
from under the table

§ 96. *Prepositions and the cases which they govern.*

(1) *Prepositions governing the Genitive case:*

без, without
близ, near
вдоль, along
вме́сто, instead of
внутри́, inside of
вне, outside of
во́зле, near (by)
вокру́г, around
для, for (intended for)
до, up to, as far as
из, from, out of
из-за, because of, from behind
из-под, from under
кро́ме, beside
ме́жду, between, among (motion)
ми́мо, by
насчёт, on account of

насу́против, opposite, facing
о́коло, about
относи́тельно, concerning
от, away from
позади́, at the back of
по́дле, near (by)
поперёк, across
посре́дством, by means of
по́сле, after
пре́жде, before
про́тив, opposite
ра́ди, for the sake of
сверх, beside
снару́жи, from outside
среди́, in the midst of
у, by, at, near
с, from, from off

§ 96a.   (2) *Prepositions governing the Dative case :*

вопреки, contrary to
к [ко], towards
назло, to spite
наперекор, in spite of, against
  the will of
сообразно ⎱ according to, in
согласно ⎰   conformity with

по, along, according to
  (Also with nouns, and numerals:
  один, одна, -о, and from пять on
  in the sense of distribution, see
  § 47, 6, Note.)   For по with
  numerals 2, 3, 4, see § 96b.

§ 96b.   (3) *Prepositions governing the Accusative case :*

про, about, concerning
сквозь, through
через, across, through
в [во], in (motion)
на, on (motion)
о, об, against
с, approximately

по, up to, as far as
  (Also with numerals 2, 3, 4, 200, 300,
  400 in the meaning of distribution.)
за, behind (motion), for (in place of,
  in exchange for)
под, under (motion)
пред, in front of (motion)

§ 96c.   (4) *Prepositions governing the Instrumental case :*

над, over
под, under (rest)
между, among
за, behind (rest)

пред, in front of (rest)
перед, before
с, with

§ 96d.   (5) *Prepositions governing the Locative (Prepositional) case :*

при, by, in the presence of
о, об, about
в [во], in (rest)

на, on (rest)
по, after

§ 96e.

NOTE 1.   It will be seen that the greater number of
prepositions govern the genitive case.   Of these, у is the
most frequently used in the meaning of : at, near,
of, by.

NOTE 2.

за, behind
под, under
пред, in front of
⎱ (govern the accusative case when the idea
⎰   of motion is implied, and the instru-
    mental case when the idea of rest is
    implied)

в [во], in на, on	(govern the accusative case (motion) and the locative case (rest))
о [об, обо], about, against	(govern the accusative in the meaning of 'against' and the locative in the meaning of 'about,' 'concerning')
мéжду, among	(governs the genitive (motion) and the instrumental (rest))
с [со], from	(govern the genitive)
с, approximately	(governs the accusative)
с [со], with	(govern the instrumental)
по, along	(governs the dative)
по, as far as, up to	(governs the accusative)
по, after	(governs the locative)

NOTE 3. Nearly all the adverbs which are used as prepositions govern the genitive case :

Genitive :

вдоль, along	напрóтив, opposite
вмéсто, in place of	óколо, about
внутрú, inside	пóдле, near
вне, outside	позадú, behind
вóзле, near	поперёк, across
вокрýг, around	пóсле, after
близ, near	прóтив, in front, opposite
крóме, beside	рáди, for the sake of
кругóм, around	снарýжи, from outside
мéжду, between { gen. (motion) { instr. (rest)	Dat. вопрекú, contrary to Acc. сквозь, through

§ 96f. *The Accent of Prepositions.*

A. Proclitics. Normally prepositions have no stress of their own : the word which follows them takes the stress. (See § 14.)

на столé,	on the table
óколо дóма,	near the house
перед чáем,	before tea

B. Enclitics. Some Russian nouns (mainly monosyllabic and dissyllabic) have, however, a tendency to throw their accent back on the preceding prepositions[1] :

[1] The stressed preposition and noun form an adverbial expression.

на, по, под, за, без, до. The nouns that most frequently throw their accent back, and so lose their own stress, are :

час,	hour	мо́ре,	sea
пол,	floor	двор,	yard
нос,	nose	во́лос,	hair
день,	day	по́яс,	waist (belt)
год,	year	стол,	table
бок,	side	бе́рег,	shore (bank of river)
дом,	house	гора́,	hill
лес,	forest	зима́,	winter
род,	birth	нога́,	leg
ночь,	night	рука́,	arm, hand
не́бо,	sky	смерть,	death

also : голова́, head, and a few others.

NOTE. A noun with a tendency to become enclitic after one preposition usually shows the same tendency after other prepositions.

(1) *Enclitics* with на (governing the accusative singular) :

на́ бок,	aside
на́ берег,	on to the bank
на́ волос,	within a hair's breadth
на́ воду,	on to the water
на́ голову,	on the head
на́ гору,	up the hill
на́ зиму,	for the winter
на́ пол,	on the floor
на́ море,	on the sea
на́ ухо,	into the ear (in a whisper)

(2) *Enclitics* with по (governing dative and accusative singular) :

по́ городу (*dat.*),	over the town
по́ двору (*dat.*),	over the yard
по́ воду (*acc.*),	after some water
по́ уши (*acc.*),	up to the ears
по́ пояс (*acc.*),	up to the waist (belt)

(3) *Enclitics* with под (governing the accusative singular and plural) :

	пóд вечер,	towards evening
	пóд гору,	down the hill
	пóд голову,	under the head
	пóд руку,	into the hand ; opportune
but :	под рукóй,	handy
	пóд ноги,	under the feet
	пóд нос,	under one's nose
	пóд стол,	under the table

(4) *Enclitics* with за (governing the accusative singular and plural) :

зá волосы,	by the hair
зá ноги,	by the legs
зá год,	for a year
зá голову,	by the head
зá гору,	beyond the hill (motion)
зá день,	for a day
зá море,	beyond the sea (motion) etc.

Sometimes also with the instrumental :

зá морем,	beyond the sea (rest)
зá лесом,	beyond the woods (rest)
зá городом,	outside the town (rest) etc.

(5) *Enclitics* with из, без, до (governing the genitive singular) :

úз лесу,	out of the wood
úз дому,	out of the house
бéз толку,	without sense
дó верху,	right to the top
дó низу,	right to the bottom
дó земли,	down to the ground

NOTE 1. The prepositions у, от, про, при, о, об, над, ко, во, со very seldom take the stress. The

following are practically the only *enclitics* in current use :

о́т роду (*gen.*),	from birth
при́ смерти (*loc.*),	dying, in a dying state
о́ землю (*acc.*),	against the ground
о́б пол (*acc.*),	against the floor
во́ время (*acc.*),	in time
but : во вре́мя,	during the time
со́ двора (*gen.*),	from the yard away
со́ ста (*gen.*),	from hundred
рука́ о́б руку (*acc.*),	hand in hand [arm in arm]
час о́т часу (*gen.*),	one hour from another

NOTE 2. The prepositions бе́зо, и́зо, на́до, о́бо, по́до, пре́до, пе́редо (which usually stand before nouns beginning with two consonants), also для, ра́ди, кро́ме, че́рез, сквозь, пред, пе́ред, never make the noun *enclitic*.

NOTE 3. Primary monosyllabic numerals after the prepositions по, за, на always become *enclitic :*

за́ три,	for three
за́ пять,	for five
за́ сто,	for hundred
по́ два, две,	two each
по́ три,	three each etc.

NOTE 4. Monosyllabic verbs in the past tense and past passive participles have also a tendency to become *enclitic* after the negative particle не :

не́ был,	but :	не была́
не́ дал,	,,	не дала́
не́ жил,	,,	не жила́
не́ взят, not taken,	,,	не взята́
не́ дан, not given,	,,	не дана́
не́ зван, not called, not invited,	,,	не звана́

also : не́хотя, unwillingly
       не́чего,   there is no need to . . .

(See § 135, sub-section 7.)

§ 97.. 8. *Conjunctions.* (Indeclinable sentence-words, showing connection between words and sentences.)

(NOTE. On the use of conjunction in the complex
sentence see §§ 124-129.)

(1) *Co-ordinative (copulative) Conjunctions :*

и, and; also; even   ещё, yet
и . . . и, both . . . and   даже, even
да, and   то, then
также, as well   то . . . то, now . . . then
тоже, also   отчасти, partly
притом, at the same time   как, так, as well as
сверх того, besides   не только . . . но и, not only
к тому, and then   . . . but also

(2) *Alternative :*

или ⎫ or   или . . . или ⎫ either . . . or
либо ⎭   либо . . . либо ⎭
ли . . . ли, whether . . . or

(3) *Interrogative :*

ли [ль] . . . или [иль], whether . . . or

(4) *Explanatory :*

что, that   так что, so that
будто, as if   так как, as, since
будто-бы, as it were ; supposed   тогда, когда, then, when
   to   там, где, there, where
ведь, indeed, but   куда, туда, where to, there
тогда как, whereas   to

(5) *Temporal* (Conjunctions of Time) :

сперва, at first   наконец, at last
сначала, at the beginning   далее, further
во-первых, firstly   прежде чем ⎫ prior to
во-вторых, secondly   прежде нежели ⎭
в-третьих, thirdly   пока, meanwhile
едва, hardly   лишь только ⎫ as soon as
потом, afterwards   чуть только ⎭
затем, then   то . . . то, now . . . then

(6) *Comparative* :

как, так, аs, so
нѣжели, than
чем, than, rather than (with infinitive)
как, as
чем . . . тем, the . . . the
слóвно, as if
тóчно, exactly
бýдто, as it were
так же, как, exactly as

(7) *Conditional* :

ѐжели, то⎫ if . . . then
ѐсли, то ⎭

когдá бы ⎧ if (verb after бы
ѐсли бы ⎨ stands in the past
⎩ tense)

когдá, тогдá, if . . . then
лишь-бы, only to, if only

(8) *Hypothetical (Suppositional)* :

бы, ежели-бы, если-бы, if (with verb in the past tense); had it been

(9) *Concessive* :

хотя́ [хоть], although, though ; at least, at any rate
хотя́ бы, if only ; even though
хоть и, even if
хоть, но [однáко], though . . . yet
пусть, но [а], though . . . yet
лишь, if only
всё-таки, nevertheless, all the same
пусть ⎫ let
пускáй ⎭
прáвда, true

впрóчем, however
пожáлуй ⎫ admitted
полóжим ⎭
допýстим, allowing
несмотря́ на то, notwithstanding that
скóлько ни, however much, no matter how much
как ни, no matter how
что ни, no matter what
что-ли? perhaps?, shall we say?

(10) *Conjunctions of Purpose* :

чтóбы [чтоб], дабы́, in order to ; that (with verb, either in the past or in the infinitive)
(When чтóбы introduces a subordinate clause expressing *desire* or *wish*, the verb in the subordinate clause stands in the past tense.)

(11) *Conjunctions expressing opposition or antithesis* (adversative) :

а, but [and]
но, but
же, but, also
да, but [and]

однáко, however
тóлько, only
напрóтив, on the contrary

(12) *Conjunctions of cause, of effect, or of result* (causative) :

и́бо, because (not often used in the spoken language)

потому́ что, because

так как, as

для того́ же, it is for this . . .

за тем что ⎱ for this reason
за то что ⎰

оттого́ что, for the reason that . . .

(13) *Concluding Conjunctions* :

ита́к, and so

так, so

посему́, consequently

сле́довательно, consequently

зна́чит, it means

ста́ло-быть, it follows

почему́, why

§ 98.　9. *Interjections.*　(Sentence-words, expressing various emotions.)

Joy :　　　ура́! hurrah!

Grief :　　　ах! ah!
　　　　　　　ох! oh!
　　　　　　　увы́! alas!
　　　　　　　о! oh!

Contempt :　фи! фу! phew! fie!

Fright :　　　ух! ough!
　　　　　　　ах! oh!

Surprise :　　а! ah!
　　　　　　　ба! here comes!
　　　　　　　тфу! фуй! phew!

Call :　　　эй! гей! eh there!

Curt dismissal :
　　　　　　　прочь! away!
　　　　　　　доло́й! down!
　　　　　　　по́лно! enough! that will do!

Thanks :　　спаси́бо! thanks!

Threat :　　вот ужо́! you wait!

Reproach :　э! эх! eh!
　　　　　　　ну! indeed!

Indication :　вон! out! there!

Approbation :　бра́во! well done!
　　　　　　　сла́вно! glorious!

Assurance :　ей-ей! ⎱ indeed!
　　　　　　　пра́во! ⎰

Offer :　　　на! на-те! here!

Sound imitation :
　　　　　　　бац! slap!
　　　　　　　хлоп! pop!
　　　　　　　бух! pop!
　　　　　　　цап! snap!

SECTION III

SYNTAX

§ 99. *Essentials of Russian Syntax.*

It is not the purpose of this work to deal at length with Russian syntax, but as no study of Russian can be pursued without at least some minimum knowledge of syntax, it will be within the scope of this little work to supply that minimum in order to assist the beginner to keep his bearings in the various forms of construction of the rich Russian language.

In dealing with complex sentences the simpler forms have been treated. The few indispensable rules of general syntax are marshalled here, in so far as they have any bearing on Russian syntax, with a view to assisting the student to foster an appropriate grammatical consciousness which is essential for acquiring the knowledge of a language so highly inflected as Russian.

§ 100. *The Sentence.*

(1) A sentence is a word or group of words which express a complete thought or meaning.

(2) In any sentence one must distinguish at least two ideas which make up a thought : (*a*) what we think of ; (*b*) what we think concerning it.

The first is called the **subject** of the sentence.

The second is called the **predicate** of the sentence.

(3) Subject and predicate are joined together in various ways, and the relation between them is modified in various other ways.

(4) The principal content of a sentence is made up of words which denote either a subject (a person or object), or an action or state, or a property, or a number. These are supplied by nouns, pronouns, verbs, adjectives, and numerals.

(5) The manner of combination of various words in a sentence is indicated either by various inflexions (declensions and conjugations) of the principal words of the sentence, or by other words which connect the principal words or show their relation to each other. This function is performed by pronouns, some adverbs, prepositions, and conjunctions.

(6) Other parts of a sentence, besides the subject and predicate, are : (1) the **object** (object-complement) ; (2) **qualifying words** (qualifiers) ; (3) **adverbial expressions** : (*a*) of place, (*b*) of time, (*c*) of manner, (*d*) of cause, (*e*) of purpose.

§ 101. *Relation between Words in the Sentence.*

The various parts of the sentence can stand to each other either in the relation of co-ordination or of subordination. These relations can be shown either by word-order alone (very rarely in Russian) or by concord where two words (head-word and adjunct-word) agree in whatever grammatical form they have in common : inflexion, number, case. The head-word governs the adjunct-word. (See § 116.)

§ 102. The **Subject** (principal object of our thought in the sentence) can be expressed :

   (*a*) by a noun in the nominative case, answering to the questions : кто ? who ?, что ? what ? ;

   (*b*) by a pronoun or numeral in the nominative ;

   (*c*) by a verbal infinitive or participle ;

   (*d*) by any indeclinable part of speech when it is used in the sense of a noun in the nominative. Such words when used as the subject of the sentence are treated as if they were neuter nouns as regards their co-ordination. (See § 119.)

§ 103. The **Predicate** (part of the sentence which denotes what is stated about the subject of the sentence).

The predicate can be expressed :

   (*a*) by a verb in any tense ;

   (*b*) by a short adjective ;

   (*c*) by a short past passive participle ;

(*d*) by a noun, when the verbal idea is only implied, and the **present tense** of the auxiliary verb быть is omitted :

Он мой брат.   He is my brother.

(есть—present tense—is omitted, but the past and future are not omitted : он был мой друг, he was my friend ; он будет моим учителем, he will be my teacher.)

NOTE. Besides the auxiliary verb быть, the verbs стать, сделаться (to become), are also used as a copula for the same purpose. The nouns which they govern stand either in the nominative or the instrumental case (see above example).

§ **104.** The predicate can be either a simple one or a compound one (see § 103). The declinable part of a compound predicate is called the name-part.

(1) The name-part of a predicate can be expressed by all the declinable parts of speech : nouns, adjectives, pronouns, and numerals.

(2) The name-part of a predicate can stand in the nominative, instrumental, or genitive case :

Я столяр (*nom.*).   I am a joiner.

Наши берёзы стали высокими деревьями (*instr.*). Our birch trees have become tall trees.

Он был тихого нрава (*gen.*). He was of a quiet disposition.

Он был среднего роста (*gen.*). He was of medium height.

Он был моим другом (*instr.*).   He was my friend. (It implies the idea of a defined, limited time.)

Он был мой друг (*nom.*, always).

§ 105. *Irregular use of Tenses in Sentences for the sake of expressiveness.*

(1) Use of **present** instead of **past** tense :

Прибежа́ли в и́збу де́ти,
второпя́х зову́т отца́ . . .
The children ran into the house, hurriedly they call
father . . .

(2) Use of **present** instead of **future** tense :

Меня́ занима́л вопро́с : куда́ он е́дет ? . . .
I was preoccupied with the question : where is he
going to ? (instead of : пое́дет).

(3) Начина́ет одно́, че́рез мину́ту возьмётся за дру-
го́е . . .
He begins one thing, in a minute he will take up
something else . . .

§ 106. *Peculiarities in the use of Moods.*

(1) First person plural of the present tense instead of
imperative (in the sense of : let us) :

Идём, пойдём гуля́ть.
(colloquially : Идёмте, пойдёмте гуля́ть).
Let us go for a walk.
Забу́дем э́то. Let us forget this.

(2) Conditional mood (which is always in the past tense
and is either preceded or followed by the particle бы), used
in the sense of giving advice :

Ты бы пое́хал к дя́де. You should go to uncle's.
Ты бы ра́ньше напи́лся ча́ю. You might have tea first.

(3) Imperative singular instead of conditional :

Не приди́ он, я бы не пое́хал с ва́ми. Had not he
come, I would not have gone with you (instead of :
Е́сли бы он не пришёл).

Знай я э́то ра́ньше, я бы не дал кни́ги. Had I known this before, I would not have given the book (instead of : Е́сли бы я знал э́то ра́ньше).

Не будь нас там, все бы скуча́ли. If it had not been for us [but for us] everybody would have felt bored (instead of : Е́сли бы мы не бы́ли там). (See § 123b, sub-section (2).)

(4) **Infinitive** mood instead of **indicative** mood :

Я ему́ сде́лал вы́говор, а он пла́кать (instead of : стал пла́кать). I rebuked him, and he started crying.

Не вида́ть тебе́ мои́х книг. You will not see my books (instead of : Не уви́дишь мои́х книг).

(5) **Infinitive** instead of **imperative** (particularly in case of urgency) :

посла́ть сейча́с,	send at once
вы́дать неме́дленно,	hand over at once
не писа́ть,	don't write

(6) Frequently any tense of the **indicative** mood can be replaced by verbal interjections for greater expressiveness :

а он с во́зом — бух в кана́ву (instead of бу́хнул), and he with the cart — flop right into the ditch.

This is a form much favoured by popular usage.

§ 107. The Object (Object-complement) can be expressed by any declinable part of speech in any oblique case (noun, adjective, pronoun, numeral, and participle) :

Я ви́жу реку́. I see the river (*acc.*).

Я рад слу́чаю поговри́ть.
I am glad of the occasion to have a talk (*dat.*).

Я пишу́ перо́м. I write with a pen (*instr.*).

Сытый **голодного** не разумеет (*gen.*).

The well-fed one does not comprehend the hungry one.

Мне **прошлого** не жаль (*gen.*).

I am not regretful of the past.

NOTE. An object can also be expressed by a verbal infinitive :

Мы готовы ехать. We are ready to start.

Мы хотим быть там рано (see also § 123*a*).

We want to be there early.

§ 108. *The Direct Object.*

(*a*) An object which stands in the accusative case after a transitive verb is called a **direct object** :

Он купил корову. He bought a cow.

(*b*) Any other object is called an **indirect object** :

Он торгует скотом (*instr.*). He deals in cattle.

Мы ждём ночи (*gen.*).

We are waiting for the night to come [for nightfall].

Он отказался от вина (*gen.*). He refused wine.

§ 108*a*.

(*c*) A direct object stands in the genitive instead of the accusative if the verb implies negation :

Он знает урок (*acc.*).	He knows the lesson.
but : Он не знает урока (*gen.*).	He does not know the lesson.
Он купил дом (*acc.*).	He bought a house.
but : Он не купил дома (*gen.*).	He did not buy a house.

(*d*) If the direct object is used in a partitive sense (implying not the whole quantity of an object, but only part of it), it stands in the genitive instead of accusative :

Дай мне воды́.   Give me some water.

Пожа́луйста, да́йте мне хле́ба.

Please give me some bread.

Он принёс хле́ба.   He fetched some bread.

but :   Он принёс хлеб.

He fetched the bread (all that there was of it).

Да́йте мне вина́.   Give me some wine.

but :   Принеси́те вино́.   Fetch the wine.

§ 108*b*.

Note 1. An indirect object is often expressed in the nominative plural (used as an accusative) if it denotes a change of personal condition :

Он вы́шел в лю́ди.   He became a man of standing [he succeeded in life].

Его́ взя́ли в изво́щики.   He was taken [given a job] as a cab-driver.

Он стал изво́щиком.   He became a cab-driver. (Adverbially : Он [состои́т] в изво́щиках.   He holds a position as cab-driver.)

Её взя́ли в гуверна́нтки.   She has been taken as a governess. (Adverbially : Она́ в гуверна́нтках. She is a governess [serves as a governess].)

В музыка́нты не годи́тесь.   You are no good as musicians (Krylov).

Он стал музыка́нтом, or : он поступи́л в музыка́нты (*nom. pl.* instead of *instr. sing.*). He became a musician.

Он стал сто́рожем, or : он поступи́л в сторожа́ (*nom. pl.*). He became a porter, he took a position as a porter.

Его́ взя́ли в солда́ты (*nom. pl.*). He was taken as soldier.

Его́ произвели́ в офице́ры.   He has been promoted [gazetted] an officer.

Она поступила в горничные (or Она стала горничной).
  She took a post as chambermaid.

Я пойду в няни. I shall become a nurse. (Adverbially :
  Она няней. She serves as a nurse. Он солдатом.
  He is a soldier.)

By analogy the nominative plural is also used on other
occasions :

Мы поедем в гости. We shall go on a visit (as guests).

Мы были в гостях (adverbially). We were on a visit.

Мы приехади из гостей (adverbially). We came back
  from a visit (as guests).

NOTE 2. If a direct object is expressed by a verbal
infinitive followed by a noun-complement, the noun (or
any other declinable word) stands in the instrumental
case :

  Я хочу быть солдатом. I want to be a soldier.

  Она не хочет быть горничной.
  She does not want to be a chambermaid.

The instrumental is also required after : стать, стано-
виться, сделаться, to become ; считаться, слыть, to
be known as, to be reputed as.

§ 109. Qualifying Words (*Qualifiers*).

These denote the quality or any other definition of
nouns in a sentence :

  Богатый купец жил в **большом** доме.
  The rich merchant lived in a big house.

  С **той** поры **моё** положение переменилось.
  Since that time my position has changed.

  Он держал **двух** поваров.
  He kept two cooks (men).

  Дом моего **дяди** сгорел.
  The house of my uncle is burned down.

NOTE 1. Qualifying words usually answer to the questions : каков ? what kind ? ; какой ? which ? ; чей ? whose ? ; сколько ? how much ?, how many ? They are expressed by adjectives, pronouns, numerals, and participles, and they stand *in concord* with the word which they qualify :

Бе́лый дом ви́ден и́здали.
The white house is visible in the distance (*adj.*).

Мой сад с ка́ждым днём стано́вится гу́ще.
My garden (with) every day becomes thicker [denser] (*prons.*).

Восьмо́й день прошёл.
The eighth day has passed (*ord. num.*).

Мы ви́дели игра́ющих дете́й.
We saw playing children (*part.*).

In the above examples the qualifiers agree with the qualified word in gender, case, and number.

NOTE 2. If the qualifier is expressed by a noun or any other declinable part of speech, it can stand in various cases (but mostly in the genitive) :

Его́ спасла́ темнота́ но́чи.
[Он был спасён темното́й но́чи.]
He was saved by the darkness of the night.

Не́мцы бежа́ли с по́ля би́твы.
The Germans ran from the field of battle.

Не́мцы разру́шили их сёла.
The Germans destroyed their villages.

NOTE 3. A qualifying word can also be expressed by an infinitive :

Не́мцев лиши́ли возмо́жности разруша́ть.
The Germans were deprived of the possibility to destroy.

Пришло́ вре́мя расста́ться.
The time for parting has come.

§ 110. The **apposition** is a qualifying word expressed by a noun which stands in the same case as the qualified word :

Пришёл Пётр, **старйк**, которого мы вйдели вчерá.
Came Peter, the old man whom we saw yesterday.

В гóроде жил старйк, по имени **Мирóнов**.
In the town lived an old man by the name of Mironov.

Ты дóлжен доверять мне, своемý дрýгу.
You must trust me, your friend.

Appositions are frequently joined to the qualified words by means of conjunctions, or other words which serve as conjunctions, such as : как, as ; йли, or ; тó-есть, that is ; йменно, namely ; как-то, as follows ; etc.

Он мне, как дрýгу, всегдá доверяет.
He always confides in me as in a friend.

Степь, то-есть, безлéсная равнйна . . .
The steppe, that is a woodless plain . . .

Степь, йли безлéсная равнйна . . .
The steppe, or a woodless plain . . .

The apposition can stand either before or after the qualified word.

NOTE 1.   The subordination of the apposition to its head-word is so slight that the two are almost *co-ordinated.*

NOTE 2.   The apposition usually stands within commas as a parenthetic sentence, if it follows the head-word.

NOTE 3.   Occasionally an apposition is expressed by an adjective, particularly after a personal pronoun :

Он, беспокóйный, всегдá кудá-то бежйт.
He, the restless one, always runs somewhere.

Adverbial Expressions

§ 111. (*a*) **Adverbial expressions of place,** answering to the questions : где? where?; куда? where to?; откуда? where from?:

Я живу́ в Ло́ндоне.	I live in London.
Мы е́дем в Москву́.	We are going to Moscow.
Он прие́хал из Ленингра́да.	He arrived from Leningrad.

§ 112. (*b*) **Adverbial expressions of time,** answering to the questions : когда́? when?; как до́лго? how long?; с како́го вре́мени? since when?; до како́го вре́мени? till when?:

Она́ ждала́ с утра́ до ве́чера.
She waited from morning till evening.

Он про́был здесь две неде́ли.
He stayed here two weeks.

Он пробу́дет здесь до о́сени.
He will remain here till autumn.

Он до́лго не мог реши́ться.
For a long time he could not decide [make up his mind].

§ 113. (*c*) **Adverbial expressions of manner,** answering to the questions : как? how?; каки́м о́бразом? in what manner?; ско́лько? how much?; в како́м разме́ре? to what extent?:

Он мно́го тру́дится, да по́льзы в э́том нет.
He labours much, but there is no profit in it.

Он полива́ет огоро́д два ра́за в день.
He waters the kitchen garden twice a day.

Мы пое́хали ры́сью.   We went at a trot.

Он двумя́ года́ми ста́рше меня́ (*also* моего́).
He is older than I by two years.

G

§ 114.　(*d*) **Adverbial expressions of cause**, answering to the questions : почему́ ? why ? ; по како́й причи́не ? for what reason ? ; отчего́ ? because of what ? ; за что ? what for ? :

　　Я остаю́сь до́ма **по боле́зни.**
　　I remain at home owing to illness.

　　Он просну́лся **от внеза́пного шу́ма.**
　　He woke up because of the sudden noise.

　　Он был расстро́ен **с доса́ды.**
　　He was upset from aggravation [annoyance].

　　Я был нака́зан **за свою́ го́рдость.**
　　I was punished for my pride.

　　Я чуть не вскри́кнул **со стра́ха.**
　　I nearly cried out from fear.

§ 115.　(*e*) **Adverbial expressions of purpose**, answering to the questions : заче́м ? for what object *or* what for ? ; для чего́ ? to what purpose ? ; с како́й це́лью ? with what object ? :

Он был по́слан [его́ посла́ли] в го́род **за вино́м.**
He was sent to town to fetch wine.

Они́ останови́лись в корчме́ [на постоя́лом дворе́] **для ночле́га.**
They stopped at the inn for the night [to stay for the night].

Мой сосе́д пригласи́л меня́ **обе́дать** с ним.
My neighbour invited me to dine with him.

　　Note.　The most frequently used words for expressing adverbials of all classes are : adverbs, gerunds, nouns, and infinitives.

§ 116.　*Co-ordination and Subordination.*

The student must bear in mind that in the study of a language so highly inflected as Russian he will have to familiarize himself with the right mode of joining the various parts that go to make up the sentence, in order to join them into a coherent and correct whole.

Words are joined into a sentence in two ways :

        (1) by *Co-ordination.*
        (2) by *Subordination.*

§ 117. (1) *Co-ordination*, where parts of the sentence are placed in the same form as far as number, gender, and person are concerned :

Старик ловил рыбу. The old man was catching fish. (Subject and predicate are in the same number and gender.)

Старуха пряла. The old woman spun. (Co-ordination of gender and number.)

Я иду гулять. I go for a walk. (Co-ordination of person and number.)

Co-ordination mainly affects :

        (*a*) predicate and subject ;
        (*b*) qualifying word and qualified word.

(*a*) **Predicate**, when expressed by a verb, agrees with the subject of the sentence in person, number, and in gender (if in the past tense) :

Весело сияет месяц.	Brightly [gaily] the moon is shining.
Прибежали дети.	The children came running.
Старик ловил рыбу.	The old man caught fish.
Птица летала.	The bird was flying.
Хлеб стал дорог.	Bread has become dear.
Щука жадная рыба.	The pike is a greedy fish.

(*b*) **Qualifying word** agrees with the qualified word in gender, number, and case :

Белый снег сверкает.	The white snow glitters.
Белка там живёт ручная.	A tame squirrel lives there.

§ 118. (2) *Subordination.*

By subordination we mean such a manner of joining two words in a sentence where one word stands in the particular case which is required by the other word :

Осёл увидел соловья́. The donkey saw the nightingale. (Direct object in the genitive, instead of accusative, is required in the case of an animate noun.)

Лиса́ зале́зла в сад. The fox got into the orchard. (Accusative with в answering to the question куда́ ?.)

Он досто́ин ва́шего внима́ния. He is deserving of your attention.

The word which requires that the other word should stand in a particular case, thus deciding the particular case in which that word should stand, is called the **governing word.**

The word which conforms in the particular case (the modified word) in accordance with the requirement of the governing word, is called the **governed word.**

Governing words in the sentence are mostly verbs, but occasionally they can also be nouns and adjectives :

Я ви́дел бра́та. I saw brother. (Governing word is a verb).

У него́ привы́чка к труду́. He has a bent for work. (Governing word is a noun.)

Он досто́ин внима́ния. He is deserving of attention. (Governing word is a short adjective.)

Governed words are nearly always nouns.

Subordination can be effected both with and without a preposition :

Осёл увидел соловья́. The donkey saw the nightingale.
Над осло́м смею́тся. The donkey is laughed at.
Лиса́ зале́зла в сад. The fox got into the orchard.

The relation between the governing and the governed words can be either (1) an indirect one, or (2) a direct one : that is, (1) with a preposition, or (2) without a preposition.

1. Лиса́ зале́зла в сад.
2. Осёл уви́дел соловья́.

§ 119. 1. *Peculiar Cases of Co-ordination between Subject and Predicate.*

(1) If the subject is expressed by a cardinal numeral or the words : мно́го (much), ма́ло (little), мно́жество (a large quantity), не́сколько (a few), then the verb (predicate) can stand either in the plural or in neuter singular :

Остава́лось семь вёрст до Москвы́.

It was [remained] se'ven versts to Moscow. (Verb in neuter singular.)

Не́сколько каза́ков встре́тили капита́на.

A few Cossacks met the captain. (Verb in the plural.)

На столе́ бы́ло мно́го буты́лок вина́.

On the table there were many bottles of wine.

Мно́жество соба́к встре́тило нас гро́мким ла́ем.

A large number of dogs met us with loud barking. (Verb in neuter singular.)

Мно́жество но́вых до́миков мелька́ло из-за дере́вьев.

A large number of new small houses glimmered through [from behind] the trees. (Verb in neuter singular.)

(2) If the auxiliary verb быть (usually omitted in the present tense if used as a copula) is used as an ordinary predicate, the singular есть can be used even when plurality is expressed (see § 134a) :

У нас есть кни́ги. We have books.

§ 120. 2. *Peculiar Cases of Co-ordination between Qualifier and Qualified word.* (See § 137, sub-section 7.)

(1) Cardinal numerals два, о́ба, три, четы́ре, полтора́ do not conform in case with their noun (that is, they do not

take the nominative or accusative plural), but require the genitive singular :

два[1] рубля́,	two roubles
о́ба стола́,	both tables
три сту́ла,	three chairs
четы́ре бра́та,	four brothers
полтора́[1] фу́нта,	1½ pounds

(2) Cardinal and collective numerals, and also adverbial pronouns denoting an indefinite quantity (пять, шесть, etc. ; дво́е, тро́е, etc. ; мно́го, ма́ло, не́сколько), require the genitive plural, except when мно́го, ма́ло are used with partitive nouns, such as butter, sugar, tea, etc., in the sense of ' much,' ' little ' :

ма́ло столо́в,	few tables
мно́го сту́льев,	many chairs
не́сколько книг,	a few books
but : ма́ло ма́сла,	little butter
мно́го са́хару,	much sugar

(3) In the oblique cases cardinal numerals (and adverbial pronouns denoting quantity) agree with the noun :

Gen.	двух столо́в
Dat.	двум стола́м
Instr.	мно́гими стола́ми

NOTE. In Russian the expressions *five, six, a few, how many people*, are rendered as :

пять челове́к	
шесть челове́к	
не́сколько челове́к	not люде́й
ско́лько челове́к	

(see §§ 20, group 9 ; 54*b*) ;

---

[1] две, полторы́, if used with a feminine noun.

but the expressions *few people, many people*, are rendered as :

мáло людéй	мнóго людéй

or in the popular forms :

мáло нарóду	мнóго нарóду

PERSONAL AND IMPERSONAL SENTENCES

§ 121. (1) *Personal sentences* have either a clearly defined (apparent) or a latent (implied) subject :

травá растёт,	grass grows
я пишý,	I write

§ 122. (2) *Impersonal sentences* have no apparent grammatical subject :

Морóзит.	It freezes.
Светáет.	It is daybreak [it is becoming light].
Рассвелó.	It is daybreak [it has become light].
Мне хóчется есть.	I feel hungry.
Мне хотéлось есть.	I felt hungry.
По ýлицам слонá водѝли.	

An elephant was being led along the streets.

In the first three sentences, which express natural phenomena, both the formal subject and the predicate are merged in one word. In the second three sentences the grammatical subject is inverted (turned into an object). (See § 56b.)

To the same class belong :

мне дýмается,	I seem to think ; I am thinking ; it occurs to me
мне дýмалось,	I was thinking ; it occurred to me
говоря́т,	they say
нет [не есть],	no
темнéет,	it is becoming dark
мне не спѝтся,	I cannot sleep
мне кáжется,	it seems to me
мне казáлось[*по-],	it seemed to me ; I thought

NOTE. The predicate of an impersonal sentence can be expressed :

(a) By the second person of the present tense of the indicative mood or by the second person of the imperative mood :

Тише éдешь, дáльше бýдешь.
The slower you travel, the farther you will be [get].
Хлеб-соль ешь, а прáвду режь.
Eat bread and salt, and be truthful [cut the truth].

(b) By the third person singular (neuter) of the indicative mood (both past and present) :

Рассветáет.	It is the beginning of daybreak.
Рассвелó.	It is daybreak.
Морóзит.	It freezes.
Морóзило.	It was freezing.

Крышу сорвáло бóмбой.
The roof has been torn off by a bomb.
Меня сильно толкнýло вперёд.
I was forcibly pushed forward.

Мне хóчется есть.	I feel hungry.
Мне не хотéлось есть.	I did not feel hungry.
Мне не спится.	I cannot sleep.
Мне не спáлось.	I could not sleep.
Егó нет [не есть] дóма.	He is not in [at home].
Егó нé было дóма.	He was not in [at home].
У меня нé было дéнег.	I had no money.

В лес дров не вóзят.
Wood (fire-wood) is not carted into the forest.

NOTE. The tendency to turn a personal construction into an impersonal one is one of the peculiarities of the Russian language. This frequently happens even when the grammatical subject is not quite hidden. Some of the above sentences could be expressed as personal sentences with a formal subject :

я хочу́ есть ; я не хоте́л есть ; я не могу́ спать ; я не мог спать ; он не до́ма ; он не́ был до́ма ; я не име́л де́нег ; etc.

But these personal constructions would imply too much individual deliberate *volition*, which it is the intention of the impersonal sentence not to express too prominently. (See § 56*b*.)

(*c*) By the infinitive :

Мне не́когда вози́ться. I have no time to bother.

(*d*) By means of the auxiliary verbs : быть (to be), станови́ться, стать, сде́латься (to become), in compound predicates, with an adverb. In the present tense the auxiliary verb is omitted :

Мне ску́чно.	I feel bored [dull].
Мне бы́ло ску́чно.	I felt bored.
Мне ста́ло ве́село.	I began to feel cheerful.
Мне ста́ло хо́лодно.	I began to feel cold.
Мне стано́вится жа́рко.	I begin to feel hot.

(*e*) By a neuter verb with the reflective particle ся in the passive sense :

дом стро́ится [дом стро́ят],	the house is being built
э́то де́лается [э́то де́лают],	this is done
э́то называ́ется [э́то называ́ют],	this is called

(See § 131.)

Note. The sentences in this group are only logically impersonal ; grammatically they have the character of personal sentences.

(*f*) An impersonal character is lent to a sentence by the use of the second person singular of the present tense

σ *

(or future in perfectives) preceded by the past tense
of the semi-iterative verb бывáть — бывáло :

бывáло, скáжешь,	it often happened one would say
бывáло, éдешь,	it often happened one would go [travel]
бывáло, спрóсишь,	it often happened one would ask

NOTE. Other persons can also be used with
бывáло :

бывáло, говорят,	it often happened ⎫	they would
бывáло, спрóсят,	it often happened ⎭	say, ask

(g) By the use of any form of an active verb for the
passive form :

его убúло грóмом instead of он был убúт грóмом
he was killed by lightning [thunder]

(h) By the use of the past tense in the neuter with the
formal subject turned into an object, usually in the
genitive :

приéхало мнóго гостéй,	many guests arrived
собрáлось мнóго нарóду,	many people gathered

NOTE. мнóго in these two sentences is the formal
subject (*neuter*).

§ 123. *Negative Sentences* (see § 135, sub-section 6).

Double and treble negations are usual in Russian :

никогó не вúдно,	no one to be seen
никогó не видáть,	one cannot see anybody
никогó нет,	no one is in ; there is nobody
я никогдá не забýду,	I shall never forget
он ничегó не сдéлал,	he did nothing
ничегó нет,	there is nothing
он никогдá ничегó не дéлает,	he never does anything
я нигдé не был,	I was not anywhere
я никудá не поéду,	I shall not go anywhere

я совсе́м не зна́ю,	I don't know at all
ниско́лько не зна́ю,	I don't know in the least
совершённо не зна́ю ⎫ нима́ло не зна́ю ⎭	I absolutely do not know
я во́все не хочу́,	I do not at all wish [want]

NOTE. Negative pronouns and adverbs always stand before the particle не which precedes the verb.

§ 123a. *Use of the Infinitive* as an object-complement. (See § 107.)

ду́маю пойти́,	I think of going
ду́маю нача́ть,	I think of beginning
ду́маю писа́ть,	I think of writing
ду́маю посла́ть,	I think of sending
¹ начну́ рабо́тать,	I shall begin to work
¹ на́чал писа́ть,	began to write
¹ стал проси́ть,	began to ask

§ 123b. *Use of the Imperative.*

(1) The affirmative imperative (when requesting or ordering someone to do a thing) is often expressed in the imperfective form even if the verb is used in the perfective aspect in the indicative mood. An order or command thus expressed is less abrupt :

сади́тесь здесь (sit down here) is less definite, but is also less abrupt than ся́дьте здесь.

In the negative imperative the same tendency is noticed :

не говори́, не ска́зывай (do not speak, do not tell) instead of не скажи́.

NOTE. But if a verb is used with a prepositional prefix, which often alters the general meaning of the verb by giving it a modified direction, the imperative is used in the perfective form :

принеси́те кни́ги,	fetch the books
унеси́те всё э́то,	take all this away
позови́те дво́рника,	call the porter

---

¹ After verbs denoting beginning or termination of an action, the imperfective of the complement verb is used.

(2) Often the imperative singular takes the place of a conditional clause :

зна́й я э́то ра́ньше, я бы не дал кни́ги, had I known this before, I would not have given the book (instead of е́сли бы я знал э́то ра́ньше).   (See § 106, subsection (3).)

(3) The imperatives of дать, дава́ть : дай[те], дава́й[те] mean : let us . . .

дава́йте игра́ть в пря́тки, let us play at hide-and-seek.

бу́дем, бу́демте also have the meaning of 'let us . . . '

(4) The imperatives of пусти́ть, пуска́ть (to let, to allow) : пусть, пуска́й, followed by another verb, mean : let him, let them :

пусть, пуска́й пи́шет,   let him write
пусть, пуска́й де́лают,   let them do

пусть, пуска́й, used alone, mean : 'all right,' 'I don't care.'

(5)

здра́вствуй[те] { customary form of greeting instead of : good morning, good day, good evening } how do you do ?

literal meaning : keep well

проща́й[те],   good-bye

are imperatives which are used almost adverbially.

§ 124. *Complex Sentences.*

It is frequently found necessary to elucidate some part of a simple sentence by expressing it in a whole sentence instead of one word. When this is done a **complex sentence** is formed. Two or three simple sentences can be joined together into one **complex sentence**. The simple sentences thus joined are called **clauses**. There is usually a principal clause and one or more subordinate clauses. The **principal clause** is that which expresses the main thought of the complex sentence. Any other clauses which form a part of the main sentence are called **subordinate clauses**. The dependent clause, or clauses, may be either *co-ordinate* or *subordinate*:

Порá вставáть : ужé седьмóй час ;   or
Порá вставáть, потомý что ужé седьмóй час (co-ordination).
It is time to get up : because it is already past [gone] six (the seventh hour).

Нам не нужнá постéль : мы бýдем спать на дворé ;   or
Нам не нужнá постéль, потомý что мы бýдем спать на дворé (co-ordination).
We need no bed as [because] we will sleep in the yard [outside].

Сfirst шёл дождь, потóм тýчи разогнáло вéтром, и наконéц нéбо прояснúлось (co-ordination).
At first it was raining, then [afterwards] the clouds were dispersed by the wind, and finally the sky cleared.

Дверь отворúлась, и человéк вошёл в кóмнату (co-ordination).
The door opened, and a man entered the room.

Кóмната, где лежáл Ильá Ильúч, казáлась прекрáсно ýбранной (subordination).
The room in which Ilya Ilyich was lying appeared to be beautifully decorated [furnished].

Он указáл на стол, на котóром Облóмов обéдал (sub-ordination).
He pointed to the table at which Oblomov was having dinner [was dining].

Никтó не знáет, бýдет ли он зáвтра жив úли умрёт (subordination).
No one knows whether he will be alive to-morrow or he will be dead.

Европейцы долго не знали, что существует Америка ; or Европейцы долго не знали того, что существует Америка (subordination).

Europeans did not know for a long time about the existence of America. (Here the subordinate clause answers to the question чего ? what ? The clause stands as a direct object complementing a negative predicate.)

Besides these two categories of clauses, there are also **inserted** and **parenthetic** clauses :

Когда он говорит, а он почти всегда говорит, его лицо выражает досаду (inserted clause).

When he talks, and he almost always talks, his face expresses vexation [annoyance].

Ты, говорят, большой мастер петь (parenthetic clause).

They say, thou art a great master of [good at] singing.

Он, я полагаю, приедет завтра (parenthetic clause).

He, I suppose, will arrive to-morrow.

Он, говорят, ранен ⎰ They say ⎱
Говорят, он ранен ⎱ he is ⎰ (parenthetic clauses).
Он ранен, говорят ⎰ wounded ⎱

Спорили, как водится, очень долго (parenthetic).

They argued a very long time, as usual.

Inserted and parenthetic clauses can stand in the relation of co-ordination or subordination to the principal clause. They usually stand between commas if in the middle of the principal sentence. They are separated by a comma if they stand at the beginning or at the end of the sentence.

Clauses can stand in the same relation to each other and to single words as words do to one another in the sentence.

Subordinate clauses, either in an apparent or in an implied way, can be made to answer to the same questions

as the word in the principal sentence, which they supplant
for the purpose of greater elucidation :

Я нé был в клáссе, потомý что я был бóлен.
I was not at the class because I was ill.

This sentence can answer to the questions : почемý ? why ? ;
по какóй причи́не ? for what reason ? The sentence can
be paraphrased as : Я нé был в клáссе по болéзни (by
reason of illness).

Я прилёг, чтóбы вздремнýть [я прилёг вздремнýть].
I lay down in order to have a little sleep.

This subordinate clause can answer to the question : for
what purpose ?

Что прошлó, тогó не ворóтишь [прóшлого не ворó-
    тишь] ; не ворóтишь тогó, что прошлó.
That which is past [gone] thou wilt not turn back [cannot
    be recalled].

The question is here : чегó не ворóтишь ?

§ 125. *Simple subordinate clauses* which form part of a
complex sentence fall under the three main heads of :

(1) **Noun-clauses** ; (2) **adjective-clauses** ; and (3) **adverb-
clauses.**

(1) A noun-clause can stand to its principal clause in the
relation of : (*a*) subject ; (*b*) predicate ; (*c*) direct object.

(2) An adjective-clause always qualifies a noun (as
qualifier).

(3) An adverb-clause stands to its principal clause in the
same relation as an adverb.

NOTE. Noun-clauses and adjective-clauses cannot
take the inflexions of nouns or adjectives ; they merely
stand in place of nouns or adjectives. These clauses are
frequently preceded by pronouns with the functions of

conjunctions. These take the case of the noun or adjective which is supplanted, in accordance with the grammatical demand of the word in the principal sentence to which the clause is subordinated (see last example of § 124). Subordinate clauses are also introduced by adverbs and conjunctions.

§ 126. (a) *Subject-clauses.*

A subject-clause is a clause which has the function of a subject to the principal clause. It answers to the questions: кто? who?; что? what? and is joined to the principal clause by the conjunction-words: кто, что, who, which, that:

Кто победи́л, тот прав.
[Тот прав, кто победи́л.]
He is (in the) right who conquered [won].

Что с во́зу упа́ло, то пропа́ло.
[То пропа́ло, что с во́зу упа́ло.]
What has fallen off the cart is lost.
[That is lost which has fallen off the cart.]

Кто сыт, тот голо́дного не понима́ет.
[Тот, голо́дного не понима́ет, кто сыт.]
[Сы́тый голо́дного не понима́ет.]
He who is well-fed does not understand the hungry one.

Кто бога́т, тот ча́сто забыва́ет бе́дных.
[Бога́тый ча́сто забыва́ет бе́дных.]
He who is rich often forgets the poor.

§ 127. (b) *Predicate-clauses* are not so frequent, but they are occasionally used as an elucidating predicate to the principal clause. They answer to the questions: како́в, -а́, -о́, -ы́?, кто?, что?; how is?, who?, what? They are joined to the principal clause by the conjunction-words: како́в, -а́, -о́, -ы́; како́й, -а́я, -о́е, -и́е, as, exactly as не кто ино́е как, none other than; не что ино́е как, nothing else but:

Какова́ я́блоня, тако́в и плод.

[Тако́в плод, какова́ я́блоня.]

As is the apple-tree, so is the fruit.

Был он [э́то был] не кто ино́й, как наш сосе́д Петро́в.

He was [it was] none other than our neighbour Petrov.

(c) *Object-clauses* have the same function as an ordinary object and are usually connected with the principal clause by the conjunction-word что, and also by other conjunction-words :

Тепе́рь все зна́ют, что не́мцы свире́пы.

[Все зна́ют свире́пость не́мцев.]

Now everyone knows that the Germans are cruel [ferocious].

Что во́лки жа́дны, вся́кий зна́ет.

[Вся́кий зна́ет, что во́лки жа́дны.]

[Все зна́ют о жа́дности волко́в.]

Everyone knows that wolves are ravenous.

Что посе́ешь, то и пожнёшь.

[То пожнёшь, что посе́ешь.]

[Посе́янное пожнёшь.]

What thou wilt sow thou wilt also reap.

§ 128. *Qualifier-clauses* (adjective-clauses) serve as detailed (descriptive) qualifiers to any noun in the principal sentence. They are usually joined to the principal sentence by the pronouns кто, who ; како́й, -а́я, -о́е, -и́е, what kind ; кото́рый, -ая, -ое, -ые, which ; чей, чья, чьё, чьи, whose ; что, what ; and also by conjunction-words, such as где, where ; когда́, when ; куда́, whither :

Наста́л день, когда́ я по́нял значе́ние его́ слов.

The day arrived when I understood [realized] the meaning of his words.

Есть таки́е лю́ди, кото́рые ничего́ не зна́ют.

There are such people who know nothing.

Найди письмо, которое я вчера получил от брата.
Find the letter which I received yesterday from brother.

Человек, который здоров, может работать.
[Здоровый человек может работать.]
A man who is healthy can work.

Тот, кто глуп, осудит [глупый осудит].
He who is stupid will condemn.

Тот, кто умён, поймёт [умный поймёт].
He who is wise will understand.

§ 129. *Adverb-clauses* have the function of adverbs in relation to the principal clause. According to their meaning adverb-clauses are classed as adverb-clauses : (1) of time ; (2) of place ; (3) of cause ; (4) of manner ; (5) of purpose.

These clauses are joined to the principal clause in the following way :

§ 129a. (1) *Adverb-clauses of time* answer to the questions : когда ? when ? ; как долго ? how long ? ; с каких пор ? since when ? They are joined by : когда, when ; в то время, как, at the time when (as) ; с тех пор, как, since the time when ; после того, как, after :

Когда восходит солнце, становится светло.
When the sun rises it becomes light.

В то время как [когда] это случилось, его уже не было в живых.
At the time when this happened he was no longer alive [among the living].

С тех пор, как началась война, жить стало трудно.
Since [the time that] the war started, life has become difficult [it has become difficult to live].

После того, как он объяснил нам суть дела, всё стало ясно.
After he had explained to us the pith [gist] of the matter, everything became clear.

§ 129b. (2) *Adverb-clauses of place* answer to the questions : где ? where ? ; куда ? whither ? ; откуда ? whence ? They are joined by : куда, whither ; где, where ; откуда, whence :

Его нашли на том же месте, где он и раньше был.

He was found on the very spot where he had also been before.

Я оттуда, где струится [течёт] тихий Дон.

I am from [thence] where the quiet Don flows.

§ 129c. . (3) *Adverb-clauses of manner* answer to the questions : как ? how ? ; каким образом ? in what manner ? They are joined by : как, as, in the manner of ; что, that :

Пусть другие живут, как хотят.

Let others live as [in the manner] they like

Он так много работает весь день, что к вечеру у него уж нет больше сил работать.

He works so much all day that towards the evening he has no more strength to work.

День был ясен, как душа младенца.

The day was as clear as the soul of a babe.

Он поёт, как соловей [поёт соловьём].

He sings like a nightingale [sings in the manner of a nightingale].

Он свернулся, как калач [свернулся калачом].

He rolled himself up like a roll [round cake] [in the manner of a roll].

§ 129d. (4) *Adverb-clauses of cause* answer to the questions : почему ? for what reason ? ; отчего ? why ? ; за что ? what for ? They are joined by : потому-что, because ; оттого-что, за то что, for the reason that :

Я оттого могу помогать бедным, что всегда был бережлив.

I can help the poor because I have always been frugal.

Я за то на тебя сердит, что ты ничего не делаешь.

I am angry with you because you are not doing anything.

Я не поеду заграницу, потому что решил поступить
в университет.

I shall not go abroad because I have decided to enter
the university.

§ 129e. (5) *Adverb-clauses of purpose* answer to the questions : зачем ?, для чего ? for what purpose ? They are
joined by [для того], чтобы, in order to :

Дровосек пошёл [отправился] в лес, чтобы рубить
дрова.

The wood-cutter has gone to the forest in order to cut
[chop] wood.

Мальчик пошёл к реке [на реку] с удочкой, чтобы
удить. [Для того, чтобы ловить рыбу.]

The boy went to the river [on the river] with a fishing-
rod in order to angle.

§ 130. *Function of the Participle in the Complex Sentence.*

Participles can replace the predicate of a qualifying
subordinate clause. The joining conjunction-word is
dropped, and a participle takes the place of the verb-
predicate in the same tense :

(1) Костёр пылал и освещал лица наших людей,
которые сидели около него. The camp fire
burned brightly and lit up the faces of our men
who sat round it.

This sentence can be turned into :

Костёр пылал и освещал лица наших людей,
сидевших около него. (Past active participle in
genitive plural to conform with the case of наших
людей.) (The sentence is thereby shortened.)

(2) Няня немедленно послала на почту письмо, которое она написала. The nurse sent to the post-office the letter which she had written.

This can be turned into :

Няня немедленно послала на почту письмо, написанное ею. (Past passive participle in the accusative (neuter) to conform with письмо.)

§ 130a. *Function of the Gerund (Verbal Adverb) in the Complex Sentence.*

. Gerunds can replace verb-predicates in some subordinate adverb-clauses. The joining conjunction-word is dropped and the verb-predicate is supplanted by a gerund :

(1) **Present gerund** (verbal adverb) is used when the actions (or states) in both the principal and the subordinate clauses takes place at the same time :

Когда я брожу вблизи реки, я слышу выстрелы. When I stroll [wander] near the river I hear shots [firing].

This can be turned into :

Бродя вблизи реки, я слышу выстрелы (present gerund).

Когда мы будем в Москве, мы посетим все музеи. When we are [shall be] in Moscow we shall visit all the museums.

This can be turned into :

Будучи в Москве, мы посетим все музеи.

(2) **Past gerund** (verbal adverb) is used when the action of the subordinate clause precedes that of the principal clause :

Когда он написал письмо, брат отнёс его на почту. Brother, after he had written the letter, took it to the post-office.

This can be turned into :

Написав письмо, брат отнёс его на почту.

§ 131. *The Passive Voice.*

The long form of the passive participle (both present and past) is mainly used in subordinate clauses :

Дом, построенный моим отцóм, сгорéл.
The house built by my father has been burned down.

Старйк, уважáемый всéми жйтелями нáшего гóрода, вы́бран мэ́ром.
The old man who is respected by all the inhabitants of our town, has been elected mayor.

The short passive participle is frequently used as a predicate, either by itself or with the auxilary verb быть :

Он вы́бран мэ́ром:	He has been elected mayor.
Он был вы́бран мэ́ром.	He was [had been] elected mayor.
Дом постróен.	The house has been built.
Дом был постróен.	The house was [had been] built.
Он всéми уважáем.	He is respected by everybody.
Он был всéми уважáем.	He was respected by everybody.

But the paraphrased expressions :

его все уважáют   его все уважáли

are more frequently used.

A great number of passive constructions are rendered by reflexive verbs.   (See §§ 69 ; 122, note (e).)

это называется⎫
[это называют]⎭ this is called

это называлось⎫
[это называли]⎭ this was called

зóлото добывáется⎫
[зóлото добывáют]⎭ gold is procured [found]

вопрóс обсуждáется⎫
[вопрóс обсуждáют]⎭ the question is discussed

обсуждáлся [обсуждáли], was discussed

он считáется богáтым ⎱ he is considered rich
[егó считáют богáтым] ⎰

он считáлся [егó считáли], he was considered

они́ считáлись ⎱ they were considered
[их считáли]. ⎰

бельё стирáется прáчкой, linen is laundered by a
    laundress

газéта издаётся instead of издавáема, the news-
    paper is published

концéрт кончáется   instead of   кончáем
концéрт начинáется   „   начинáем

The passive voice is frequently expressed by the impersonal use of a transitive verb :

          Егó уби́ло грóмом
instead of Он был уби́т грóмом.
          He was killed by lightning.

          Кры́шу сорвáло вéтром
instead of Кры́ша былá сóрвана вéтром.
          The roof has been torn away by the wind.

          Все дорóги занеслó снéгом
instead of Все дорóги бы́ли занесены́ снéгом.
          All the roads have been covered with snow.

§ 132. *Subjunctive and Conditional Moods.*

(1) In Russian there is no subjunctive mood (thought
mood) for indirect narration. Subordinate sentences of
indirect narration are often introduced by the adverbs:
де, дéскать, мол (as if to say ; said he [she]; says he,
etc.), and the verb is in the present, past, or future of the
indicative mood, as required by the sense of the sentence.
The above three adverbial expressions and also the parenthetic verb ' говори́т,' although very frequent in colloquial
speech, are not so often used in the literary, or everyday,
language of the educated Russian. The adverbs бýдто,

[бу́дто-бы] (as if) is very often used to introduce a subordinate sentence of reported speech when the narrator is not quite convinced of the truth of what he had been told :

Он говори́т, бу́дто его́ обокра́ли.
He says he has been robbed.
(This may be so, but I refrain from commenting on it.)

If there is no room for such doubt, the subordinate clause of indirect narration is simply introduced by что :

Он говори́т, что его́ обокра́ли.
He says he has been robbed.

In subordinate sentences which are a paraphrased rendering of an interrogative or a negative sentence, the English words ' whether,' ' if,' are rendered in Russian by the particle ли, which is placed immediately after the verb of the subordinate clause :

Я не зна́ю, е́дет ли он в Ло́ндон, и́ли нет.
I do not know whether [if] he goes [is going] to London or not.

Вы не зна́ете, до́ма-ли он ?
You do not know if he is at home ?

(For the use of the imperative in a conditional or subjunctive sense see § 106, sub-section (3), and § 123b, subsection (2).)

(2) *Conditional sentences* are introduced by е́сли and е́сли бы (popular : е́жели, коли́, е́жели бы). Е́сли (if) can be followed by a verb in any tense :

Е́сли он придёт, то я бу́ду его́ ждать.
If he is coming, I shall wait for him.

Е́сли он е́дет сюда́, то ну́жно пригото́вить ко́мнату для него́.
If he is coming here, then it is necessary to prepare a room for him.

Если он уже приехал, то я пойду к нему.
If he has already arrived, then I will go to him.

After **если бы**, which means 'if . . . had,' and after **бы**,
'would,' the verb can stand only in the past tense :

Если бы я знал, что вы приедете сюда, то я бы
послал вам лошадь.
If I had known [had I known] that you were coming
here, I would have sent you a horse.

(See also § 106, sub-section (3), and § 123*b*, sub-section (2).)

(3) *Indirect (reported) sentences.*

The tense of the verb in an indirect (reported) sentence
is that in which the verb has been used in the actual
direct statement. It does not conform to the tense of
the verb in the principal clause :

Он сказал, что придёт. He said he *will* come (not
would come, which would be пришёл-бы, and therefore incorrect).

Он сказал, что знает всё об этом. He said he *knows*
all about it (not *knew*, which would be знал and
would mean in Russian *had known*).

Он писал, что приедет завтра. He wrote that he *will*
come to-morrow (not *would* come, which would be
incorrectly приехал-бы with the Russian meaning
of *might, would have come*).

NOTE. This is characteristic of the exactness of
Russian speech, which does not subordinate logical
correctness to grammatical forms.

For example, a Russian says : Я приеду, если брат
будет там, I shall come if brother *will* be there, not : Я
приеду если брат там, which would mean : I shall come
if brother is *there now*.

(4) *Subordinate sentences of wish or request.*

A subordinate sentence which represents a wish or request is introduced in Russian by the conjunction **чтобы** followed by the verb in the past tense :

Я хочу, чтобы вы приехали завтра.

I wish that you should come to-morrow.

Он просил, чтобы вы сделали это.

He asked that you should do this.

But when чтобы means *in order to* it is followed by the infinitive :

Я приехал [для того] [за тем], чтобы познакомиться с вами.

I came in order to make your acquaintance.

Я приехал сюда, чтобы отдохнуть.

I came here to have a rest.

§ 133. *Word Order.*

There is a greater freedom of word order in Russian than in English. This is made possible by the manifold inflexions. About the word order in Russian the following can be said :

(1) Although the subject of a simple sentence usually stands before the predicate, these can change places in accordance with the *position-emphasis* which it is desired to put on the predicate or the subject :

весна пришла   Spring has arrived

пришла весна . . . Came the spring . . .

(2) Attributive adjectives stand before the noun which they qualify. So do pronouns and numerals if they have an attributive function :

белый дом,	white house
мой брат,	my brother
пять книг,	five books
в это время,	at this time
весь город,	the whole town

(3) Adverbial expressions have a greater freedom of order:

приду́ за́втра ⎱
за́втра приду́ ⎰ I will come to-morrow

скажу́ пото́м ⎱
пото́м скажу́ ⎰ I will tell afterwards

§ 134. *Function of the Auxiliary verbs,* **быть** (to be), **име́ть** (to have) *in the Russian sentence.*

1. Быть.

(1) The present tense of the verb **быть** is not used in colloquial speech; it is usually omitted. In the written language the third person singular and, less often, plural, **есть, суть** are occasionally used when special emphasis is needed. Есть is also used when it means: there is, there are:

Он мой брат.	He is my brother.
Он до́ма.	He is at home.
Он здесь.	He is here.
Я бо́лен.	I am ill [not well].
Она́ весела́.	She is gay.
Они́ бе́дны [ы́].	They are poor.
Мы за́няты.	We are engaged [occupied].

In these examples есть and суть are omitted. (See § 103, group (d).)

But: Есть у меня́ та́кже . . . I also have . . .
Есть таки́е лю́ди . . . There are such people . . .
Есть там так мно́го но́вого.
There is so much novel [new] there.
Там нет [не есть] ничего́ но́вого.
There is nothing novel [new] there.

(2) But in the past and future tenses the verb **быть** *is not omitted* in similar constructions:

Он был здесь.	He was here.
Она́ бу́дет до́ма.	She will be at home.
Ты бу́дешь рад.	You will [thou wilt] be glad.
Вы бу́дете у нас.	You will be at our house.

Егó нé было дóма.   He was not at home [in].

Меня́ не бу́дет дóма.   I shall not be at home.

This form is used more frequently than я не бу́ду дóма. The latter form would seem to sound too precise, as if to say: I will make a point of not being at home; it would denote too much definite purpose, whereas меня́ не бу́дет дóма is just a casual statement that I shall not be in. The same applies also to the preceding example: егó нé было дóма.

(3) The present tense of быть 'есть' is also omitted in impersonal sentences formed from short adjectives:

> мóжно,   it is possible
> дóлжно,   it is necessary
> прия́тно,   it is pleasant
> полéзно,   it is useful. (See §§ 45, 90 (2) (a).)

Note. долgiven бытьжнó быть means: probably.

But in the past and future it is:

> мóжно бы́ло, мóжно бу́дет
> бы́ло прия́тно, бу́дет прия́тно
> бы́ло бы полéзно, it would [might] be useful
> бу́дет полéзно,   it will be useful

(4) Есть is omitted in the expressions жаль, it is a pity; and лень, too lazy!, laziness, indolence:

> мне лень,   I am lazy, I feel lazy [indolent]
> мне жаль,   I feel sorry
> мне бы́ло жаль, I felt sorry
> ему́ бы́ло лень, he felt lazy [indolent]

also in the expression нельзя́, it is not possible (from the obsolete form льзя). This expression is only used by itself in the present tense. In the past and future it is used with бы́ло or бу́дет: нельзя́ бы́ло, нельзя́ бу́дет.

§ 134a.   2. Имéть.

Имéть is not used as an auxiliary verb for the formation of verbal tenses as in English. Its ordinary meaning is: to possess.

я имѣю means : I am in the possession of :

Он имѣет дом на Ту́льской у́лице.

He has [possesses] a house in Tula street.

It is also used in such expressions as :

Дом имѣет пять ко́мнат.

The house has five rooms.

Кварти́ра имѣет ва́нную ко́мнату [ва́нну].

The flat has a bathroom [bath].

Гости́ница имѣет хоро́ший рестора́н.

The hotel has a good restaurant.   (But also :

При гости́нице имѣется хоро́ший рестора́н.

A good restaurant is attached to the hotel.)

У него́ имѣются [во́дятся, есть] де́ньги.

He has [possesses] money.

In colloquial speech the place of—

я имѣю, etc., is taken by у меня́ есть.

он имѣет —— у него́ есть.

ты имѣл —— у тебя́ был, -а́, -о, -и.

мы бу́дем имѣть —— у нас бу́дет [бу́дут].

я имѣю мно́го книг —— у меня́ есть мно́го книг, I
have many books.

> Note.   Есть is used for both singular and plural
> in such constructions.   (See § 119.)

я имѣл мно́го книг —— у меня́ бы́ло (*neuter*) мно́го
книг, I had many books.

он имѣл хоро́ший сад —— у него́ был хоро́ший сад,
he had a good garden.

кто имѣет мой нож? —— у кого́ мой нож?, who has
my knife ?

кто имѣет ло́шадь? —— у кого́ есть ло́шадь?, who
has a horse ?

мы не имѣем ло́шади —— у нас нет ло́шади, we have
no horse.

In all the sentences where the verb имѣть is replaced by a corresponding tense of быть, the logical subject is turned into a grammatical object. In the negative the sentence is turned into an impersonal one, also with the inverted subject as object. The inverted form is frequently used, as this is more in consonance with the spirit of the Russian language. (See §§ 122-123.)

§ 135. *Tautological and other expressions and particles used in Russian sentences.*

1.

чуть-чуть,	just a little
мáло-помáлу,	little by little, by degrees
давны́м-давнó,	a very long time ago
тóчь-в-тóчь,	exactly as
друг дрýга	{ each other / one another
друг от дрýга	{ one from the other / from each other
друг к дрýгу	{ one to the other / to each other
друг с дрýгом	{ one with the other / with each other
друг о дрýге	{ one about the other / about each other

2. Pronouns (and adverbs) with the particle **то** (see § 53) :

кто-то, someone
что-то, something } implying some uncertainty as to
как-то, somehow } who, or what, or how
то-то, indeed ; yes, indeed

NOTE. The particle то attached to a noun means, particularly in popular speech : but as regards . . . or, as for . . .

отéц-то ничегó . . ., as for father, he is all right . . .
да мáчеха-то, не дай Бог . . ., but as for step-mother, God help us [God forbid] . . .

3. Pronouns and adverbs with the particles : **кóе [кой]**, **нибýдь, лѝбо** (see § 53) :

кóе-кто, someone ⎫
кóе-что, something ⎬ with a certain degree of definite-
кóе-как, somehow ⎭ ness

ктó-нибýдь, someone or other, anyone
чтó-нибýдь, something or other, anything
кáк-нибýдь, somehow or other, anyhow

гдé-нибýдь ⎫
кудá-нибýдь ⎬ somewhere

когдá-нибýдь, sometime or other

ктó-лѝбо ⎰someone ⎱ ⎫
　　　　⎱anyone ⎰ ⎬ certainty is immaterial or
чтó-лѝбо ⎰something⎱ ⎭ problematical
　　　　⎱anything ⎰

(See §§ 47, 6 ; 91, group *B* (*c*).)

NOTE. The adverbial particles то, нибýдь, лѝбо, placed *after* the interrogative-relative pronouns кто, что, чей, какóй, скóлько, and the adverbs как, где, кудá, откýда, когдá ; also the particle кóе [кой] placed *before* the same pronouns and adverbs, while they all indicate indefiniteness, yet each one conveys a particular degree of indefiniteness :

то expresses less indefiniteness than нибýдь.

кóе conveys the idea that the person who says : кóе-что, кóе-кто, кóе-где, кóе-как, knows exactly what the something, somebody, somewhere, somehow is, but that he prefers not to specify it.

лѝбо expresses even less certainty than нибýдь : ктó-лѝбо, чтó-лѝбо means anyone, anything—immaterial who or what. The who or what is given a problematical character by the particle лѝбо.

In adverbial expressions of time, когдá-то means : some time ago, once upon a time ; когдá-нибýдь means : at some time or other in future.

In an interrogative sentence, когда́-нибу́дь may mean :
at any time in the past :

> Вы когда́-нибу́дь там бы́ли ?
> Were you there at any time [ever] ?

In adverbial expressions of place, где́-то means :
somewhere, at some definite place ; где́-нибу́дь means :
somewhere or other :

> Мы переночева́ли где́-то, недалеко́ от реки́.
> We stayed for the night somewhere, not far from
> the river.
> Мы переночу́ем где́-нибу́дь.
> We shall stay for the night somewhere or other.

ко́е-где́ means: somewhere; where exactly is known to
the speaker, but he does not bother to specify. ко́е-где́
is also used in the sense of : in places, here and there.

4. Adverbs with **по** (see § 90 (2) (*f*)) :

> по-ру́сски,　　in Russian
> по-англи́йски, in English
> по-дру́жески,　in a friendly manner
> по-де́тски,　　in the manner of a child
> по-ребя́чески, in a childish manner

5. Numerals with **во** (used as adverbs) (see § 91 (*b*)) :

> во-пе́рвых, firstly
> во-вторы́х, secondly
> в тре́тьих, thirdly

6. Pronouns and adverbs with the negative particle ни
(see § 123) :

никто́,	no one	ниотку́да,	from nowhere
ничто́,	nothing	никогда́,	never
никако́й,	not any	ника́к,	not in any way
ниче́й,	not anybody's	нисько́лько,	not in the
ничего́,	nothing		least
нигде́ } нику́да }	nowhere		

NOTE 1. Pronouns with the particle ни are declined as the original pronouns from which they are formed (see § 51):

Nom.	никто́	[ничто́][1]	
Gen. {	никого́	ничего́	
	ни от кого́	ни от чего́	When used with a
Dat. {	никому́	ничему́	preposition the con-
	ни к кому́	ни к чему́	struction is split up
Acc.	никого́	ничего́	in declension
Instr. {	нике́м	ниче́м	
	ни с кем	ни с чем	
Loc.	ни о ком	ни о чём	

ни ... ни used as a conjunction means: neither ... nor:

> ни я, ни он, neither I nor he

ни used by itself can mean : not a ...

> У него́ ни копе́йки не оста́лось.
> He has been left with not a copeck.

> У меня́ нет ни гро́ша[а́]. I have not a farthing left.

NOTE 2. Pronouns and adverbs with the particle ни are always followed by the particle не, which stands immediately before the verb which it negates. These negative expressions, together with the particle не, constitute a double negation, which is usual in Russian.

NOTE 3. ни after a relative pronoun or adverb can form indefinite expressions with the meaning of 'no matter ...':

кто ни прика́зывай,	no matter who gives the order
что ни говори́те,	no matter what you say
ско́лько ни дава́й,	no matter how much you give
како́й он ни есть,	no matter what kind of man he is
дава́й, что ни попа́ло,	give anything that comes [falls] into your hands (no matter what)

[1] Ничего́ is more frequently used.

н

кто-бы он ни́ был,   no matter who he might be
с кем бы то ни́ было, with anybody, no matter who
как во́лка ни корми́, no matter how [however much]
                 you may feed a wolf . . .

It will be noted that the negative meaning of ни in these sentences is absorbed in the meaning of ' no matter who,' ' no matter how,' ' no matter when,' etc. Not only is the negative meaning gone, but such sentences even express a degree of emphasis and they are, consequently, not followed by the particle не.

7. *Pronouns and adverbs with the negative particle* не (contraction of нет=не есть). (See § 91, *B* (*c*).)

This particle, which has the meaning of нет (there is not), when joined with a pronoun or adverb *and used with a verbal infinitive,* is capable of forming an impersonal sentence. The logical subject usually stands in the dative as an inverted object :

Мне не́кого [нет кого́] посла́ть. I have no one to send.
Мне не́когда [нет когда́] писа́ть.
I have no time to write.
Мне не́где [нет где] сиде́ть. I have nowhere to sit.
Мне не́куда [нет куда́] е́хать. I have nowhere to go.
Мне не́ от кого́ ожида́ть по́мощи.
I have no one from whom to expect help.

NOTE 1. The pronouns most used for such negative predicative expressions are the oblique cases of кто, что, and the adverbs где, куда́, отку́да, когда́. The pronoun can be used either with or without a preposition. If a preposition is used it usually stands between the particle не and the required oblique case of the pronoun :

не́ с кем . . .   there is no one with whom . . .
не́ о чём . . .   there is nothing about . . .
не́ о ком . . .   there is no one about whom . . .
не́ от кого . . .   there is no one from whom . . .

не́ к кому . . .	there is no one to whom . . .
не́ к чему . . .	there is nothing to which . . .
не́ на что . . .	there is nothing on which . . .
не́ за что . . .	there is nothing for which . . .
не́зачем . . .	there is no need [occasion] . . .
не́откуда . . .	there is nowhere from . . .

It will be noted that as negative definitions these impersonal expressions have no nominative case, but they have all the oblique cases (accusative is merged in the genitive):

Gen.-Acc.	не́кого	не́чего
Dat.	не́кому	не́чему
Instr.	{ не́кем	не́чем
	{ не́ с кем	не́ с чем
Loc.	не́ о ком	не́ о чём

не́чего can mean:

1. there is nothing to . . .
2. there is no need to . . .
3. there is no use . . .

не́чего писа́ть,	there is nothing to write
не́чего де́лать,	nothing to be done
не́чего беспоко́иться,	no need to worry
не́чего боя́ться,	no use, no need to fear

NOTE 2. All these expressions with the particle не́ have the value of a negative predicate. In the present tense нет is implied; in the past and future tenses бы́ло (*neuter*) and бу́дет are used respectively:

мне не́когда,	I have no time
мне не́когда бы́ло,	I had no time
мне не́когда бу́дет,	I shall have no time
не́чего де́лать,	there is nothing to be done
не́чего бы́ло де́лать,	there was nothing to be done
не́чего бу́дет де́лать,	there will be nothing to be done
не́кого посла́ть,	there is no one to send

некого было послать,   .there was no one to send
некого будет послать,   there will be no one to send
не с кем будет говорить, there will be no one to talk to
[with]

Note 3.   The negative expressions treated in sub-division 7 *are not followed* by the particle не.

Note 4.   The negative predicative particle не should not be confused with the particle не in—

некто,   someone   ⎫
нечто,   something   ⎬ The particle не in these
некоторый, a certain person or ⎭ words has no implied
              thing   predicative meaning

(See § 47, 6.)

§ 136. *Use of the Reflexive Possessive Pronouns* свой, -я, -ё, -й *instead of* мой, твой, наш, ваш, его, её, их ; my (mine), thy (thine), our(s), your(s), his, her(s), their(s).

If these possessive pronouns refer to anything belonging to the person named as the subject of the sentence, then they are replaced by свой, -я, -ё, -й :

Я взял свою книгу (instead of мою книгу).
I took my book.

Ты забыл свой зонтик (instead of твой зонтик).
You forgot your umbrella.

Она потеряла свою шляпу (instead of её шляпу).
She has lost her hat.

Они оставили свой дом (instead of их дом).
They (have) left their house.

Он прислал свою лошадь (instead of его лошадь).
He (has) sent his horse.

Вы знаете свой характер (instead of ваш характер).
You know your nature.

Note.   There are, however, deviations from this rule in colloquial speech, when the ordinary possessive is used.   (See § 49, note 2.)

§ 136*a*. *Peculiarities in the use of Personal Pronouns.*

In colloquial speech the personal pronoun expressions :

я и ты		мы с тобóй
я и вы		мы с вáми
я и он	are changed into	мы с ним
я и онá		мы с нéю
я и онú		мы с нúми

if the action performed, or to be performed, is expressed by the same verb. The verb stands in the first person plural.

Thus, instead of я и ты пойдём — мы с тобóй пойдём.
Similarly the pronouns :

ты и он		вы с ним
ты и онá	are changed into	вы с ней
ты и онú		вы с нúми

The verb stands in the second person plural. Thus, instead of ты и он (онá, онú) пойдёте — вы с ним (с ней, с нúми) пойдёте.

In the oblique cases of pronouns similar changes occur.

Thus, | меня и тебя | are changed into | нас с тобóю |
       | тебé и ему | | вам с ним etc. |

§ 136*b*. *The Function of the Personal Reflexive Pronoun :*
себя.

себя (oneself) can be used with all persons, genders, and numbers :

Я вúжу себя. I see myself.
Ты не знáешь себя. You do not know yourself [thyself].
Он считáет себя ýмным. He considers himself clever.

Онá имéет дéньги при себé.
She has the money on her [with her].

Она привелá с собóю сестрý.
She brought (her) sister with her.

Мы не знаем, что делать с собою.
We do not know what to do with ourselves.

Он о себе высокого мнения.
He has a high opinion of himself.

Он звал меня к себе домой.
He asked me to (come to) his house.

Он у себя в комнате.　He is in his room.

The unstressed себе (*dat.*) is often used to indicate an independent and carefree attitude of the person to whom it refers :

Живёт себе как барин и ни с кем не считается.
He lives like a squire and takes no account of anybody.

In a somewhat similar meaning себе is used in the expressions :

　　　　　　　ничего [себе], 　not so bad
　　　　　　　так себе, 　　　so-so

Word Subordination

The Meaning and Uses of Oblique Cases of Nouns,
Pronouns, etc.

§ 137. Genitive is used :

1. To express **possession**, and also certain properties and characteristics :

	дом дяди,	uncle's house
	человек доброго нрава,	a man of kind disposition
or	высокого роста,	of high stature (a tall person)

2. To express **state, quality,** or **number** of object or objects ; also when a part of a quantity is referred to :

у меня много работы,	I have much work (to do)
набралось воды,	some water got collected (impersonal sentence)

	хлѣба хватит для всех,	there will be enough bread for all
	я принёс воды,	I have brought some water
but :	я принёс воду,	I brought water (in a general sense)
	он купил ржи,	he bought some rye
but :	он купил рожь,	he bought the rye (the whole quantity)

3. To express **comparison** :

свѣтлѣе солнца,	brighter than the sun
темнѣе ночи,	darker than night

4. To express **negation**. When a noun stands after verbs with the particle не :

(*a*) in impersonal sentences :

нé было дождя,	there was no rain
не будет обѣда,	there will be no dinner
у меня нет дéнег,	I have no money
у них нет хлѣба,	they have no bread

(*b*) in negative constructions, after a transitive verb, as a direct object :

не читал письма,	did not read the letter
ничего не дѣлает,	does nothing
я не видел сада,	I did not see [have not seen] the garden

NOTE. A double negation is usual. (See § 123.)

(*c*) in negative constructions, after an intransitive verb, in conjunction with adverbial expressions of time or place :

не спит ночей,	does not sleep (whole) nights
не прошёл версты,	did not cover a verst (by walking)

5. In constructions éxpressing time and dates :

трéтьего дня,	the day before yesterday
двадцáтого мáя,	on the 20th of May
сегóдня [сегó дня],	to-day
седьмóго января тысяча девятьсóт пятнáдцатого гóда [1915-го],	on the 7th of January 1915
пéрвого мáя,	on the 1st May
тóй-же нóчи,	on that night
вчерáшнего дня,	yesterday

6. Generally the genitive is used in constructions after verbs which denote striving for, aiming at, or wishing for something ; also in the sense of being deprived of something. The following verbs belong to this class :

желáть, to wish for	ждать, to await
просить, to ask for	искáть, to seek
хотéть, to want, to wish	трéбовать, to demand
лишиться, to be deprived of, to lose	боя́ться, to fear
стыдиться, to be ashamed of	опасáться, to be apprehensive
	избегáть, to avoid

7. Genitive is also used after cardinal and collective numbers :

(a) Genitive singular : after два [две], три, четы́ре, óба, мнóго (in the meaning of ' much '), мáло (in the meaning of ' little ').

(b) Genitive plural : after пять, шесть, семь, вóсемь, дéвять, дéсять, двáдцать, etc. мнóго (in the meaning of ' many '), мáло (in the meaning of ' few '), нéсколько, a few.

Also after collective numerals : двóе, трóе, чéтверо, etc. (See § 55b.)

Note. The numerals of this sub-section require the genitive plural of the qualified noun if they stand in the nominative or accusative. If they stand in any of the other cases the qualified noun stands in the same case as the numeral :

два стула,	two chairs
две чашки,	two cups
три книги,	three books
четыре стола,	four tables
оба брата,	both brothers
мало чая,[1]	little tea
мало воды,[1]	little water
пять столов,	five tables
шесть стульев,	six chairs
много книг,[1]	many books
несколько столов,[1]	a few tables
достаточно,[1]	sufficient
недостаточно,[1]	insufficient
пять человек,	five people
много людей,[1]	many people

but :
двух столов	четырёх столов
трёх книг	обоих братьев etc.

(See §§ 20 (9), 54*b*, 120.)

8. After prepositions governing the genitive.   (See § 96.)

§ 138. Dative is used:

1. In impersonal constructions the logical subject (inverted as grammatical object) is usually in the dative case :

что нам делать,	what are we to do
мне кажется,	it seems to me [I think]
ему хочется,	he would like to
мне можно,	it is permissible to me
ему нельзя,	he must not [to him it is not permissible]
мне надо [нужно],	I have to
нам пора ехать,	it is time for us to go [to start]
мне некогда,	I have no time

[1] Adverbs and adverbial pronouns, denoting indefinite quantity.

н *

мне не́куда е́хать,   I have nowhere to go
ему́ поле́зно,   it is useful to him
нам вре́дно,   it is harmful to us

2. Generally in the dative stands the person or object in whose direction the action is meant to take place :

я ему́ подари́л,   I gave him as a present
он мне говори́л \   he spoke to me
   [сказа́л] /   ·he told me
мы им слу́жим,   we serve them
они́ нам помога́ют,   they help [assist] us
я хоте́л ему́ помо́чь,   I wished to help him
я дал ему́,   I gave him
он писа́л мне,   he wrote me [to me]
я им сде́лал предложе́ние,   I made them an offer
он мне друг,   he is a friend to me.

3. Dative is also used with the short (predicative) adjectives : мил, до́рог, прия́тен, рад, ну́жен, поле́зен, etc. :

я вам всегда́ рад,   I am always glad to see you
мы вам ра́ды,   we are glad to see you
она́ нам дорога́ [мила́],   she is dear to us
мне прия́тно слы́шать,   I am glad to hear
они́ нам до́роги,   they are dear to us
вы мне нужны́,   I need you
он мне был поле́зен,   he was useful to me
э́то нам бу́дет поле́зно,   this will be useful to us
вам изве́стно,   it is known to you

4. After prepositions governing the dative case. (See § 96a.)

§ 139. Accusative is used:

(1) When the declinable word serves as a direct object to a transitive verb :

Я купи́л коро́ву.   I bought a cow.
Я про́дал дом.   I sold the house.

(2) When a declinable word stands as an adverbial expression of time or place, etc., and answers to the questions : как до́лго? how long?; как далеко́? how far?; ско́лько? how much?; etc.

Мы спа́ли весь день.	We slept all day.
Мы прошли́ пять вёрст.	We covered [went] five versts.
Он сиде́л це́лый час.	He sat a whole hour.

NOTE. If the verb in the sentences of the above subdivisions (1 and 2) expresses negation, the accusative is supplanted by the genitive. (See § 137.)

(3) After prepositions governing the accusative case. (See § 96b.)

§ 140. The **instrumental case** is an 'adverb case,' and is mostly used in adverbial expressions of manner. (See § 16.)

1. It denotes the instrument, or means, by which, or through which (or the person by whom), an action is performed :

Я рабо́таю рука́ми.	I work with (my) hands.
Я пишу́ перо́м.	I write with a pen.
Я ре́жу ножо́м.	I cut with a knife.
Я плачу́ деньга́ми.	I pay with money [in cash].
Я по́льзуюсь слу́чаем.	I make use of the occasion.
Я воспо́льзовался его́ сове́том.	I made use of his advice.

2. It denotes the person (or thing) who (or which) is the logical subject of the sentence (inverted indirect object) in a passive construction :

Письмо́ бы́ло напи́сано бра́том, The letter was written by (my) brother (instead of брат написа́л письмо́).

Э́то бы́ло сде́лано мно́ю, This was done by me (instead of я э́то сде́лал).

3. Nouns stand in the instrumental after the verbs :
владеть, управлять, пользоваться [*вос-], заниматься
[*заняться], гордиться [*воз-], to be proud of; кома́-
ндовать, to command, etc. (as an indirect object) :

Я управля́ю де́лом.	I manage the business.
Он владе́ет фа́брикой.	He owns the factory.
Я по́льзуюсь слу́чаем.	I make use of the opportunity.
Я занима́юсь му́зыкой по вечера́м.	I am engaged with music in the evenings.

4. In the instrumental case stand nouns used in the
sense of an attribute or state, in a qualified predicate in
conjunction with the verbs быть, стать, сде́латься,
каза́ться (particularly if the qualifying state is not permanent) :

Он был на́шим учи́телем.
He was our teacher (during a particular period).

Он стал [его́ сде́лали] чле́ном управле́ния.
He became [was made] a member of the administration.

Он каза́лся у́мным челове́ком.
He seemed [appeared] to be a clever [sensible] man.

5. The instrumental case is used in adverbial expressions of quality, relation, manner ; also of time and
place :

слаб здоро́вьем,	weak in health
слаб глаза́ми,	weak in his eyes
хоро́ш ⎫ хороша́ ⎭ собо́ю,	good looking
высо́к, -а́ (ро́стом),	tall
е́хать ша́гом,	to travel at a slow pace (go, drive)
лета́ть (лете́ть) стрело́й,	to fly as quick as an arrow
е́хать ле́сом,	to drive by way of [through] the forest

итти́ бе́регом,	to go along [by way of] the bank of the river
выть во́лком,	to howl as a wolf
петь соловьём,	to sing as [in the manner of] a nightingale
у́тром,	in the morning
ве́чером,	in the evening
днём,	in the day-time
но́чью,	in the night

6. It is used after prepositions governing the instrumental case. (See § 96c.)

§ 141. 1. The **locative** (prepositional) case expresses place, and can. be regarded as an ' adverb case ' (see § 16). It answers to the question где ? (where ?), and is mostly used in adverbial expressions of place :

Мы живём в го́роде.	We live in town.
Мы жи́ли в дере́вне.	We lived in the country [in a village].
Зве́ри живу́т в лесу́.	Beasts live in the forest.
Я был в теа́тре.	I was at [in] the theatre.

2. It is used after prepositions governing the locative case. (See § 96d.)

§ 142. *Punctuation.*

The rules of punctuation in Russian are generally the same as in English, with the exception of those governing the comma. The place of the comma in the Russian sentence is determined by concrete rules, and is not subject to considerations of ' logic,' or used for the sake of a more convenient flow of words.

The beginner's task will be to acquire an elementary knowledge of the position of (1) the comma, (2) the semicolon, and (3) the full-stop.

(1) **A comma is used:**

(*a*) before and after an apposition (see § 110) ;

(*b*) before and after parenthetic words and phrases (see § 124) ;

(*c*) to separate similar words following one another in the same sentence ;

(*d*) to separate the adverbs да, нет, from the sentence that follows them, when they imply special emphasis ;

(*e*) to separate words of address and words of interjection from the rest of the sentence ;

(*f*) to separate the words : кро́ме (besides), вме́сто (instead), сверх (besides, above), when, together with other words attached to them, they form a contrast to the part of the sentence which they serve ;

(*g*) to separate adverbial expressions which elucidate other adverbial expressions in the sentence ;

(*h*) to separate parts of a sentence which are themselves qualified by other words ;

(*i*) to separate independent clauses in a complex sentence (see §§ 124-129*e*) ;

(*j*) to separate a subordinate clause, or clauses, from the principal clause.

(2) **A semicolon is used:**

(*a*) to separate independent sentences in a complex sentence, when these have been considerably expanded ;

(*b*) to separate words and phrases within the same sentence when these have been considerably expanded by qualifying words.

(3) **A full-stop is used:** to separate sentences which have a completed, independent meaning.

§ 143. *Patronymics.*

Russians address each other by their Christian name alone, if they are related to each other, or if they are intimately acquainted. Acquaintances are usually addressed by their Christian name followed by the Christian name of their father, which has an adjectival termination. (See § 37.)

. The father's name is called óтчество, patronymic :

Ивáн Петрóвич [1]	— Ivan, son of Peter
Пётр Ивáнович	— Peter, son of Ivan
Пáвел Андрéевич	— Paul, son of Andrew
Áнна Петрóвна	— Anne, daughter of Peter
Áнна Андрéевна	— Anne, daughter of Andrew
Áнна Ивáновна	— Anne, daughter of Ivan

When introducing a person, the introducer usually says :

Семёнов, Ивáн Петрóвич
Семёнова, Áнна Петрóвна

NOTE. The feminine surname will end in **ова, ева, ына, ииа, ая, ская** if the same masculine surname ends in **ов, ев, ын, ин, ой, скпй.**

If a person introduces himself by his surname alone, he is often politely asked :

Как вáше ймя и óтчество ?

or : Как вас зовýт по ймени и óтчеству ?

What is your name and patronymic ?

How are you called by name and patronymic ?

NOTE. Russians have only one Christian name.

The suffixes for patronymics are :

ович, евич for masculine (often shortened into **ыч ич**) ;

овна, евна for feminine.

---

[1] Both name and patronymic are declined as nouns.

Christian names ending in **a**, **я** form their patronymic with the suffixes **ич** for masculine :

Кузьма́	—	Кузьми́ч
Фома́	—	Фоми́ч
Илья́	—	Ильи́ч
Са́вва	—	Са́ввич
Ники́та	—	Ники́тич

ишична for feminine :

	Кузьма́	—	Кузьми́нична
	Фома́	—	Фоми́нична
	Илья́	—	Ильи́нична
or **ична [ишна]**	Са́вва	—	Са́ввична
	Ники́та	—	Ники́тична

LESSON I

Vocabulary

кто, who
что, what

э́тот (*masc.*)
э́та (*fem.*) } this
э́то (*neut.*)

э́ти, these (all genders)

я, I
ты, thou
он, he
она́, she
оно́, it
мы, we
вы, you
они́, they

мой (*masc.*)
моя́ (*fem.*)
моё (*neut.*) } my, mine
мои́ (*pl.*)

твой (*masc.*)
твоя́ (*fem.*)
твоё (*neut.*) } thy, thine
твои́ (*pl.*)

наш (*masc.*)
на́ша (*fem.*)
на́ше (*neut.*) } our, ours
на́ши (*pl.*)

ваш (*masc.*)
ва́ша (*fem.*) } your,
ва́ше (*neut.*) } yours
ва́ши (*pl.*)

тот (*masc.*)
та (*fem.*) } that
то (*neut.*)

те, those (all genders)
где ? where ?

тут } here
здесь }

там, there
его́, his (for all genders and numbers)
её, her, hers (for all genders and numbers)

их, their, theirs (for all genders and numbers)

чей ? (*masc.*)
чья ? (*fem.*) } whose ?
чьё ? (*neut.*)
чьи ? (*pl.*)

(For pronouns, their functions and declensions, see §§ 47-53.)

дом, house
сад, garden, orchard
до́ма, at home (*adv.*)
в саду́, in the garden (*loc. case*)
у́лица, street
на у́лице, in the street
двор, yard
на дворе́, in the yard, outside
оте́ц, father
мать, mother
брат, brother
двою́родный брат, cousin

сестра́, sister
двою́радная сестра́, cousin (*fem.*)
друг, friend
дочь, daughter
сын, son
дед } grandfather
де́душка }
ба́бушка, grandmother
внук, grandson
вну́ки, grandchildren
вну́чка, granddaughter
дя́дя, uncle

тётя, aunt
мáльчик, boy
дéвочка, girl
дитя́, child
дéти, children
кóмната, room
в кóмнате, in the room
бумáга, paper
кни́га, book
перó, pen, nib
карандáш, pencil
ли, whether, if
вот, here, there
вон, there
хлеб, bread

мáсло, butter, oil
сыр, cheese
мя́со, meat
соль, salt
стол, table
на столé, on the table
человéк, man, human being
лю́ди, people
сосéд (*masc.*) ⎫
сосéдка (*fem.*) ⎬ neighbour
сосéди, neighbours
быть, to be
не, not
нет, no
и́ли, or

(See Section I, on nouns, their genders and declensions, §§ 15-33.)

Notes

1. There is no definite or indefinite article in Russian.

2. The present tense of the verb быть,[1] 'to be,' is usually omitted when it has the function of a copula in the meaning of : I am, he is, it is, they are, etc. (See § 134.)

3. Нет, in the meaning of 'no' (no, it is not), is followed by a comma.

4. Это is ordinarily the demonstrative pronoun for neuter nouns : это перó, 'this pen,' etc., but when it is used in the meaning of 'this is,' etc., it can be used for nouns of all genders in both singular and plural :

это мой брат,　　this is [it is] my brother
это моя́ сестрá,　this is [it is] my sister
это мои́ кни́ги,　these are [it is] my books

5. Russian possessive pronouns make no distinction between **conjoint** and **absolute** forms :

мой means both my and mine
её 　,,　　,, her 　,, hers
наш 　,,　　,, our 　,, ours
ваш 　,,　　,, your ,, yours

[1] The only persons of быть used in the present tense are : есть, is ; суть, are. (See Appendix IV, p. 313.)

6. The particle ли, 'whether,' 'if,' is not often used in direct interrogative sentences in colloquial speech: дóма-ли он? 'is he at home?' is better expressed by дóма он? or он дóма? with the sentence-stress on дóма. In indirect interrogative sentences ли appears more often. (See § 132.)

Exercises

Что э́то?	What is this?
Э́то моя́ кни́га.	It is my book.
Кто там?	Who is there?
Мой брат там.	My brother is there.
Чей э́то дом?	Whose house is this?
Э́то мой дом.	It is my house.
But : Чей э́тот дом?	Whose is this house?
Э́тот дом наш.	This house is ours.
Чья э́та кни́га?	Whose is this book?
Чьи э́ти кни́ги?	Whose books are these?
Э́то мой кни́ги.	These are my books.
Я тут.	I am here.
Он там.	He is there.
Она́ здесь.	She is here.
Они́ не здесь.	They are not here.
Они́ там.	They are there.
Э́то его́ сад?	Is this his garden?
Нет, э́то мой сад.	No, it is my garden.
Э́то ваш дом?	Is this your house?
Нет, э́то его́ дом.	No, it is his house.
Где ва́ша сестра́?	Where is your sister?
Моя́ сестра́ в саду́.	My sister is in the garden.
Где его́ брат?	Where is his brother?
Он на дворе́.	He is in the yard (outside).
Дóма он?	Is he at home?
Нет, он на дворе́.	No, he is in the yard (outside).
Нет, он не дóма ⎫ Нет, его́ нет дóма ⎭	No, he is not at home. (See Lesson II.)

Её мать дома.
Her mother is at home.

Его отец здесь.
His father is here.

Мой дядя и моя тётя в саду.
My uncle and my aunt are in the garden.

Где ваша книга?
Where is your book?

Она тут на столе.
It is here on the table.

Вот наш дом.
Here is our house.

Вон [там] наш сад.
There is our garden.

Тот сад наш.
That garden is ours.

Те книги наши.
Those books are ours.

Это молоко наше.
This milk is ours.

Это наше молоко.
This is our milk.

Это его сыр.
This is his cheese.

Этот сыр его.
This cheese is his.

Это наш хлеб.
This is our bread.

То масло наше.
That butter is ours.

Где его карандаш?
Where is his pencil?

Его карандаш на столе.
His pencil is on the table.

Моя книга и моё перо на столе.
My book and my pen are on the table.

Дедушка и бабушка в саду.
Grandfather and grandmother are in the garden.

Она их внучка.
She is their granddaughter.

Я и моя сестра их внуки.
I and my sister are their grandchildren.

Наша мать их дочь.
Our mother is their daughter.

На столе хлеб, мясо, сыр и масло.
On the table there are bread, meat, cheese, and butter.

Где бумага и перо?
Where is the paper and the pen?

Бумага и перо на столе.
The paper and the pen are on the table.

Кто тот человек?
Who is that man?

Кто те люди?
Who are those people?

Это наш сосед [наша соседка].
This is our neighbour.

Это наши соседи.
These are our neighbours.

LESSON II

Note on the function of the auxiliary verb быть (to be) *in the sentence.*

As already stated in note 2 to Lesson I, the present tense of быть is not often used in colloquial speech : it is usually omitted.   In the written language the third person singular and, less often, plural : есть, суть, are used occasionally when special emphasis is needed.   (See §§ 119, 134.)

Present	*Past*	*Future*
он дóма	он был дóма	он бýдет дóма
he is at home	he was at home	he will be at home
онá здесь [там]	онá былá здесь [там]	онá бýдет здесь [там]
she is here [there]	she was here [there]	she will be here [there]

The colloquial negative form of the present tense of быть is нет (не есть, не суть).   This negative form нет causes the grammatical subject to change from the nominative case to the genitive case, in conformity with the tendency of a negative predicate to require its object to stand in the genitive case (see § 108a).   Thus the grammatical subject becomes a grammatical object (although it still remains the *logical* subject).   The particle не in the past and future tenses has the same effect.   Furthermore, all the tenses of the verb быть with нет and не can assume a neuter and impersonal character :

егó нет дóма	егó нé было дóма	его не бýдет дóма
he is not at home	he was not at home	he will not be at home
их нет здесь	их нé было здесь	их не бýдет здесь
they are not here	they were not here	they will not be here
её нет там	её нé было там	её не бýдет там
she is not there	she was not there	she will not be there

(See § 122 on the meaning and purpose of an impersonal sentence.)

For purposes of simple negation, if the sentence is not turned into an impersonal one, the negative particle не precedes all the persons of present (where the verb itself is dropped), past, and future tenses :

| он не до́ма | он не́ был до́ма | оп не бу́дет до́ма |

The past of быть has the function of the verb-part of a compound predicate (see § 104) :

> Он был мой друг.   He was my friend.

The future of быть can also have the same function. Its main function, however, is as that of an auxiliary verb for the formation of the future tense of the principal (imperfective) verb.   (See § 57.)

Conjugation of the Past and Future Tenses of быть

Past	*Future*
я был, -а́	я бу́ду
ты был, -а́	ты бу́дешь
он был	он ⎫
она́ была́	она́ ⎬ бу́дет
оно́ бы́ло	оно́ ⎭
мы ⎫	мы бу́дем
вы ⎬ бы́ли	вы бу́дете
они́ ⎭	они́ бу́дут

Note.   я бу́ду means : (1) I shall ; or (2) I shall be :

(1) Я бу́ду чита́ть.   I shall read [be reading].

(2) Я бу́ду дома.   I shall be at home.

Vocabulary

слу́шать [*по-], to listen
слу́шать му́зыку, to listen to music
чита́ть [*по-], to read
гуля́ть [*по-], to stroll, to go for a walk
ку́шать [*по-], to eat
знать [*у-], to know

за́втракать [*по-], to have breakfast
[по́лдничать] [1] [*по-], to have lunch
обе́дать [*по-], to have dinner
у́жинать [*по-], to have supper
пить чай [*вы́-], to have [drink] tea

---

[1] Not often used.

играть [*по-], to play
играть в карты, to play cards
играть на скрипке, to play the violin
работать [*по-], to work

спать [*по-], to sleep { сплю
                         спишь
                         спят

писать [*на-], to write { пишу́
                          пи́шешь
                          пи́шут

итти́ спать
[*пойти́ спать]   } to go to bed,
ложи́ться [*лечь]   to go to sleep
  спать   (see § 73)

у́тро, morning
у́тром, in the morning (adv.)
день, day
днём, in the day-time (adv.)
ве́чер, evening
ве́чером, in the evening (adv.)
ночь, night
но́чью, in the night, at night (adv.)
ра́но, early
по́здно, late   } (adv.)
ра́ньше, earlier
по́зже, позднее, later (adv.)
за́втрак, breakfast
до за́втрака, till [until] breakfast
пе́ред за́втраком, before breakfast
по́сле за́втрака, after breakfast
обе́д, dinner
до обе́да, till [until] dinner
пе́ред обе́дом, before dinner
по́сле обе́да, after dinner
чай, tea [tea-time]
до ча́я, till [until] tea-time
пе́ред ча́ем, before tea
по́сле ча́я, after tea
у́жин, supper
до у́жина, till [until] supper
пе́ред у́жином, before supper
по́сле у́жина, after supper
к за́втраку { for breakfast
             to breakfast

за за́втраком (adv.), at breakfast
к обе́ду { for dinner
          to dinner
за обе́дом (adv.), at dinner
к ча́ю { for tea
        to tea
за ча́ем (adv.), at tea
к у́жину { for supper
          to supper
за у́жином (adv.), at supper
в холо́дный день, on a cold day
в тума́нное у́тро, on a misty morning
в нена́стный ве́чер, on a rainy evening
в тёмную ночь, on a dark night
в тот-же день, on the very day
в ту ночь, on that night
в э́тот ве́чер, on this evening
в то у́тро, on that morning
сего́дня, to-day
сего́дня ве́чером, this evening
за́втра, to-morrow
раз, once
ещё раз, once again
когда́?, when ?
тогда́, then
тепе́рь, now
всегда́, always
иногда́, sometimes
уже́, already
ещё, yet
ещё не, not yet
ско́ро, soon
                        } (adv.)
дово́льно по́здно, pretty late
до́лго, long, a long time
о́чень ра́но, very early
о́чень по́здно, very late
никогда́ [не], never
нигде́ [не], nowhere
никто́ [не], no one
ничего́ [не], nothing
никуда́ [не], not anywhere
                        } (adv.)
что, that (conj.)

щи, cabbage soup
селя́нка, stew
жарко́е, roasted meat
с ма́слом, with butter
с варе́ньем, with preserves, jam
пото́м, afterwards
зате́м, and then
опя́ть, again
весь, вся, всё, все, the whole, all

це́лый, the whole
яйцо́, egg
я́йца, eggs
ветчина́, ham
ры́ба, fish
жа́реная ры́ба, fried fish
копчёная груди́нка   { smoked
копчёные рёбрышки   { [cured]
               { bacon [1]

Notes

1. For the conjugation of the verbs of this lesson (except спать, писа́ть, итти́) see § 75, sub-division (d). Present tense of итти́ : я иду́, ты идёшь, он, она́, оно́ идёт, мы идём, вы идёте, они́ иду́т. For the formation of the past tense of all these verbs see § 83.

2. All the verbs of this lesson can have both the **imperfective** and the **perfective** aspects. For the respective meaning and functions of the two aspects see §§ 58-60. The preposition which can be prefixed to each imperfective verb in order to turn it into a perfective one is given in brackets, thus : [*по-] (see § 65) :

     слу́шать,   to listen, to be listening
   *послу́шать, to listen for a short time, or once

The asterisk denotes verbs of the perfective aspect throughout this book.

3. An extensive list of adverbs of time, place, manner, etc., will be found in §§ 90-92.

4. A full statement on prepositions, their meaning and functions, and the cases which they govern, will be found in §§ 93-96.

5. Negative pronouns and adverbs : никто́, ничего́, никогда́, нигде́, etc., are followed by the particle не,

---

[1] There is no specific word for bacon in Russian. Ветчина́, ham, is mostly used. Where bacon, as cured in England, is used, it is referred to as above.

which completes the negation. It stands before the verb under negation :

Он ничего не делает.	He does nothing.
Я никогда не ужинаю.	I never have supper.
Я нигде не видел.	I saw nowhere. etc.

(See § 135, sub-division 6.)

6. The particle не takes the accent before был, было, были, but not before была. It also takes the accent in negative constructions where не implies the predicate :

Мне некогда.	I have no time.
Негде спать.	There is nowhere to sleep.

(See § 135, sub-division 7.)

7. The personal pronouns он, она, when they refer to an inanimate noun, have the meaning of 'it,' both in the nominative and in the oblique cases :

Где стекло ?	Where is the glass ?
Я его не видел.	I have not seen ' it ' (not ' him ').
Где бумага ?	Where is the paper ?
Я не могу найти её.	I cannot find ' it ' (not ' her ').

8. In Russian there is no construction corresponding to the English ' do,' ' does,' ' did,' etc., for negative and interrogative sentences : ' I do not write,' is rendered я не пишу (I not write) ; ' do you write ? ' is rendered вы пишете ? (you write ?), etc.

Exercises

Когда вы будете дома ?	When will you be at home ?
Я буду дома вечером.	I shall be at home (in) the evening.
Утром мы завтракаем ; днём мы обедаем [полдничаем] и пьём чай ; вечером мы ужинаем ; поздно ночью мы идём спать [мы ложимся спать].	In the morning we have breakfast ; in the day-time we dine [have lunch] and have [drink] tea ; in the evening we have supper ; late at night we go to bed [to sleep].

За за́втраком [к за́втраку] мы ку́шаем [еди́м] хлеб с ма́слом, я́йца [яйцо́], копчёную груди́нку [копчёные рёбрышки], ветчину́, жа́реную ры́бу, и пьём чай и́ли ко́фе с молоко́м. Мы иногда́ ку́шаем [еди́м] хлеб с варе́ньем.

At breakfast [for breakfast] we eat bread and [with] butter, eggs [an egg], bacon, ham, fried fish, and we drink tea or coffee with milk. We sometimes eat bread and [with] jam.

За обе́дом и за у́жином [к обе́ду и к у́жину] мы пре́жде всего́ ку́шаем суп, затем еди́м ры́бу, щи, борщ и́ли селя́нку, жарко́е, котле́ты, ка́шу. Пото́м мы ку́шаем пирожки́ [пиро́жное] и фру́кты: я́блоки, гру́ши, сли́вы, ви́шни.

At dinner [for dinner] we first of all eat soup, then we eat fish, cabbage soup, borsch or stew, roast, cutlets, gruel [black gruel]. Afterwards we eat pies [pastry] and fruit: apples, pears, plums, cherries.

По́сле обе́да и по́сле у́жина мы всегда́ пьём ко́фе.

After dinner and after supper we always drink coffee.

За ча́ем [к ча́ю] мы всегда́ ку́шаем хлеб с ма́слом и варе́ньем [и с варе́ньем] и ра́зное пече́нье.

At tea [for tea] we always eat bread and butter and preserves, and various pastries.

По́сле ча́я мы идём гуля́ть.

After tea we go for a walk.

Пе́ред обе́дом мы рабо́таем.

Before dinner we work.

Мы чита́ем и пи́шем.

We read and write.

Я никогда́ не рабо́таю по́сле обе́да.

I never work after dinner.

Пе́ред у́жином я иногда́ слу́шаю му́зыку, и́ли игра́ю в ка́рты.

Before supper I sometimes listen to music, or play cards.

Я зна́ю, что он тепе́рь де́лает.

I know what he is doing now.

Я бу́ду чита́ть по́сле, тепе́рь я иду́ пить чай.

I shall read afterwards, now I am going to have [drink] tea.

Мы ско́ро пойдём обе́дать.	We shall soon go to have dinner.
Сего́дня ве́чером я бу́ду до́ма.	This evening I shall be in.
Сего́дня я бу́ду до́ма весь [це́лый] день [всё у́тро, весь ве́чер, всю ночь].	To-day I shall be at home [in] all day [the whole morning, the whole evening, the whole night].
За́втра ве́чером я бу́ду игра́ть в ка́рты [в ша́хматы], [в ша́шки].	To-morrow evening I shall play cards [chess], [draughts].
По́сле у́жина я пойду́ домо́й.	After supper I shall go home.
Когда́ вы бу́дете обе́дать?	When will you have dinner?
Когда́ вы у́жинаете?	When do you have supper?
Я никогда́ не у́жинаю.	I never have supper.
Он никогда́ не обе́дает до́ма: он обе́дает у бра́та.	He never dines at home: he dines at his brother's.
Мы за́втракаем о́чень ра́но, но у́жинаем о́чень по́здно.	We have breakfast very early, but have supper very late.
Мы чита́ем до за́втрака, рабо́таем до обе́да, и игра́ем в те́ннис до ча́я.	We read till breakfast, work until dinner, and play tennis till tea.
Иногда́ он игра́ет на скри́пке и́ли на роя́ле; мы всегда́ слу́шаем его́ игру́ [как он игра́ет].	Sometimes he plays the violin or the piano; we always listen to his playing.
Он дово́льно хорошо́ понима́ет му́зыку.	He understands music pretty well.
Когда́ вы идёте спать?	When do you go to bed?
Мы всегда́ идём спать о́чень по́здно, но встаём (see § 64, group 4) о́чень ра́но.	We always go to bed very late, but (we) get up very early.
Тепе́рь ещё дово́льно ра́но.	It is still pretty early now.
Нет, уже́ по́здно.	No, it is already late.

Ещё не óчень пóздно.	It is not very late yet.
Он вчерá был здесь.	He was here yesterday.
Егó вчерá нé было здесь⎫ Он нé был здесь вчерá ⎭	He was not here yesterday.
Он бýдет здесь пóздно вéчером.	He will be here late in the evening.
Мы бýдем там рáно ýтром.	We shall be there early in the morning.
Я бýду здесь до обéда.	I shall be here till dinner.
Они зáвтра не бýдут здесь⎫ Их зáвтра не бýдет здесь ⎭	They will not be here to-morrow.
Я придý после чáя.	I will come after tea.
Он придёт пéред ýжином.	He will come before supper.
До ýжина ещё дóлго.	It is a long time yet till supper.
Он ужé был здесь.	He was here already.
Он ещё нé был здесь ⎫ Егó ещё нé было здесь⎭	He was not yet here.
Онá былá дóма.	She was at home [in].
Её нé было дóма.	She was not in.
Её не бýдет дóма до вéчера.	She will not be in till the evening.
Я читáл и писáл всю ночь.	I was reading and writing the whole night.
Мы ужé бы́ли здесь рáньше.	We were here before.
Он всегдá спит до чáя.	He always sleeps [has a nap] till tea-time.
Он придёт потóм [пóсле чáя].	He will come afterwards [after tea].
Я её вúдел тóлько раз.	I saw her only once.
Они не спáли до утрá.	They did not sleep till morning.
Мы рабóтаем весь [цéлый] день.	We work all day.

· LESSON III

Vocabulary

чёрный ⎫
бѣлый ⎬ -ая, -ое, -ые ⎰ black
красный ⎭ ⎱ white
⎰ red

синій, -яя, -ее, -не, blue
большой, -ая, -ое, -іе, large, big
малый, -ая, -ое, -ые ⎫
маленькій, -ая, -ое, -не ⎬ small

новый ⎫ ⎰ new
старый ⎬ -ая, -ое, -ые ⎱ old

слабый, -ая, -ое, -ые, weak

сильный, -ая, -ое, -ые ⎫ strong
крѣпкій, -ая, -ое, -не ⎭

глупый ⎫ -ая, -ое, -ые ⎰ foolish, silly
умный ⎭ ⎱ wise, clever

что за ? what kind ? what a . . .

какой ? ⎫ -ая, -ое, -іе ⎰ what kind ?
такой ⎭ ⎱ such a one

каков [1] ⎫ -а, -о, -ы ⎰ of what kind
таков [1] ⎭ ⎱ of such a kind

For the short (predicative) form of these adjectives and for their comparative form, see § 45.

слабое здоровье, delicate health
слаб, -а, -о, -ы, здоровьем, delicate (in health) (adv.)

покупать ⎫ to buy (see § 66)
*купить ⎭

давать ⎫ to give
*дать ⎭

продавать ⎫ to sell (see § 64, group 2)
*продать ⎭

болѣ-ть, to be ailing, to ache ⎫
*заболѣ-ть, to be taken ill ⎬ (see p. 258)

жить [*по-], живу, живёшь, живут, to live
варить [*с-], варю, варишь, варят, to cook, to boil
имѣть, to have
бывать, to happen ; to be (iter.) ; to frequent
видеть [*у-], вижу, видишь, видят, to see
ѣхать [*по-] ⎫ to travel (see § 63)
ѣздить [*с-] ⎭

когда-то, once (before)
часто, often
рѣдко, seldom
чаще, more often
рѣже, less often
ещё раз, once more
ни разу, not once

два ⎫ ⎰ twice
три ⎬ раза ⎨ thrice
четыре ⎭ ⎱ four times

много раз, many times
нѣсколько раз, a few times
совсѣм, entirely
не совсѣм, not quite, not entirely
довольно, fairly, moderately, pretty
гораздо, much (used with a comparative adjective)
кажется, it seems, I think, I believe
сейчас, this minute
через час, in an hour
сію минуту, this moment
через минуту, in a minute
скоро, soon, quickly

[1] These correspond to the short adjectives and imply a predicate.

чем, than (*conj.*)

недáвно, not long ago

давнó, long ago ; a long time

сюдá, here (motion) [hither]

тудá, there (motion) [thither]

зáвтра ýтром, to-morrow morning

зáвтра вéчером, to-morrow evening

вчерá вéчером, last night

сегóдня вéчером, to-night

день, day

кáждый день, every day

раз в день, once a day

год, a year. *Pl.:* летá; гóды (see note 7 to this lesson)

кáждый год, every year

раз в год, once a year

чéрез год, in a year's time

чéрез два дня, in two days' time

чéрез час, in an hour's time

мéсяц, a month

чéрез мéсяц, in a month's time

кáждый мéсяц, each month, every month

раз в мéсяц, once a month

недéля, a week

чéрез недéлю, in a week's time

кáждую недéлю, each week, every week

раз в недéлю, once a week

в э́том годý, this year

в прóшлом годý, last year

в бýдущем годý, next year

óсень, autumn

óсенью, in the autumn (*adv.*)

зимá, winter

зимóю, in the winter (*adv.*)

прóшлой зимóй, last winter (*adv.*)

веснá, spring

веснóю, in the spring (*adv.*)

бýдущей веснóй, next spring (*adv.*)

лéто, summer

лéтом, in the summer (*adv.*)

э́тим лéтом, this summer

к óсени, towards autumn

к зимé, towards winter

к веснé, towards spring

к лéту, towards summer

в концé гóда, at the end of the year

к концý гóда, towards the end of the year

в начáле гóда, at the beginning of the year

к начáлу гóда, towards the beginning of the year

в начáле мéсяца, at the beginning of the month

к начáлу мéсяца, towards the beginning of the month

в концé мéсяца, at the end of the month

в концé недéли, at the end of the week

к концý мéсяца, towards the end of the month

к концý недéли, towards the end of the week

томý назáд, ago

мéсяц томý назáд, a month ago

год томý назáд, a year ago

недéлю томý назáд, a week ago

две недéли томý назáд, two weeks ago

трéтьего дня, the day before yesterday.

два	} дня томý {	two days ago
три	} назáд {	three days ago
четы́ре		four days ago

час томý назáд, an hour ago

в э́том мéсяце, this month

в бýдущем мéсяце, next month

в прóшлом мéсяце, last month

на бýдущей недéле, next week

на прóшлой недéле, last week

на э́той недéле, this week

на другóй день, next day

рýсский, a Russian

рýсская, a Russian woman

англичáнин, an Englishman

англичáнка, an Englishwoman

францу́з, a Frenchman
францу́женка, a Frenchwoman
америка́нец, an American
америка́нка, an American woman
кита́ец, a Chinaman
китая́нка, a Chinese woman
не́мец, a German
не́мка, a German woman
япо́нец, a Japanese
япо́нка, a Japanese woman
Сове́тский Сою́з, Soviet Union
Росси́я, Russia
А́нглия, England
Фра́нция, France
Кита́й, China
Герма́ния, Germany
Япо́ния, Japan
в Сове́тском Сою́зе, in U.S.S.R.
в Росси́и, in Russia
в А́нглии, in England
в Кита́е, in China
в Аме́рике, in America
в Герма́нии, in Germany
в Япо́нии, in Japan (loc.)
в Сове́тский Сою́з, to U.S.S.R.
в А́нглию, to England
в Кита́й, to China
во Фра́нцию, to France
в Герма́нию, to Germany
в Япо́нию, to Japan (acc.)
ко́мната, a room

кварти́ра, a flat
на кварти́ре, at the flat
у меня́ на кварти́ре, at my flat
у нас на кварти́ре, at our flat
у них на кварти́ре, at their flat
у вас на кварти́ре, at your flat
у него́ на кварти́ре, at his flat
у неё на кварти́ре, at her flat
столо́вая (n.), dining-room
спа́льня, bedroom
прихо́жая, entrance-hall
де́тская, nursery
ва́нная [ко́мната], bathroom
гости́ная, sitting-room
ку́хня, kitchen
гости́ница, hotel
но́мер, room (at hotel)
у меня́ в но́мере, in my room (at the hotel)
у меня́ в спа́льне, in my bedroom
у нас в [на] ку́хне, in our kitchen
у них в столо́вой, in their dining-room
го́род, town
дере́вня, village
у нас в го́роде } in our town
в на́шем го́роде
у нас в дере́вне } in our village
в на́шей дере́вне
состоя́ние, estate, fortune ; condition ; state (of health, of weather)

Notes

1. The verb быва́ть is the iterative form of быть. In its iterative form it is only used in the past tense (see § 62). It can be used as an imperfective verb in the meaning :

(1) to frequent ; (2) to visit occasionally ; (3) to happen.

Я там быва́ю иногда́. — I go there sometimes.
Он быва́ет здесь [прихо́дит сюда́] о́чень ча́сто. — He comes here very often.
Э́то быва́ет. — This happens [can happen].
Быва́ли таки́е слу́чаи. — Such cases did happen.

(On the meaning and function of the neuter singular past, бывáло, see § 122 (*f*).)

2. The short (predicative) comparative degree of an adjective requires the indirect object (the object of comparison) to stand in the genitive :

(*a*) Мой брат богáче меня́.   My brother is richer than I.

But the sentence can be paraphrased so as to conform to the English pattern :

(*b*) Мой брат богáче, чем я.

The first pattern is the most frequently used in colloquial speech.

(*c*) A popular variation of the first pattern is the use of the genitive of the possessive pronoun instead of the personal pronoun :

богáче моегó instead of богáче меня́ ;
лýчше твоегó   ,,   лýчше тебя́ ;
      etc.

3. The verb имѣть (to have) is for colloquial purposes replaced by the verb быть. The grammatical subject is then changed into an object (although it still remains the *logical* subject (see § 134*a*)).

Instead of я имѣл лóшадь (I had a horse), the colloquial form used is, у меня́ былá лóшадь :

Он имѣл сад.   — У негó был сад.
Он не имѣл сáда. — У негó нé было сáда.
He had no garden.
Кто имѣет нож ? — У когó есть нож ?
Who has a knife ?

But : У когó нож ? would mean : Who has *the* knife ?

By analogy the following indirect expressions are used :

Instead of : на моём столé   — у меня́ на столé
          в моéй кóмнате — у меня́ в кóмнате
          в нáшем садý   — у нас в садý

4. *Peculiarities in the Conjugation of a few verbs in frequent use.*

жить [*по-], to live   хотѣть [*за-], to wish, to want
ѣхать [*по-], to travel   *лечь,   to lie down
*дать,   to give   *сесть,   to sit down
ѣсть [*по-],   to eat   болѣть [*за-], to ache ; to
                                         be ailing

The asterisk (*) denotes a verb of the perfective aspect, the present form of which has a future meaning. (See §§ 58, 59.)

Present (or future in Perfective verbs).

Singular

я живу́	ѣду	*дам	ѣм	хочу́	*ля́гу	*ся́ду
ты живёшь	ѣдешь	*дашь	ѣшь	хо́чешь	*ля́жешь	*ся́дешь
он она́ } живёт оно́	ѣдет	*даст	ѣст	хо́чет	*ля́жет	*ся́дет

Plural

мы живём	ѣдем	*дади́м	ѣди́м	хоти́м	*ля́жем	*ся́дем
вы живёте	ѣдете	*дади́те	ѣди́те	хоти́те	*ля́жете	*ся́дете
они́ живу́т	ѣдут	*даду́т	ѣдя́т	хотя́т	*ля́гут	*ся́дут

Past.

я ты } жил он	ѣхал	дал	ѣл	хотѣ́л	лёг	сѣл
она́ жила́	ѣхала	дала́	ѣла	хотѣ́ла	легла́	сѣла
оно́ жи́ло	ѣхало	да́ло	ѣло	хотѣ́ло	легло́	сѣло
мы вы } жи́ли они́	ѣхали	да́ли	ѣли	хотѣ́ли	легли́	сѣли

Imperative.

Sing.	живи́	поезжа́й [1]	дай	ѣшь	захоти́ [1]	ляг	сядь
Plur.	живи́те	поезжа́йте	да́йте	ѣшьте	захоти́те	ля́гте	ся́дьте

[1] No imperative in use for the imperfective aspect of these verbs.

I

Present.

болеть [быть больны́м], to be ailing (*instr.* or *absolute*) :

я боле́ю,   ты боле́ешь,   он ⎫
                        она́ ⎬ боле́ет
                        оно́ ⎭

мы боле́ем,   вы боле́ете,   они́ боле́ют

болеть, to ache   он ⎫
                        она́ ⎬ боли́т, они́ боля́т
                        оно́ ⎭

NOTE. болеть (to ache) is only used in the third person singular and plural.

Past.   боле́л, боле́ла, боле́ло, боле́ли.

Imperative.   боле́й, боле́йте.

У меня́ боля́т зу́бы.	My teeth are aching; I have toothache.
У меня́ голова́ боли́т.	My head is aching.
У меня́ всегда́ но́ги боля́т [боля́т но́ги].	My legs are always aching.
Но́чью у меня́ голова́ боле́ла [боле́ла голова́].	In the night my head was aching.
Он всегда́ боле́ет.	He is always ailing.
Он боле́л [был бо́лен] ти́фом.	He was ill with typhus.
Не боле́йте.	Don't be ailing.

5. Есть and ку́шать (see Lesson II) both mean ' to eat.' Ку́шать is supposed to be a politer form when referring to another person :

Вы ку́шали ; пожа́луйста, ку́шайте.

You were eating [ate] ; please, eat.

мы еди́м, бу́дем есть ; we eat, we shall eat.

There are, however, no clear lines of distinction between the two forms. Practice and reading Russian texts will help the student to decide which form is more suitable on a given occasion.

6. Nationality of a person is written with a small letter ; his country, with a capital letter :

ру́сский	— Росси́я
не́мец	— Герма́ния
англича́нин	— А́нглия etc.

7. Год (year) has a double plural: лета́, го́ды. The colloquial form is лета́ :

пять лет тому́ наза́д,	five years ago
ему́ де́сять лет,	he is ten years old
в его́ лета́х,	at his age
сре́дних лет,	of middle age

but : Он ста́рше меня́ тремя́ года́ми (or на́ три го́да).
He is older than I by three years.

When years in general, or a particular period, are referred to, the plural го́ды is used :

в те го́ды,	in those years
в сороковы́х года́х,	in the forties
в ста́рые го́ды,	in old times
молоды́е го́ды,	youth

Exercises

У него́ но́вая шля́па.	He has a new hat.
Его́ шля́па нова́.	His hat is new.
Моя́ шля́па нове́е, чем его́ шля́па.	My hat is newer than his.
У неё [есть] большо́й дом.	She has a large house.
Её дом вели́к.	Her house is large.
Мой дом бо́льше, чем её дом.	My house is larger than her house.
У него́ ста́рое пальто́.	He has an old overcoat.
Его́ пальто́ ста́ро.	His overcoat is old.
Моё пальто́ гора́здо старе́е.	My overcoat is much older.
Его́ ру́ки бы́ли кра́сны.	His hands were red.
Мои́ ру́ки бы́ли красне́е.	My hands were redder.

У негó [есть] мáленький брат

Он имéет мáленького брáта

He has a little brother.

У нас есть глýпые лю́ди. — We have stupid people.

Он глупéе своегó брáта

Он глупéе, чем егó брат

He is more stupid than his brother.

Егó дом совсéм бéлый. — His house is entirely white.

Их дом белéе. — Their house is whiter.

[Мне] Кáжется, егó дом не совсéм бéлый. — I believe [I think] his house is not entirely white.

Наш сад óчень велúк. — Our garden is very large.

Их сад горáздо бóльше. — Their garden is much larger.

Их дом óчень [довóльно] велúк. — Their house is very [pretty] large.

Каковó [состоя́ние] егó здорóвье [-я] ? — How is the state of his health ?

Каковó егó состоя́ние ? — How is his state [estate] ?

Онó не óчень великó. — It is not very great.

Зимóю иногдá бывáет óчень хóлодно. — In the winter it sometimes happens to be very cold.

Мы бывáем у них чáсто. — We visit them [we go to them] frequently.

Онú бывáют у нас рéдко. — They visit us seldom.

[Это] Всегдá так бывáет. — It always happens so.

Когдá-то, я бывáл у них кáждый день. — Some time ago [at one time] I used to visit them every day.

Рáньше онú бывáли у нас чáсто. — Before they used to come to us [visit us] often.

Он óчень ýмный человéк. — He is a very clever [wise] man.

Онú весьмá ýмные лю́ди. — They are very clever [wise] people.

Эти лю́ди умны́. — These people are clever.

Эта дáма умнá. — This lady is clever.

Я у них был два рáза. — I visited them [was at their house] twice.

Я ни разу не был у них.	I have never [not once] visited them.
Я ещё ни разу не был у них.	I have not yet been to see them once.
Я пойду к ним опять } Я ещё раз пойду к ним }	I shall visit them [go to them] again [once more].
Я давно не был у него.	I have not been at his house for a long time [it is a long time since I have been at his house].
Я недавно был у них.	I was at their house not long ago.
Я приду сию минуту [через минуту], [сейчас].	I will come this minute [in a minute], [immediately].
Он сейчас будет здесь.	He will be here presently.
Он скоро придёт.	He will soon come.
Я никогда не знал.	I never knew.
Он нигде не был.	I was not anywhere.
Мы никого не видели там.	We saw nobody there.
Он недавно приехал сюда.	He arrived here not long ago.
Он будет у нас зимою.	He will be at our house in the winter.
Я буду у них летом.	I shall visit them [be at their house] in the summer.
К весне я поеду в Англию.	Towards [by] spring I shall go to England.
К осени мы будем дома [приедем домой].	Towards [by] autumn we shall be at home [will return home].
Зимою мы живём в городе; летом они живут в деревне [на даче].	In the winter we live in town; in the summer they live in the country [at the country-house].
Мы живём здесь в гостинице.	We live here at an hotel.
У нас [Мы имеем] очень хороший номер.	We have a very good room (at the hotel).

У них [есть] хорóшая, не-
большáя квартúра
[Онú имéют хорóшую, не-
большýю квартúру]

They have a good, small [not
very large] flat.

Онú имéют столóвую, две
спáльни [спáльню], кýх-
ню, небольшýю гостúную,
вáнную кóмнату, дéт-
скую и прихóжую.

They have a dining-room,
two bedrooms [bedroom],
kitchen, small sitting-
room [drawing-room],
bathroom, nursery, and
entrance-hall.

Вчерá вéчером ваш брат
был у нас.

Last night your brother was
at our house.

Зáвтра ýтром мы бýдем у
негó.

To-morrow morning we shall
be at his house.

Я бывáю у негó иногдá
[кáждый день].

I visit him sometimes [every
day].

К концý гóда [в начáле
новóго гóда], [в бýдущем
годý] мы поéдем в Россúю
[в Совéтский Сою́з].

Towards the end of the year
[at the beginning of the
new year], [in the next
year] we shall go to Russia
[to U.S.S.R.].

Онú бы́ли у нас мéсяц томý
назáд [две недéли томý
назáд], [час томý назáд],
[недéлю томý назáд].

They were at our house a
month ago [a fortnight
ago], [an hour ago], [a
week ago].

Я егó вúдел трéтьего дня.

I saw him the day before
yesterday.

У нас в гостúнице живýт
рýсские [трóе рýсских],
два англичáнина, два
французá, и одúн нéмец.

At our hotel reside [live]
Russians [three Russians],
two Englishmen, two
Frenchmen, and one Ger-
man.

Онú все бýдут у нас [по-
сетя́т нас] на бýдущей
недéле.

They will all visit us in the
coming week.

Мы бы́ли у них на прó-
шлой недéле.

We were at their house
[place] last week.

Они́ бу́дут у нас че́рез два дня [че́рез ме́сяц], [че́рез год], [че́рез две неде́ли].	They will be at our house in two days' time [in a month's time], [in a year], [in a fortnight].
Я его́ уви́жу на э́той неде́ле [в э́ту неде́лю], [на бу́дущей неде́ле].	I will see him during this week [this week], [during next week].
Он был здесь в про́шлом ме́сяце, на той неде́ле.	He was here last month, last week [in the past month, in the past week].
Он пришёл на друго́й день [на друго́й день он пришёл].	He came the next day [the next day he came].

(For the conjugation and aspect of the verbs of this lesson not shown in the Vocabulary, see §§ 65-66.)

LESSON IV

Vocabulary

воскресе́нье, Sunday
понеде́льник, Monday
вто́рник, Tuesday
среда́, Wednesday
четве́рг, Thursday
пя́тница, Friday
суббо́та, Saturday
в воскресе́нье, on Sunday (*acc.*)
до воскресе́нья, till, until Sunday (*gen.*)
к воскресе́нью, by, for Sunday (*dat.*)
по воскресе́ньям, on Sundays (*dat. pl.*)

в понеде́льник, on Monday ⎫
во вто́рник, on Tuesday ⎪
в сре́ду, on Wednesday ⎬ (*acc.*)
в четве́рг, on Thursday ⎪
в пя́тницу, on Friday ⎪
в суббо́ту, on Saturday ⎭

до понеде́льника, till, until Monday ⎫
до вто́рника, till, until Tuesday ⎪
до среды́, till, until Wednesday ⎪
до четверга́, till, until Thursday ⎬ (*gen.*)
до пя́тницы, till, until Friday ⎪
до суббо́ты, till, until Saturday ⎭

к понеде́льнику, for, by Monday ⎫
к [ко] вто́рнику, for, by Tuesday ⎪
к среде́, for, by Wednesday ⎬ (*dat.*)
к четвергу́, for, by Thursday ⎪
к пя́тнице, for, by Friday ⎪
к суббо́те, for, by Saturday ⎭

по понедѣльникам, on Mondays
по вторникам, on Tuesdays
по средамъ, on Wednesdays (dat. pl.)
по четвергамъ, on Thursdays
по пятницам, on Fridays
по субботамъ, on Saturdays
январь,[1] January
февраль, February
мартъ, March
апрѣль, April
май, May
іюнь, June
іюль, July
августъ, August
сентябрь, September
октябрь, October
ноябрь, November
декабрь, December
въ январѣ [мѣсяцѣ], in January
въ февралѣ [,,], in February
въ мартѣ [,,], in March
въ апрѣлѣ [,,], in April
въ маѣ [,,], in May
въ іюнѣ [,,], in June
въ іюлѣ [,,], in July
въ августѣ [,,], in August
въ сентябрѣ [,,], in September
въ октябрѣ [,,], in October
въ ноябрѣ [,,], in November
въ декабрѣ [,,], in December
въ теченіе января, during January etc.
съ воскресенья, from Sunday on
съ понедѣльника, from Monday on etc.
съ марта, from March on
отъ марта до мая, from March till May
отъ субботы до среды, from Saturday till Wednesday
въ теченіе зимы, during winter
въ теченіе лѣта, during summer
въ теченіе весны, during spring
въ теченіе осени, during autumn

въ будущую зиму, [in the] next winter
въ будущее лѣто, [in the] next summer
въ будущую весну, [in the] next spring
въ будущую осень, [in the] next autumn
въ началѣ января, at the beginning of January
въ концѣ января, at the end of January
къ началу января, towards the beginning of January
къ концу января, towards the end of January
въ часъ, at one o'clock
въ два часа, at two o'clock
къ часу, by one o'clock
къ двумъ часамъ, by two o'clock
въ пять часовъ, at five o'clock
въ пятомъ часу, between four and five
на дняхъ, shortly; also; the other day, lately
на этихъ дняхъ, one of these days [soon]
на досугѣ, at leisure
въ полдень, at midday
въ полночь, at midnight
въ какое время? at what time?
въ скоромъ времени, soon
въ половинѣ перваго, at half-past twelve
въ половинѣ втораго, at half-past one
въ половинѣ третьяго, at half-past two etc.
въ которомъ часу? at what hour? [at what time?]
который часъ? what is the time?
который теперь часъ? what time is it now?
сутки (pl.), day and night
цѣлыя сутки, a whole 24 hours

[1] Names of months ending in -ь are of masculine gender.

магазин, store

лавка, shop

банк, bank

ресторан, restaurant

граница, boundary, frontier

за-границу,[1] abroad (motion)

за-границей,[1] abroad (rest)

из за-границы,[1] from abroad

вход, entrance

касса, cash-desk, booking-office (at theatre, etc.)

праздник, holiday

праздники, holidays

на праздниках, during the holidays

святки, Christmas holidays

на святках, during the Christmas holidays

Святая неделя, Easter week

на Святой [неделе], during Easter week

Пасха, Easter

Рождество, Christmas

театр, theatre

в театре, at the theatre

в театр, to the theatre

опера, opera

в опере, at the opera

в оперу, to the opera

концерт, concert

на концерте, at the concert

на концерт, to the concert

из театра, from the theatre

из оперы, from the opera

с концерта, from the concert

кинематограф, cinema

в кинематографе, at the cinema

в кинематограф, to the cinema

из кинематографа, from the cinema

станция, railway station

на станцию, to the station

на станции, at the station

со станции, from the station

почта, post office

на почте, at the post office

на почту, to the post office

с почты, from the post office

вокзал, railway station

на вокзал, to the railway station

на вокзале, at the railway station

с вокзала, from the railway station

поезд, train

вагон, carriage

поезд отходит, train leaves

поезд прибывает, train arrives

прибытие поезда, arrival of train

отход поезда, departure of train

уставать, to grow tired, weary

*устать, to get tired (see § 64, group 4)

вид, appearance

очки, eye-glasses

угол, corner; в углу, in the corner

на углу, at the corner (of street)

на конце улицы, at the end of the street

дверь (*fem.*), door

окно, window

лестница, staircase, steps

спускаться } по лестнице, to go

*спуститься } down the stairs

подниматься } по лестнице, to go

*подняться } up the stairs

наверху, at the top

внизу, at the bottom

наверх, up } (motion)

вниз, down }

открыва-ть,
  -ю, -ешь, -ют } to open, to
*откр-ыть, } uncover
  -ою, -оешь, -оют

открытый, -ая, -ое, -ые, uncovered

открыт, -а, -о, -ы, opened, open

закрыва-ть,
  -ю, -ешь, -ют } to close, to
*закр-ыть, } cover
  -ою, -оешь, -оют

закрытый, -ая, -ое, -ые, covered

закрыт, -а, -о, -ы, closed

[1] Also : за границу, за границей, из-за границы.

I *

занятóй, -áя, -óе, -ы́е, busy, engaged (*adj.*)

за́нятый, -ая, -ое, -ые⎫ occupied
за́нят, -á, -о, -ы (*instr.* ⎬ (*part.*)
or *absolute*) ⎭

больнóй, -áя, -óе, -ы́е⎫ ill, ailing
бóлен, больнá, -о, -ы́ ⎬ (patient)
(*instr.* or *absolute*) ⎭

здорóвый, -ая, -ое, -ые⎫ healthy,
здорóв, -а, -о, -ы   ⎬ strong

Notes

1. In Russian the days of the week and the names of
the months are *not* written with a capital letter. Feasts
are written with capital letters.

2. The relation between words in a Russian sentence
is shown more by inflexions than by word order (see
§ 133). The case-endings and other terminations are, therefore, of great importance. The student should familiarize
himself with the uses of the various cases, as every case
has a distinct function in the making of a Russian sentence.
In the section of this book which treats of the Russian
Syntax, the use of the various cases is dealt with in greater
detail (see §§ 117-120, 137-141). A few hints as we go
along may be useful. We will begin with the

**Genitive case of nouns, adjectives, pronouns, numerals,
and participles.**

The genitive case shows that the word used in this case is
an adjunct, or qualifying word, or part-object, to another
word. It is used :

(*a*) to express possession or certain other characteristics
(see § 137, sub-section 1) ;

(*b*) to denote a direct object used in a partitive sense
(see § 137, sub-section 2) ;

(*c*) to denote a direct object if the predicate is in the
negative (see §§ 108*a*, 137, sub-section 4) ;

(*d*) to express comparison (see § 137, sub-section 3) ;

(*e*) in constructions which express days and dates (see
§ 137, sub-section 5) ;

(*f*) after cardinal numerals (see § 137, sub-section 7) ;

(*g*) after the prepositions enumerated in § 96 ;

(*h*) after verbs which have the meaning of striving for, aiming at, or wishing for, something (see § 137, sub-section 6) ;

(*i*) in a few expressions of greeting or leave-taking :

до свида́ния,	good-bye
до ско́рого свида́ния,	to an early meeting
всего́ хоро́шего всего́ лу́чшего	} all the best
до́брого у́тра,	good morning [but also : до́брое у́тро, good morning ; до́брый ве́чер, good evening]
споко́йной но́чи,	good night [restful night]
счастли́вого пути́,	happy journey

NOTE. In the expressions of this group the word жела́ю [-ем] (I [we] wish) is implied.

(*j*) in a few adverbial expressions of time :

от поры́ до вре́мени от вре́мени до вре́мени	} from time to time
с утра́ до ве́чера,	from morning till evening
с каки́х пор ?	since when ?
до каки́х пор ?	till when ?
с тех пор,	since then
с тех пор, как,	since
с мое́й стороны́,	on my part, as for me
до тех пор, пока́ [не],	till, until
до того́,	to such an extent
кро́ме того́ сверх того́	} besides, over and above
из-за́ моря,	from beyond the sea
из-за грани́цы,	from abroad
снача́ла,	at first (*adv.*)
сра́зу,	at once (*adv.*)

Exercises

Это сад моего дяди.	This is my uncle's garden [orchard].
Я дал ему чаю.	I gave him some tea (see § 20).
У меня нет чая.	I have no tea.
Я купил сукна.	I bought some cloth.
Я купил сукно хорошего качества.	I bought cloth of good quality.
Пожалуйста, принесите вина [воды], [пива].	Please fetch [bring] some wine [water], [beer].
Я не знал урока.	I did not know my lesson.
У нас нет стола.	We have no table.
Вчера не было дождя.	Yesterday it did not rain [there was no rain].
У меня нет работы.	I have no work.
У меня не было работы.	I had no work.
Нужно купить сахару.	It is necessary to buy some sugar (see § 20).
Какая теперь цена сахара?	What is the price of sugar now?
Сегодня не будет обеда.	To-day there will be no dinner.
Вчера не было ужина.	Yesterday there was no supper.
Завтра не будет завтрака.	To-morrow there will be no breakfast.
Такой беды мы не ожидали.	We did not expect such a misfortune.
Я жду письма от моего брата.	I expect a letter from my brother.
Мы ждали его приезда.	We were waiting for his arrival.
Я боюсь такого исхода.	I am afraid of such a sequel.

Я желаю вам успéха.	I wish you success.
Я сегóдня ýтром был у вáшего отцá.	This morning I was at your father's house.
Мы покупáем кни́ги у кни́гопродáвца.	We buy books at a bookseller's.
До обéда я рабóтаю ; пóсле обéда я отдыхáю.	I work till dinner ; after dinner I rest.
Убери́те тарéлки со столá.	Clear away the plates from the table.
Я приéхал из дерéвни.	I came [arrived] from the country.
Без очкóв я не могý читáть	Without glasses I cannot read.
Я ничегó не получáю от брáта.	I receive nothing from my brother.
Я не получáю никакóй пóмощи от негó.	I receive no help whatever from him.
Мы приéхали со стáнции. [с вокзáла], [с концéрта], [с собрáния].	We arrived [came] from the railway station [from the concert], [from the meeting].
Стул стои́т у столá ; стол стои́т у окнá.	The chair stands near the table ; the table stands near the window.
Я сижý у столá.	I am sitting at the table.
[Врéмя от врéмени] От врéмени до врéмени мы получáем пи́сьма из Росси́и.	[Occasionally] From time to time we receive letters from Russia.
С каки́х пор вы знáете [знáли] óто ?	Since when have you known this ?
С тех пор, как я вернýлся из Лóндона.	Since I came back from London.
До каки́х пор вы бýдете здесь ?	Till when [how long] will you be here ?

До тех пор, пока я не кончу свою работу.

Until I have finished [will finish] my work.

Я только вчера приехал из за-границы.

I came from abroad only yesterday.

Я не увижу его до понедельника, я буду занят.

I shall not see him till Monday; I shall be busy [occupied].

Комната была занята его братом.

The room was occupied by his brother.

Мы скоро поедем на станцию [на вокзал].

We shall soon go to the railway station.

Поезд прибывает в пять часов вечера.

The train arrives at five o'clock in the evening.

Он приедет со своим младшим братом в среду вечером.

He will arrive with his younger brother on Wednesday evening.

Девятнадцатого июня мы поедем в Англию. Сегодня двадцатое мая.

On the 19th of June we shall go to England. To-day is the 20th of May.

Они ездят на станцию каждый день.

They travel to the railway station every day.

Мы туда приедем за час до отхода поезда [перед отходом поезда].

We shall arrive there an hour before the departure of the train.

Он весьма [очень] занятой человек.

He is a very busy man.

Эти люди всегда заняты.

These people are always busy [occupied].

В начале марта мы поедем за-границу (acc.).

At the beginning of March we shall go abroad.

Мы пробудем за-границей около трёх месяцев.

We shall remain abroad about three months.

Отнесите письмо на почту; потом идите на станцию; там ждите прихода [до прихода] поезда.

Take the letter to the post office; then go to the station; there wait until the arrival of the train.

На дворе́, ка́жется, хо́-
лодно тепе́рь : возьми́те
пальто́ [наде́ньте паль-
то́].

I think it is cold outside
now: take an overcoat
[put on an overcoat].

Ве́чером мы все пойдём в
теа́тр [в о́перу], [в кине-
матогра́ф], [на конце́рт].

In the evening we shall all
go to the theatre [opera],
[to the cinema], [to the
concert].

Мы пробу́дем в теа́тре [в
о́пере], [на конце́рте], [в
кинематогра́фе], о́коло
трёх часо́в.

We shall stay [remain] at
the theatre [at the opera],
[at the cinema], [at the
concert], about three
hours.

Мы прие́дем [вернёмся] из
теа́тра [из о́перы], [с
конце́рта], [из кинема-
то́графа] о́коло одинна-
дцати часо́в ве́чера [но́чи].

We shall arrive [return]
from the theatre [from
the opera], [from the con-
cert], [from the cinema]
about 11 o'clock in the
evening [night].

Мы там бу́дем до двух
часо́в но́чи, до полови́ны
тре́тьего [ча́са], [но́чи],
до че́тверти четвёртого
[ча́са].

We shall be there till 2 o'clock
in the morning [till half-
past two], [till 3.15].

К нам пришли́ [пришло́]
тро́е из его́ друзе́й.

Three of his friends came to
our house [to us].

Мы заказа́ли у́жин для
двои́х [трои́х], [четве-
ры́х].

We have ordered supper for
two, three, four [for a party
of two, of three, of four].

За́втра [бу́дет] пра́здник.

To-morrow is [will be] a
holidáy.

Все магази́ны, ла́вки и
ба́нки бу́дут закры́ты ;
теа́тры и кинематогра́фы
бу́дут откры́ты то́лько
ве́чером с [от] шести́ до
одинна́дцати часо́в.

All stores, shops and banks
will be closed ; theatres
and cinemas will be open
only in the evening, from
six till eleven o'clock.

Рестораны будут открыты весь [целый] день.

Restaurants will be open all [the whole] day.

Ваш брат, кажется, болен ; у него больной [болезненный] вид.

Your brother, I think, is ill ; he has a sick [sickly] appearance.

Нет, он вполне здоров ; он только устал ; он ехал [был] в поезде целые сутки.

No, he is quite well ; he is only tired ; he was in the train a whole day and night.

Теперь я у них буду по субботам ; раньше я у них никогда не бывал по субботам.

Now I shall be at their house [visit them] on Saturdays ; before I was never at their house on Saturdays.

Мы всегда бываем у них по воскресеньям.

We are always at their house [go to see them] on Sundays.

Раньше четверга не ждите меня.

Do not expect me before Thursday.

Может быть я пробуду у вашего брата до пятницы.

Maybe I shall stay at your brother's till Friday.

Я купил собаку у соседа [от соседа].

I bought the dog from my neighbour.

Мы всегда берём деньги у брата [от брата]; он очень богат.

We always take money of brother [from brother] ; he is very rich.

Вон [вот] он стоит у входа [у кассы].

There [here] he stands near the entrance [near the booking office].

Он был возле [около] театра.

He was near the theatre.

Я видел его недалеко от вашего дома.

I saw him not far from your house.

После концерта мы будем ужинать у моего дяди.

After the concert we shall have supper at my uncle's.

Мы поедем туда прямо с концерта.

We shall go there straight from the concert.

Он живёт недалеко от театра.	He lives not far from the theatre.
Кроме нас там также будут наши соседи.	Besides us, our neighbours will also be there.
Вы будете сидеть возле меня.	You will sit next to me.
Без вас я не поеду ; я еду ради вас.	Without you I shall not go ; I go for your sake.
Мы там пробудем около часа.	We shall stay there about an hour.
Моя мать [матушка] ждёт письма от нашей тёти.	My mother expects a letter [waits for a letter] from our aunt.

LESSON V

Vocabulary

становиться }	to become, to get	заказывать }	to order (see § 64,
*стать }	(see § 64, group 4)	*заказать }	group 1)

For adverbs formed from adjectives which can have a predicative meaning see §§ 43, 90 (2) (a), 134, sub-section (3) :

темно, dark	безопасно, safe
темнее, darker	безопаснее, safer
светло, light	плохо, bad
светлее, lighter	хуже, worse
тепло, warm	дурно, bad
теплее, warmer	недурно, not bad
холодно, cold	не так плохо, not so bad
холоднее, colder	не так дурно, not so bad
прохладно, cool	хорошо, well
прохладнее, cooler	нехорошо, bad(ly)
свежо, fresh [cool]	лучше, better
свежее, fresher [cooler]	приятно, pleasant
жарко, hot	приятнее, pleasanter
жарче, hotter	неприятно, unpleasant
трудно, difficult, hard	неприятнее, more unpleasant
труднее, harder, more difficult	весело, jolly
опасно, dangerous	веселее, jollier
опаснее, more dangerous	скучно, dull, boring

скучнѣе, duller
грустно, sad
грустнѣе, sadder
пасмурно, dull (weather)
вѣтрено, windy (weather)
темнота, darkness
в темнотѣ⎫ in darkness
впотьмах⎭
обыкновенно, usually
должно быть, probably
прежде чем, before, prior to (with *infin.*)
непременно, without fail
особенно, particularly
не особенно, not particularly
совсѣм, entirely
не совсѣм, not quite
потому что, because
гораздо хуже, much worse
гораздо лучше, much better
ужасно, terrible
ужаснѣе, more terrible

жаль ⎫ a pity; it is a pity
жалко⎭
нельзя, it is impossible
нельзя было, it was impossible
нельзя будет, it will be impossible
слишком, too much
не слишком, not too much
чересчур, overmuch
нужно ⎫
надо ⎬ it is necessary (see § 45, note 1)
надобно⎭
видно, visible
не видно, not visible
ясно, clear
не ясно, not clear
неясно, obscure, cloudy
видать, to be seen
не видать, not to be seen
совсѣм не, not at all
вовсе не, not at all
так как, as

Exercises

Теперь очень темно.	It is very dark now.
Стало темно.	It has become dark.
Становится темно.	It is getting dark.
Нам вдруг стало холодно.	Suddenly [of a sudden] we began to feel cold.
Мне жаль [жалко] его (with *gen.*).	I am sorry for him.
Мне было жаль [жалко] его.	I was sorry for him.
Мне приятно слышать.	I am glad to hear.
Мне было неприятно слушать, что он говорил.	I was sorry to hear [to listen to] what he said.
Который теперь час?	What time is it now?
Теперь половина второго [часа], [два часа], [без четверти два], [пять минут третьего].	It is half-past one now [two o' clock], [a quarter to two], [five minutes past two].

Уже́ [ста́ло] темно́.
 It is already dark.

Тепе́рь ещё совсе́м светло́.
 It is still quite light now.

Ещё не совсе́м темно́.
 It is not quite dark yet.

Стано́вится темне́е.
 It is getting darker.

Пото́м бу́дет гора́здо темне́е.
 It will be much darker afterwards.

В полови́не шесто́го утра́.
 At half-past five in the morning.

В во́семь часо́в ве́чера.
 At eight o'clock in the evening.

Я встаю́ в семь часо́в [без че́тверти семь], [в че́тверть восьмо́го].
 I get up at seven o'clock [at a quarter to seven], [at a quarter past seven].

Тепе́рь без десяти́ мину́т во́семь.
 It is now ten minutes to eight.

По утра́м тепе́рь [быва́ет] о́чень хо́лодно.
 In the mornings it is now very cold.

В по́лдень [к полу́дню] стано́вится тепле́е.
 At midday [towards midday] it becomes warmer.

По вечера́м мы обыкнове́нно сиди́м до́ма, так как [потому́ что] на дворе́ темно́ и опа́сно выходи́ть.
 In the evenings we usually stay [sit] at home, as [because] it is dark outside and it is dangerous to go out.

Ничего́ нельзя́ ви́деть⟩
[Ничего́ не вида́ть] ⟩
 One cannot see anything.

Никуда́ нельзя́ пойти́ в темноте́.
 One cannot go anywhere in the dark.

Но́чью в темноте́ опа́сно ходи́ть по у́лицам.
 In the night, in the dark, it is dangerous to walk in the streets.

Днём гора́здо прия́тнее и удо́бнее.
 In the day-time it is much more pleasant and more comfortable.

Вчера́ ве́чером бы́ло сли́шком темно́ : ничего́ не́ бы́ло ви́дно [вида́ть].
 Last night it was too dark : one could not see anything [nothing was visible].

Я черезчу́р хорошо́ [я́сно] ви́жу. — I see too well [too clearly].

Когда́ пого́да ста́нет тепле́е, мы пое́дем. — When the weather will get [become] better [warmer], we will start.

Стано́вится свежо́ [прохла́дно]. — It is getting fresh [cool].

Бы́ло па́смурно. — It was cloudy [dull, overcast].

Мы прие́дем домо́й [бу́дем до́ма] в полови́не второ́го. — We shall arrive home [we shall be home] at half-past one.

LESSON VI

Vocabulary

вещь (*fem.*), thing
ве́щи, things
ры́нок, market
на ры́нок, to the market
на ры́нке, at the market
крова́ть (*fem.*), bedstead
поднима́ться, to go up, to rise
*подня́ться, to rise (see § 64, group 7)
гора́, hill, mountain
под го́ру, downhill
на́ гору, uphill
ми́ля, mile
верста́, verst
рубль (*m.*), rouble
оставля́ть }
*оста́вить } to leave (see § 66)
благодари́ть [*по-], to thank (see § 65)
услу́га, service
себя́, oneself
пра́вый, -ая, -ое, -ые, right
ле́вый, -ая, -ое, -ые, left
рука́, hand

сторона́, side
по пра́вую сто́рону [ру́ку], to the right side [hand]
по ле́вую сто́рону [ру́ку], to the left side [hand]
по ту сто́рону, on that side [along that side]
гриб[ы́], mushroom[s]
итти́ по грибы́, to go after mushrooms
на вес, by weight
на всё, for anything
назло́, to annoy
на беду́, unfortunately
на ско́рую ру́ку, hurriedly
на [про] чёрный день, for a rainy day
на восто́к, eastward, to the east
на за́пад, westward, to the west
на се́вер, northward, to the north
на юг, southward, to the south
за́ руку, by the arm
под руку, arm-in-arm, under one's arm

под вечер, towards evening [about evening-time]
под конéц, at the end, towards the end
под мýзыку, to music
под заклáд, under mortgage
пó пояс, up to the belt

навéрх, upstairs, upward
вниз, downstairs, downward
налéво, to the left
напрáво, to the right
вперёд, forward
назáд, backward, back

Notes

Use of the accusative case.

Nouns, adjectives, pronouns, numerals, and participles stand in the accusative case :

(a) when they are used as a direct object in a sentence, completing the meaning of a transitive verb (see §§ 16, 108) ;

NOTE. In negative constructions the direct object stands in the genitive. (See §§ 108a, 137, sub-section 4.)

(b) frequently when they are used as adverbial expressions of time and place (see Lesson IV, also §§ 111, 112) :

я шёл пять миль,　I went [walked] five miles
я спал всю ночь,　I slept the whole night ;

(c) after the prepositions enumerated in § 96b, if they imply a meaning of movement or direction as given by the verbs which they serve (see § 95, sub-section (2));

(d) in many idiomatic and adverbial expressions (see Vocabulary to this lesson).

Exercises

Я éду [идý] в гóрод [на пóчту], [на стáнцию], [на рынок], [на концéрт], [на лéкцию], [на собрáние].

I go to town [to the post office], [to the station], [to the market], [to the concert], [to a lecture], [to a meeting].

Мы завтра поедем за город.	We shall go to the country [out of town], [to the outskirts] to-morrow.
Положи вещи под кровать [под стол].	Put the things under the bed [under the table].
Мы поднимаемся на гору.	We go up the hill.
Я купил это за два рубля.	I bought this for two roubles.
Я взял это за мою книгу.	I took this in exchange for my book.
Я пришлю брата за себя.	I will send my brother in my place.
Я про это знаю.	I know about this.
Мы сидели там с час.	We sat there about an hour.
Они пробыли у нас с год.	They stayed with us about a year.
Мы прошли с милю.	We went [walked] about a mile.
Два раза в год.	Twice a year.
Три раза в неделю [в месяц].	Three times a week [a month].
Я еду туда на год [на месяц], [на всё лето], [на зиму], [на ночь], [на неделю], [на короткое время].	I go there for a year [for a month], [for the whole summer], [for the winter], [for the night], [for a week], [for a (short) time].
Мы едем за-границу.	We are going [go] abroad.
Мы идём под гору.	We go downhill.
Я иду наверх [вниз].	I go up [upstairs], [down], [downstairs].
Иди направо [налево].	Go to the right [to the left].
Поезжай вперёд [назад].	Go forward [backward], [back].
Мы едем в Лондон на [целую] всю неделю, на две недели.	We go to London for the whole [for a whole] week, for a fortnight.

Мы там пробудем всю зиму [всё лето], [всю осень], [весну].	We shall stay there the whole winter [the whole summer], [the whole autumn], [the spring].
Я останусь там с неделю [с месяц].	I shall remain there about a week [about a month].
Я положил ваши вещи под стол.	I have put [placed] your things under the table.
Положите их на стол [за диван], [в ящик].	Put them on the table [behind the couch], [into the box].
Мы ездим в Лондон два раза в год.	We go to London twice a year.
Он ведёт сестру под руку.	He leads (his) sister by the arm [under his arm].
Я взял её за руку.	I took her by her hand [arm].
Мы садимся за стол.	We sit down to table.
Завтра рано утром мы пойдём в лес по грибы (also за грибами).	Early to-morrow morning we shall go to the woods after mushrooms.
Я пошёл [вошёл] в воду по пояс.	I went into the water up to my waist (belt).
Он любит ходить по ту сторону улицы.	He likes to go [walk] on that side of the street.
Хлеб продаётся [продают] на вес.	Bread is sold by weight.
Он сделал это на скорую руку.	He did this hurriedly.
На беду он не мог приехать.	Unfortunately he could not come.
Весной я поеду на Восток [на Запад].	In the spring I shall go to the East [to the West].
Придите [приходите] под вечер.	Come towards evening.
Под конец он согласился.	Towards the end [in the end] he agreed.

Пóд гору пошлá дорóга.	Things are going downhill.
Мы переéхали чéрез мост.	We drove [went] across [over] the bridge.
Они полýчат письмó чéрез два дня [чéрез недéлю], [чéрез мéсяц].	They will receive the letter in two days' time [after two days], [in a week's time], [in a month's time].
Они бýдут у нас в срéду в пéрвый раз.	They will come to us [visit us] on Wednesday for the first time.
За э́то врéмя я сдéлал [успéл] мнóго.	During this time I have done [accomplished] much.
Я бывáю у них кáждый день [раз в мéсяц].	I go to see them [visit them] every day [once a month].
Я бýду у вас в семь часóв.	I shall be at your house at seven o'clock.
Я благодарил их за книгу.	I thanked them for the book.
Мы смóтрим чéрез окнó.	We look through [out of] the window.
Он смóтрит на людéй.	He looks at the people.
Мы отвечáем на вопрóсы [на письма].	We answer questions [letters].
Они даю́т хорóший отвéт на нáши вопрóсы.	They give a good answer to our questions.

LESSON VII

Vocabulary

курить [*по-], to smoke
говорить [*по-], to speak
*сказáть, to say
дарить [*по-], to make a present of

оказывать ⎫
*оказáть   ⎬ to render

вéрить [*по-], to believe, to trust (dat.)

помогáть ⎫
*помóчь ⎬ to help, to assist (dat.)

подъезжáть ⎫
*подъéхать ⎬ to drive, up, as far (к + dat.)

обращáться ⎫
*обратиться ⎬ to apply to (к + dat.)

возвращáться ⎫
*возвратиться ⎬ to come back
*вернýться   ⎭ (gen. + с or из)

мпнова́ть⎫ to turn, to pass
*мину́ть ⎭

звони́ть ⎫ to ring
*позвони́ть⎭

позволя́ть ⎫ to allow, to permit
*позво́лить⎭ (dat.)

спеш-и́ть [*по-], -у́, -и́шь, -а́т, to hasten, to hurry ; to be in advance (clock, watch)

отстава́ть⎫ to get behind
*отста́ть ⎭

(For conjugation patterns of the above verbs, see §§ 64-66.)

вдруг, suddenly
про́сьба, request
вре́дно, harmful
поле́зно, useful
как раз, exactly
понемно́гу ⎫ little by little
ма́ло-по-ма́лу⎭
по-мо́ему, in my opinion
по-ва́шему, in your opinion
по-своему, in one's own way
по-но́вому, in the new fashion
по-ста́рому, in the old way
попола́м, by halves
так себе́, so-so
само́ по себе́, by itself
почему́ ? why ?
потому́ что, because
поэ́тому, for that [this] reason
вероя́тно, probably
по всей вероя́тности, in all probability
пора́ ⎫ time ; it is time
вре́мя⎭
па́лка, stick
услу́га, service
прогу́лка, stroll, walk
соба́ка, dog
соба́чка, little, small dog
доро́га, road, way
по доро́ге, along the road
ле́стница, staircase
по ле́стнице, down, up, the staircase
лес, forest
по́ лесу, through the forest
случай, incident, occasion

по слу́чаю, on the occasion
по э́тому слу́чаю, for this occasion
телефо́н, telephone
по телефо́ну, by [on the] 'phone
газе́та, newspaper
по газе́там, according to the newspapers
журна́л, journal
сожале́ние, regret
к сожале́нию, unfortunately, sad to say
желе́зная доро́га, railway
по желе́зной доро́ге, by rail
а́дрес, address
по а́дресу, at the address
капу́ста, cabbage
щи, cabbage soup
часы́ (pl. m.), clock
автобу́с, bus
по це́лым дням [часа́м], [неде́лям], whole days [hours], [weeks]
по утра́м, in the mornings
по вечера́м, in the evenings
по ноча́м, in the nights
по э́тим часа́м, by this clock
карма́нные часы́, (pocket) watch
буди́льник, alarm-clock
часы́ иду́т, the clock goes
часы́ спеша́т, the clock is fast
часы́ отстаю́т, the clock is slow
мои́ часы́ остановили́сь, my clock [watch] has stopped
автобу́сы иду́т, buses go
поезда́ иду́т, trains go
по́езд отхо́дит, train starts [leaves]

поезд приходит [прибывает], train arrives
скорый поезд, express, fast train
курьерский поезд, express train
пассажирский поезд, passenger train

товарный поезд, goods train
почтовый поезд, mail train
вагон ⎫
отделение ⎬ carriage, compartment,
для курящих, for smokers
для некурящих, for non-smokers

Notes

Use of the dative case:

(a) The dative case serves as an indirect object in the meaning of: where to? to whom? to what? (see §§ 16, 138):

я дал ему книгу,   I gave him the book
он купил мне подарок, he bought me a present

(b) The dative is much used in impersonal constructions where the logical subject (inverted grammatical object) is usually in the dative:

мне скучно, I feel bored
мне нельзя, I cannot, I am not allowed
мне нужно, I need

(For fuller statement on the use of the Dative, see § 138.)

(c) After the prepositions enumerated in § 96a.

(d) In many idiomatic and adverbial expressions. (See Vocabulary to this lesson.)

Exercises

Он не знает, что ему делать.	He does not know what he is to do.
Мне было очень скучно [грустно] вчера.	I felt very bored [sad] yesterday.
Мне стало вдруг весело.	Suddenly I felt cheerful.
Теперь мне совсем хорошо.	I now feel quite all right.
Вам вредно курить.	It is harmful for you to smoke.

Ему нельзя курить.	He must not smoke.
Мне можно курить; мне уже восемнадцать лет.	I can smoke; I am already 18 years (old).
Мне нужно [надо] поговорить с вами.	I must [I have to] talk to you.
Нам пора [время] было ехать.	It was time for us to go.
Ему было четырнадцать лет.	He was 14 years (old).
Мне минуло пятнадцать лет.	I am past 15 (years).
Я ему подарил свою палку.	I gave him my stick as a present.
Он мне сказал, что он очень рад этому.	He told me that he was glad of it [about it].
Ваш брат оказал мне большую услугу.	Your brother has rendered me a great service.
Они нам всегда верят.	They always trust [believe] us.
Я им иногда помогаю.	I help them occasionally.
Прогулка мне всегда полезна.	A walk is always useful [beneficial] to me.
Он писал мне, что не поедет в Советский Союз.	He wrote to me that he would not go to U.S.S.R.
Я вам всегда рад.	I am always glad to see you [you are always welcome].
Мне приятно слышать это.	I am glad to hear this.
Я поеду к брату после обеда.	I shall go to my brother's after dinner.
Я подъезжаю к его дому.	I am driving up to his house.
Мы обратимся к вам с просьбой.	We shall approach you with a request.
Я не буду дома к обеду.	I shall not be in for dinner [to dinner].

Мы вернёмся к пяти часа́м, как раз к чаю.
We shall be back by five o'clock just in time [exactly] for tea.

Соба́чка бежи́т к до́му.
The little dog runs towards the house.

Я вам дам по я́блоку.
I shall give you an apple each.

Ско́лько ему́ лет?
How old is he?

Ему́ [мину́ло] два́дцать [лет].
He is [past] 20 years.

Ему́ пошёл два́дцать пе́рвый год.
He has turned 20. [He is in his 21st year.]

Я пое́ду в Ливерпу́ль по желе́зной доро́ге.
I shall go to Liverpool by rail.

Я всегда́ е́ду домо́й по э́той доро́ге.
I always go home by [along] this road.

Пиши́те по но́вому а́дресу, не по ста́рому.
Write to [at] the new address, not to the old one.

Я вам позвоню́ по телефо́ну.
I shall ring you up (on the phone).

Я с ва́ми поговорю́ по телефо́ну.
I shall speak to you on the telephone.

По на́шим часа́м тепе́рь то́лько два часа́.
By our clock it is now only two o'clock.

К обе́ду нам всегда́ подаю́т щи [капу́сту], и́ли борщ с ка́шей.
For dinner we always get [are served] cabbage soup, or borsch with gruel.

Ра́ньше нам дава́ли к ча́ю варе́нье; тепе́рь, к сожале́нию, нет варе́нья к ча́ю.
Before we used to get jam for tea; now, unfortunately, there is no jam for tea.

LESSON VIII

Vocabulary

случá-ться, -юсь, -ешься, -ются,
to happen

*случ-и́ться, -у́сь, -и́шься, -а́тся
(*impers.* or с + *instr.*), to happen.

знакóм-иться [*по-], -люсь, -ишься,
-ятся, to become acquainted
(с + *instr.*)

здорóва-ться [*по-], -юсь, -ешься,
-ются, to greet (с + *instr.*)

прощá-ться, -юсь, -ешься, -ются,
to take leave

*прости́ться, прощу́сь, прости́шь-
ся, прости́тся, to say good-bye
(с + *instr.*)

совéт-оваться [*по-], -уюсь,
-уешься, -уются, to take counsel,
advice (с + *instr.*)

дышáть [*по-], дышу́, ды́шишь,
ды́шат, to breathe (*abs.* or
instr.)

звать [*на-], зову́, зовёшь, зову́т,
to name, to be known as (*instr.*)

казáться [*по-], to appear, to seem
(*abs.* or *instr.*) (see § 64, group 1)

занимáться, to be occupied with

*занáться, to be engaged in (*instr.*)
(see § 64, group 7)

плати́ть [*за-], to pay (*abs.* or
dat. + *instr.*) (see § 65)

ручá-ться, -юсь, -ешься, -ются,
to guarantee (for — + in —)
(за + *acc.* + в + *loc.*)

*поруч-и́ться, -у́сь, -и́шься, -а́тся,
to guarantee (за+*acc.*+в+*loc.*)

служи́ть [*по-, *у-], служу́, слу́-
жишь, слу́жат, to serve as (*abs.*
or *instr.*)

считá-ться [*по-], -юсь, -ешься,
-ются, to count, to settle; [*imperf.*,
to be reputed as (*abs.* or *instr.*)]

(For other verbs which require the instrumental case see § 140, sub-
sections 3, 4.)

за столóм, at table

зá городом, beyond the town

за рабóтой, at work

за обéдом, at dinner

за у́жином, at supper

за зáвтраком, at breakfast

за чáем, at tea

со врéменем, in time

за исключéнием, with the exception

мéжду прóчим, among the rest;
by the way

мéжду тем, in the meantime

мéжду тем, как, whilst

пéред тем [как], before

под услóвием, on condition

затéм, after that

зачéм? why?

за чем? after what?

вслед затéм, thereupon, after which

за тéм; чтóбы, in order that (with
infin.) (see also adverbial expressions in § 140, sub-section 5)

пред, пéред, before, in front of

камúн, open fireplace

спóрить [*по-], to argue (с + *instr.*)

ссóр-иться [*по-], to quarrel (с +
instr.), -юсь, -ишься, -ятся

гувернáнтка, governess

сидéлка, nurse, sick-nurse

больнóй, -áя [пациéнт], patient

сарáй, shed

огорóд, kitchen-garden

находи́ться, to be (there), to be
situated (see § 63)

рáдом, alongside

здра́вствуйте⎫ how do you do ?
здра́вствуй [1] ⎬

    Customary form of greeting
instead of : good morning, good
day, good evening (see § 123*b* (5)).

проща́йте⎫ good-bye
проща́й [1] ⎬

до свида́ния, good-bye

мы ещё уви́димся, we shall see each
    other [meet] again

да, наде́юсь, yes, I hope so.

пожа́луйста, please

спаси́бо, thanks, thank you

не сто́ит, you are welcome (lit-
    eral meaning : not worth the
    thanks)

Notes

Use of the instrumental case :

(*a*) The instrumental case is an adverb case, and is
mostly used in adverbial expressions of manner (see
§§ 16, 140) ;

(*b*) it stands after reciprocal verbs with the preposition c :

я встре́тился с бра́том,   I met (my) brother

я ссо́рился [*по-] с ним,   I had a quarrel with him ;

(*c*) it is used in many adverbial expressions of manner
(see § 140, sub-division 5) ;

(*d*) it denotes the instrument or means by which, or
through which (or person by whom), an action is
performed, and the manner in which it is performed
(see § 140, sub-section 1) ;

(*e*) it is used in passive constructions (Passive voice)
after the past passive participle, or after a reflexive
verb when it serves the purpose of a past passive
participle (see §§ 131, 122, note (*e*)) :

дом [был] постро́ен мои́м отцо́м
the house is [was] built by my father

дом, постро́енный мои́м отцо́м, сгоре́л
the house built by my father has been burned down

дом стро́ится ка́менщиками
the house is being built by bricklayers [masons] ;

(*f*) after the prepositions enumerated in § 96*c*.

[1] This form is used only when addressing intimate friends or relations.

Exercises

Я сижу́ пе́ред ками́ном.	I sit in front of the fire.
Пе́ред ча́ем я всегда́ чита́ю.	Before tea I always read.
За обе́дом я о́чень ма́ло ем.	At dinner I eat very little.
Мы сиди́м за столо́м.	We sit at table.
Кни́га за столо́м.	The book is behind the table.
Мой брат всегда́ спо́рит со мно́ю.	My brother always argues with me.
Придѝте [приходи́те] с ва́шей жено́й.	Come with [and bring] your wife.
Что с ним случи́лось ?	What has happened to [with] him ?
Мы живём за́ городом.	We live beyond the town.
Я не курю́ за рабо́той.	I do not smoke at work.
Я его́ заста́л за рабо́той.	I found him at work.
Мы посла́ли за до́ктором.	We (have) sent for the doctor.
Я вчера́ познако́мился с ва́шим сосе́дом.	I made the acquaintance of your neighbour yesterday.
Все бы́ли тут, за исключе́нием ва́шего бра́та.	Everyone was here, with the exception of your brother.
Я всегда́ здоро́ваюсь с знако́мыми, когда́ встреча́ю их, и проща́юсь с ни́ми, когда́ оставля́ю их.	I always greet acquaintances when I meet them, and say good-bye to them when I leave them.
Мы всегда́ сове́туемся с на́шими друзья́ми.	We always take counsel [advice] with our friends.
Со вре́менем вы всё узна́ете.	In time you will learn [know] everything.
Ме́жду тем ста́ло темно́.	In the meantime it became dark.
Пе́ред тем, как он пришёл [пе́ред его́ прихо́дом], мы игра́ли в ка́рты.	Before he came [arrived], [before his arrival], we played cards.
Э́то, ме́жду про́чим, не так легко́.	This is, by the way, not very easy.

Гувернáнтка смóтрит за детьмú; сидéлка смóтрит [хóдит] за больнúми [пациéнтами].

The governess looks after the children ; the nurse looks after the patients.

Нáд столóм висúт лáмпа ; над кровáтью висúт картúна.

Over the table hangs a lamp ; over the bedstead hangs a picture.

Дéти игрáют мéжду дóмом и сарáем.

The children play between the house and the shed.

За сарáем нахóдится огорóд.

Behind the shed there is a kitchen garden.

Под столóм лежúт собáка ; рúдом с ней лежúт кот [кóшка].

Under the table lies the dog ; alongside it lies the tom-cat [cat].

Онá хорошá собóй, высокá рóстом и кроткá нрáвом.

She is good-looking, tall [of tall stature], and of gentle disposition.

Он довóлен собóю, гордúтся своúм богáтством, но бóлен чем-то [слаб здорóвьем].

He is satisfied with himself, is proud of his wealth, but is suffering from something [ailing with something], [in delicate health].

Мы дúшим вóздухом.

We breathe air.

Егó зовýт Петрóм.

He is called Peter.

Мы занимáемся дéлом.

We are occupied with business.

Он смóтрит [вúглядит] больнúм.[1]

He looks [appears] ill.

Он считáется [егó считáют] богáтым.

He is considered rich.

---

[1] But : Он, кáжется, бóлен (кáжется is here used parenthetically). It seems (to me) he is ill.

LESSON IX

Vocabulary

вполнé, entirely
наканýне, on the eve
внизý, at the bottom ; downstairs
наверхý, at the top ; upstairs
при чём, by which ; at the same time ; besides which
притóм, besides
в видý, in view of, in consideration of
в такóм слýчае, in this case
во всяком слýчае, in any case
в скóрости ⎫ shortly
вскóре ⎭
в скóром врéмени, very soon
в чём дéло ? what is the matter ?
в том то и дéло, and it is just this
не в том дéло, that is not the thing [trouble]
на мойх глазáх, under my very eyes
при мне, in my presence
на сáмом дéле ⎫ in fact, in reality,
в сáмом дéле ⎭ indeed
на пóчте, at the post office

на лéкции, at the [a] lecture
на стáнции, at the station
на концéрте, at the [a] concert
на рынке, at the market
на собрáнии [мúтинге], at the meeting
у мóря, at the sea
морскóй бéрег, the seaside
на берегý мóря ⎫ at the seaside
на морскóм берегý ⎭
óвощи, vegetables
прихóд ⎫ arrival
прибытие ⎭
ухóд, departure, leave ; care, nursing
ковёр, carpet
коврый, carpets
кóврик[и], mat[s]
деревянный, of wood, wooden
кáменный, of stone
письмó, letter
заказнóе письмó, registered letter
послáть заказным [письмóм], to send by registered letter

Notes

Use of the Locative (Prepositional) case :

(a) The locative case is the 'adverb-case' which mostly expresses place, and is used in adverbial expressions of place (see § 141).

(b) It is used also after the prepositions enumerated in § 96d.

Exercises

Мы живём в Áнглии.

We live in England.

Я всегдá сижý в своéй кóмнате и читáю.

I always sit in my room and read.

к

Книга у меня в комнате на столе.

The book is in my room on the table.

На полу лежат ковры [коврики].

On the floor lie carpets [mats].

Я живу в городе в каменном доме, а они живут в деревне в деревянном доме.

I live in town in a stone [brick] house, but they live in the country [village] in a wooden house.

Мы вчера были на концерте [на собрании], [на лекции].

Yesterday we were at a concert [at a meeting], [at a lecture].

Он был всё время на станции.

He was all the time at the station.

По прибытии [приходе] поезда он пошёл домой.

On the train's arrival [after the arrival of the train] he went home.

Я скоро [вскоре], [в скором времени] поеду в Лондон.

I will soon [shortly] go to London.

В Лондоне я пробуду пять недель.

In London I shall stay [remain] five weeks.

В нашем доме спальни наверху, а столовая, гостиная и кухня внизу.

In our house the bedrooms are upstairs, and the dining-room, drawing-room [sitting-room], and kitchen downstairs.

Это случилось на моих глазах [при мне].

This happened in my presence.

[В] На самом деле я не знал, в чём [было] дело.

In fact I did not know what was [had been] the matter.

Мы всегда покупаем овощи на рынке, а хлеб, сахар и другие колониальные товары в лавке.

We always buy vegetables at the market, and [but] bread, sugar and other groceries at the shop.

LESSON X

Vocabulary

закурива-ть, -ю, -ешь, -ют, to start smoking

*закур-ить, -ю, -ишь, -ят, to light a pipe, cigarette, etc.

показывать) to show (see § 64,
*показать) group 1)

отвеча-ть, -ю, -ешь, -ют ⎫
*отве-тить, -чу, -тишь, ⎬ to answer
-тят ⎭

сидеть [*по-], сижу, сидишь, сидят, to be sitting

стоять [*по-], to stand

стоить, to cost (has no perfective aspect)

лежать [*по-], to lie, to lie down

*выспаться, to have enough sleep

покрывать[ся] ⎫
*покрыть[ся] ⎬ to cover [oneself]

мыть[ся] [*по-], моюсь, моешься, моются, to wash [oneself]

бриться [*по-], бреюсь, бреешься, бреются, to shave oneself

брать ванну ⎫ to take [have] a
*взять ванну ⎬ bath

одевать[ся] ⎫
*одеть[ся] ⎬ to dress oneself

надевать ⎫
*надеть ⎬ to put on

вставать ⎫
*встать ⎬ to get up

уставать ⎫
*устать ⎬ to get tired

(For conjugation-patterns, see §§ 63-68.)

зеркало, mirror

перед зеркалом, in front of the mirror

холодный, -ая, -ое, -ые, cold

горячий, -ая, -ее, -ие, hot

тёплый, -ая, -ое, -ые, warm

дорогой, -ая, -ое, -ие, dear, expensive

дешёвый, -ая, -ое, -ые, cheap

(For short forms and comparatives, see § 45.)

прислуга, servants (*collective noun*)

кухарка, cook

повар, cook (man)

горничная, chambermaid

бритва, razor

острая бритва, sharp razor

тупая бритва, blunt razor

квас, home-brewed beer

вино, wine

пиво, beer

кофе, coffee

водка, vodka

шоколад, chocolate

коньяк, brandy

табак, tobacco

трубка, pipe

папироса, cigarette

сигара, cigar

спичка, match

коробка спичек, box of matches

рубаха ⎫ shirt
рубашка ⎭

ночная рубаха, night-shirt

верхняя рубаха, top-shirt

нижняя рубаха, under-shirt

брюки ⎫ trousers (used in plural
штаны ⎭ only (*masc.*), see § 33)

жилет, vest

K *

пиджа́к, jacket

ку́ртка, short jacket

шу́ба, fur coat

шарф, scarf

шля́па, hat

ша́пка, cap

полушу́бок, short fur coat

причёсыва-ться, -юсь, ⎫
  -ешься, -ются   ⎬ to comb
*приче-са́ться, -шу́сь, ⎨ one's hair
  -шешься, -шутся ⎭

вытира́-ться ⎫ -юсь, -ешься, -ются,
утира́-ться ⎬ to wipe [dry] one-
         ⎭ self

*вы́-тереться ⎫ -трусь, -трешься,
          ⎬ -трутся,
*у-тере́ться ⎨ to dry [wipe] one-
          ⎭ self

посте́ль, bedding

поду́шка, pillow

одея́ло, blanket

простыня́, sheet

дрова́, firewood (used in plural only) (neut.)

у́голь (m.), coal (used in singular only in sense of fuel)

чуло́к, stocking

чулки́, stockings

носо́к, sock

носки́, socks

подтя́жки, braces (used only in pl., fem.).

сапо́г, boot

сапоги́, boots (top boots)

ту́фля, slipper

ту́фли, slippers

боти́нок   ⎫ half-boot [shoe]
[боти́нка] ⎭

боти́нки, half-boots

кало́ши ⎫ goloshes
гало́ши ⎭

воротни́к   ⎫ collar
воротничо́к ⎭

плато́к [носово́й], handkerchief

ве́жливо, courteously

из ве́жливости, out of courtesy

фа́брика, factory

заво́д, works

я́рко, brightly

во́лос ⎫ hair
волоса́ ⎭

годи́ться [*при-], to be of use (see § 68)

лицо́, face

ше́я, neck

мыть[ся] [*у-], мо́ю, мо́ешь, мо́ют, to wash [oneself]

мы́ло, soap

полоте́нце, towel

га́лстук, tie

завя́зыва-ть, -ю, -ешь, -ют ⎫ to tie
*завяза́ть, завяжу́, завя́- ⎬ up
  жешь, завя́жут   ⎭

печь (fem.) ⎫ stove
пе́чка   ⎭

гре́ться [*по-], to warm oneself

уста́лый, -ая, -ое, -ые, tired

пешко́м, on foot

трамва́ем, by tram

нра́в-иться [*по-], -люсь, -ишься, -ятся, to please, to be pleasing

и́зредка, occasionally

отдыха́-ть, -ю, -ешь, -ют ⎫
*отдохн-у́ть, -у́, -ёшь, ⎬ to rest
  -у́т   ⎭

умыва́льник, wash-basin, wash-stand

умыва́льный прибо́р, toilet-set

шкаф, wardrobe

этажёрка, shelf, whatnot

матра́ц, mattress

ро́дственник, relation

друг, friend

друзья́, friends (see § 20, subsection (6))

знако́мый [-ые], acquaintance

абажу́р, shade

про́сто, simply

лимо́н, lemon

болта́-ть [*по-], -ю, ·ешь, -ют, to chatter
уютный, -ая, -ое, -ые, cosy

удобный, -ая, -ое, -ые, comfortable
обстано́вка, set out ; equipment

Exercises

Я встаю́ о́чень ра́но.	I get up very early.
Я одева́юсь. Я снима́ю ночну́ю руба́шку и надева́ю штаны́ [брю́ки], ве́рхнюю руба́шку и жиле́т.	I dress. I take off (my) night-shirt and I put on (my) trousers, (my) top-shirt and vest.
Я бре́юсь пе́ред зе́ркалом о́строй бри́твой.	I shave in front of the mirror with a sharp razor.
Бри́твы у меня́ всегда́ о́стрые ; тупа́я бри́тва не годи́тся ; с тупо́й бри́твой бритьё продолжа́ется до́льше.	My razors are always sharp ; a blunt [dull] razor is no use ; it takes longer to shave with a blunt razor [shaving with a blunt razor].
Пото́м я мо́ю лицо́, ше́ю и ру́ки горя́чей и холо́дной водо́й и мы́лом ; я вытира́юсь [вытира́ю лицо́, ше́ю, ру́ки] [утира́юсь] полоте́нцем.	Then I wash my face, neck, and hands with hot and cold water and soap ; I [dry] wipe myself [I dry my face, neck, and hands] with a towel.
Иногда́ я беру́ горя́чую [и́ли холо́дную] ва́нну.	Sometimes I take a hot [or cold] bath.
Я причёсываюсь [причёсываю, зачёсываю волоса́], надева́ю ве́рхнюю руба́шку [руба́ху], пиджа́к [ку́ртку], воротничо́к, завя́зываю га́лстук и иду́ вниз в столо́вую [спуска́юсь по ле́стнице].	I comb my hair, I put on my top-shirt, jacket, collar, tie up my tie, and I go downstairs into the dining-room [go down the staircase], [stairs].
В столо́вой печь уже́ зато́плена [зимо́й· и о́сенью], [ками́н уже́ зато́плен ; уже́ то́пится].	In the dining-room the stove is already lit [in winter and autumn].

В камине [в печи], [в печке] весело и ярко горят дрова [горит уголь].

In the open fireplace [stove] cheerfully and brightly burns the wood [coal].

Я стою перед камином и греюсь.

I stand in front of the fireplace and warm myself.

Я греюсь у огня [у камина], и читаю газету [просматриваю газету].

I warm myself near the fire, and read the newspaper [look through the newspaper].

Мне приносят [подают] завтрак.

My breakfast is brought [served].

Прислуга [кухарка или горничная] подаёт мне завтрак.

The servant [cook or maid] serves my breakfast

Я сажусь к столу [за стол] и начинаю завтракать [завтрак].

I sit down to table and begin breakfast.

Кончив завтрак [позавтракав], [после завтрака] я закуриваю папиросу [сигару], [трубку] и курю.

Having finished [after] breakfast I light a cigarette, [cigar], [pipe] and smoke.

Я набиваю трубку [табаком]; я люблю крепкий [дорогой] табак.

I fill my pipe [with tobacco]; I like strong [expensive] tobacco.

Слабый или дешёвый табак мне не нравится. [Я не люблю слабого табаку.]

Weak or cheap tobacco is not to my liking. [I do not like weak tobacco.]

Покурив, я надеваю пальто [а зимою шубу], беру зонтик [или палку] и отправляюсь [иду, еду] в контору, [на фабрику, на завод].

Having finished smoking, I put on my overcoat [and in winter my fur coat], I take my umbrella [or stick], and set out [go, drive] to the office [to the factory, to the works].

Я éду пóездом [трамвáем], [автобýсом], [в автомобúле] или же идý пешкóм.

I go by train [by tram], [by bus] [in a car], or else I walk [go on foot].

Я рабóтаю весь [цéлый] день.

I work the whole day.

К концý дня [к вéчеру] я всегдá устаю́ [чýвствую себя́ устáлым] и рад éхать, [иттú], [пойтú] домóй обéдать.

By [towards] the end of the day [towards evening] I always get tired [I feel tired] and I am glad to drive [to go] home to dinner.

Придя́ домóй, я сажýсь за обéд.

Having arrived home I sit down to dinner.

К обéду мне подаю́т суп, ры́бу, щи или борщ, селя́нку, жаркóе, котлéты, кáшу, пирожкú, пирóжное, фрýкты.

For dinner I am served with soup, fish, cabbage soup or borsch, stew, roast, cutlets, gruel, pies, pastry, fruit.

Пéред обéдом я выпивáю рю́мку вóдки и закýсываю огурцóм, селёдкой, анчóусом, икрóй или какóй-нибудь другóй закýской.

Before dinner I drink a wine-glass of vodka, and eat (after it) some cucumber, herring, anchovy, caviar, or any other bit of snack.

За обéдом я пью вóду или квас; иногдá я пью пúво, úзредка тáкже винó.

At dinner I drink water or kvas [home-brewed beer]; sometimes I drink beer, now and then also wine.

Потóм я пью кóфе, иногдá с коньякóм.

Afterwards I drink coffee, occasionally with brandy.

Пóсле обéда [пообéдавши] я отдыхáю или читáю кнúгу.

After dinner [having dined] I rest or read a book.

Отдохнýв[ши] я идý к знакóмым [в теáтр], [в óперу], [в кинематóграф], [на мúтинг].

Having had a rest I go to see friends [to the theatre], [to the opera], [to the cinema], [to a meeting].

Иногда́ ко мне [к нам] прихо́дят друзья́ [прия́тели], [знако́мые], [ро́дственники], и мы игра́ем в ка́рты, в ша́хматы, в ша́шки.

Occasionally come to me [to us] friends [acquaintances], [relatives], and we play cards, chess, draughts.

Иногда́ кто́-нибудь игра́ет на роя́ле и мы все слу́шаем.

Occasionally someone plays the piano and we all listen.

А то про́сто сиди́м у ками́на и разгова́риваем [болта́ем], пьём чай с лимо́ном и́ли с варе́ньем.

Or else we simply sit at the [near the] fireplace and talk [chatter], drink tea with lemon or jam [preserves].

В оди́ннадцать часо́в [в полови́не двена́дцатого] я иду́ спать [ложу́сь спать].

At eleven o'clock [at half-past eleven] I go to sleep [I go to bed].

Я сплю на [в] просто́рной крова́ти, на кото́рой по́стлана посте́ль : [поду́шки, матра́ц, про́стыни, одея́ло].

I sleep on [in] a spacious bedstead, on which there is laid bedding [pillows, mattress, sheets, a blanket].

Зимо́ю я накрыва́юсь [покрыва́юсь] двойны́м одея́лом [двумя́ одея́лами].

In winter I cover myself with a double blanket [two blankets].

Ме́бель в мое́й ко́мнате проста́я : крова́ть, комо́д для белья́, стул [два сту́ла], сто́лик, кре́сло, шкаф для пла́тья, этаже́рка [по́лка], [по́лочка] для книг, зе́ркало и умыва́льник [умыва́льный прибо́р].

The furniture in my room is simple : a bedstead, a chest of drawers for linen, a chair [two chairs], a little table, an arm-chair, wardrobe for clothes, set of shelves [whatnot] for books, a mirror and wash-stand [toilet-set].

С потолка́ виси́т электри́ческая ла́мпа под абажу́ром.

From the ceiling hangs an electric lamp with a shade.

Над комо́дом виси́т карти́на.	Over the chest of drawers hangs a picture [painting].
Пол у́стлан ко́вриками [на полу́ лежи́т ковёр].	The floor is covered with mats [on the floor lies a carpet].
В о́бщем обстано́вка проста́я, но удо́бная и ую́тная.	In general the set-out is simple, but comfortable and cosy.

LESSON XI

Vocabulary

Note. A number of words in everyday use are given in the list below which are not necessarily included in the exercises to this lesson.

да́ма, lady
да́мы, ladies
для дам, for ladies
да́мский, -ая, -ое, -ие, for, pertaining to, ladies
же́нщина [ы], woman [women]
деви́ца [ы], maiden[s], girl[s], miss[es]
де́вушка [и], girl, maiden, servant girl
ба́рышня [и], young lady
де́вочка [и], little girl
жени́х, bridegroom, suitor
неве́ста, bride, engaged girl
жена́ [жёны], wife [wives]
вдова́ [вдо́вы], widow[s]
вдове́ц [вдовцы́], widower
мужчи́на [ы], man, male
муж, husband
мужско́й, for, pertaining to, men
для мужчи́н, for men
ма́льчик [и], boy
ю́ноша [и], youth
па́рень [па́рни], lad[s], youth[s] (used only colloquially)

пла́тье, clothing, wearing apparel
о́бувь (*fem.*), footwear
да́мское [же́нское] пла́тье и о́бувь, ladies' [women's] clothing and footwear
пла́тье и о́бувь для дам, для же́нщин, для деви́ц, для де́вочек, clothing [dresses] and footwear for ladies, women, maidens, and girls
ко́фточка⎱ woman's jacket
ко́фта ⎰
ю́бка, petticoat, skirt
пла́тье, dress
да́мское пальто́, lady's coat
шу́ба, fur coat
корса́ж, bodice
шля́пка, hat
блу́зка, blouse
сарафа́н, lady's sleeveless garment
боти́нки, half-boots
[боти́нка]⎱ half-boot
боти́нок ⎰
ту́фли [я], slippers
полусапо́жки, half-boots

башмáк ⎫
башмакú ⎬ lady's boot[s]

фáртук ⎫
перéдник ⎬ apron, pinafore

чулóк, чулкú, stocking[s]
шёлковые чулкú, silk stockings
шёлк, silk
шёлковая матéрия, silk material
шерстянáя матéрия, woollen ma-
.terial
шерсть (*fem.*), wool
носовóй платóк ⎫
платкú   ⎬ handkerchief[s]
носовы́е платкú⎭
полотнó, linen, linen-cloth
полотня́ный, -ая, -ое, -ые, of linen
сукнó, cloth (woollen-cloth)
сукóнн-ый, -ая, -ое, -ые, made of
(woollen) cloth
хлопчáтая бумáга, cotton
из хлопчáтой бумáги, made of
cotton
тéло, body
человéческое тéло, human body
член, member, limb
часть (*fem.*), part
члéны [чáсти] человéческого тéла,
members [parts] of the human
body
головá, head
волосá ⎫
вóлос ⎬ hair
ýхо, ear
ýши, ears
глазá, eyes
глаз, eye
лоб, forehead
гýбы, lips
губá, lip
подборóдок, chin
бородá, beard
усы́ ⎫ moustache (usually used in
ус ⎬   the plural)
нос, nose

в носý, in the nose
[бровь] (*fem.*) ⎫
брóви   ⎬ eyebrows
ресни́цы, eyelashes
[скулá] ⎫
скýлы   ⎬ cheek-bone[s]
рот, mouth
во ртý, in the mouth
грудь (*fem.*), chest
спинá, spine, back
плечó ⎫ shoulders
плéчи ⎬
[лóкоть] (*m.*) ⎫
лóкти   ⎬ elbows [forearms]
[рукá] ⎫ hands, arms
рýки   ⎬
[ногá] ⎫ leg[s], foot [feet]
нóги   ⎬
сéрдце, heart
лёгкое, lung
лёгкие, lungs
пéчень (*fem.*), liver
желýдок, stomach
живóт, belly
[жи́ла] ⎫ veins
жи́лы ⎬
кровь, blood
[пáлец] ⎫ fingers
пáльцы ⎬
[колéно] ⎫ knees
колéни   ⎬
кóжа, skin
[кость] (*fem.*) ⎫ bones
кóсти   ⎬
[нóготь] (*m.*) ⎫ nails
нóгти   ⎬
язы́к, tongue (also language)
[зуб] ⎫ teeth
зýбы ⎬
[деснá] ⎫ gums
дёсны ⎬

нёбо, palate (not to be confused with нёбо, sky)

глóтка, gullet, throat

пóяс, waist

поясни́ца, waist, loins

слáбые глазá, weak eyes

слаб, -á, -ы глазáми, weak in the eyes

близорýкость (f.), short-sightedness

близорýк-ий, -ая, -ие; -а, -и, short-sighted

очки́, spectacles

пенснэ́, eye-glasses

шкóла \
учи́лище ∫ school

ходи́ть в шкóлу \
ходи́ть в учи́лище ∫ to go to school

учи́ться в шкóле \
учи́ться в учи́лище ∫ to learn at school

учи́ться (requires dat.) рýсскому языкý, to learn the Russian language

учи́ться мýзыке, to learn music

учéбник, text-book, study book

учи́тель, teacher

учи́тельница, woman teacher

чтéние, reading

рисовáние, drawing (painting)

пéние, singing

изучá-ть, -ю, -ешь, -ют \
*изуч-и́ть, -ý, -ишь, -ат ⎬ to study
(trans. verb) ∫

учи́ть [*на-], to teach

черни́ла (in pl. only), ink

черни́льница, ink-pot

слóво, word

словáрь (m.), dictionary

дом, house

кóмната, room

крýша, roof

стенá, wall

стéны, walls

окнó, window

óкна, windows

к **

стеклó, glass, pane

стёкла, panes

дверь (fem.), door

двор, yard

на дворé, outside, out of doors

ками́н, open fireplace

пол, floor

потолóк, ceiling

лéстница, stairs, staircase; ladder

столóвая, dining-room

кýхня, kitchen

спáльня, bedroom

приёмная, reception-room

гости́ная, sitting-room

дéтская, nursery

кабинéт, study

прихóжая \
передняя ∫ entrance-hall

вáнная [кóмната], bathroom

вáнна, bath

бáня, bath-house

сарáй, shed

метлá, broom

зáступ, spade

пилá, saw

молотóк, hammer

тарéлка, plate

ми́ска, tureen

чáшка, cup

стакáн, glass, tumbler

блюдечко, saucer

чáйник, tea-pot

сáхарница, sugar basin

самовáр, tea urn

нож, knife

ножи́, knives

лóжка [и], spoon[s]

ви́лка [и], fork[s]

блюдо, dish

скáтерть [и] (fem.), tablecloth

салфéтка [и], serviette[s]

графи́н, decanter

судóк, cruet, cruet-stand

солóнка, salt-cellar

кувши́н, jug

жева́ть [*раз-], жую́, жуёшь, жую́т, to chew
дыша́ть [*по-], to breathe
осяза́-ть, -ю, -ешь, -ют, to feel
течь [*по-], теку́, течёшь, течёт, to flow
пи́ща, food
портно́й, tailor
портни́ха, tailoress
сапо́жник, shoemaker
бельё, linen
пра́чка, laundress

пра́чечная, laundry
котёл, boiler
котело́к, kettle, pot
рю́мка, small wine-glass
пе́рец, pepper
хрен, horse-radish
горчи́ца, mustard
деся́ток, a set of ten
дю́жина, dozen
фунт, pound
кило́, kilogram
полфу́нта, half a pound
полкило́, half a kilo

Exercises

Мы ви́дим [смо́трим] глаза́ми ; мы ку́шаем [еди́м] ртом ; разжёвываем [жуём] пи́щу зуба́ми ; мы слы́шим [слу́шаем] уша́ми ; рабо́таем рука́ми ; хо́дим и́ли бе́гаем нога́ми ; осяза́ем па́льцами [ко́жей] ; ню́хаем [обоня́ем] но́сом.

We see [look] with (our) eyes ; we eat with (our) mouth ; we chew food with our teeth ; we hear [listen] with our ears ; we work with our hands ; we walk or run with our legs ; we feel [touch] with our fingers [skin] ; we smell with our nose.

Мы узнаём [различа́ем] вкус пи́щи нёбом и языко́м.

We learn [distinguish] the taste of food by our palate and tongue.

Мы име́ем пять вне́шних чувств : зре́ние, слух, обоня́ние, осяза́ние и вкус.

We have five external senses : sight, hearing, smell, touch, and taste.

В на́ших жи́лах течёт кровь.

In our veins flows blood.

Близору́кие лю́ди и те, у кото́рых сла́бые глаза́, но́сят очки́ и́ли пенснэ́.

Short-sighted people and those who have weak eyes wear spectacles or glasses (pince-nez).

Мужчи́ны, взро́слые и ма́льчики, но́сят пальто́, брю́ки [штаны́], ку́ртки [пиджаки́], жиле́ты, шу́бы, полушу́бки, сапоги́, боти́нки, воротнички́, гало́ши, шля́пы, ша́пки.

Men, grown-ups, and boys, wear overcoats, trousers, jackets, vests, fur coats, short fur coats, top-boots, shoes, collars, goloshes, hats, and caps.

Же́нщины [да́мы] и де́вушки но́сят пла́тья, корса́жи, ко́фты, ю́бки, сарафа́ны, башмаки́, боти́нки, полусапо́жки, шля́пки.

Women [ladies] and girls wear dresses, bodices, jackets, skirts, [petticoats], sarafans, boots, shoes, half-boots, hats.

Дереве́нские же́нщины и де́вушки но́сят на голове́ платки́ вме́сто шля́пок.

Village women and girls wear kerchiefs on their head instead of hats.

Мужско́е пла́тье шьёт портно́й.

Men's clothing is sewn by a tailor.

Да́мское пла́тье та́кже шьёт портно́й, а иногда́ портни́ха.

Ladies' clothing is also sewn by a tailor, and sometimes by a tailoress.

Мужску́ю и да́мскую о́бувь шьёт сапо́жник.

Men's and women's footwear is sewn by a shoemaker.

Бельё шьёт портни́ха [белошве́йка].

Linen is sewn by a tailoress [seamstress].

Бельё стира́ет пра́чка.

Linen is washed by a laundress.

Лу́чшее бельё отсыла́ется в пра́чечную.

Better linen is sent to the laundry.

LESSON XII

Vocabulary

погóда, weather
хорóшая погóда, fine weather
плохáя погóда, bad weather
дождь (*m.*), rain
идёт дождь, it rains
шёл дождь, it rained
пошёл дождь, it started raining
óблако [á]⎫
тýча [п]   ⎭ cloud[s]
снег, snow
пáдает снег, it snows [snow falls]
снег пáдал, it snowed [snow fell]
град, hailstones
мóлния, lightning
сверкáет мóлния, lightning is flash-
    ing
бýря, storm
гром, thunder
гремит гром, it thunders
гремéл гром, it thundered
лёд, ice
водá, water
лёд тáет, ice melts
лёд растáял, ice has melted away
вéтер, wind
вóздух, air
нéбо, sky
óблачно, cloudy
пáсмурно, rainy
вéтрено, windy
ясно, clear
теплó, warm
хóлодно, cold
огорóд, kitchen garden
в [на] огорóде, in the kitchen
    garden
сад, garden, orchard
в садý, in the garden
пóле, field
в пóле, in the field

лес, forest
в лесý, in the forest
рекá, river
óзеро, lake
в рекé, in the river
в óзере, in the lake
на рекé, on the river
на óзере, on the lake
мóре, the sea
в мóре, in the sea
на мóре, on the sea
человéк, man
люди, men, people
зверь (*m.*), beast
живóтное, animal
лóшадь (*fem.*), horse, mare
конь (*m.*), horse
корóва, cow
собáка, dog
кóшка, cat
кот, tom-cat
птица, bird
рыба, fish
домáшняя птица, domestic
    bird
кýрица, hen
петýх, cock, cockerel
ýтка, duck
гусь (*m.*), goose
индюк, turkey-cock
индюшка⎫
индéйка ⎭ turkey
дéрево, tree
дерéвья, trees
плодóвые дерéвья, fruit trees
куст, bush, shrub
кусты, shrubs
в кустáх, in the shrubs
травá, grass
гриб [ы], mushroom[s]

я́года [ы], berry [ies]
ди́кие я́годы, wild berries
я́блоня, apple tree
ви́шня, cherry tree [cherry]
гру́ша, pear tree [pear]
сли́ва, plum tree [plum]
мали́на, raspberry
клубни́ка, strawberry
сморо́дина, currant

земляни́ка, wild (small) strawberry
крыжо́вник, gooseberry
ре́па, turnip[s]
морко́вь, (*fem.*) carrot[s]
капу́ста, cabbage
ре́дька ⎱
реди́ска ⎰ radish
карто́фель (*m.*), potato[es]
лук, onion[s]

(The above vegetables and fruits are not used in the plural, they have a collective singular only.)

бура́к [и́], beetroot[s]
ботви́нья (*sing.* only), beetroot-tops
огуре́ц, cucumber
огурцы́, cucumbers
сала́т (*sing.* only), salad [lettuce]
сади́ть [*по-], сажу́, са́дишь, са́дят, to plant
се́-ять [*по-], -ю, -ешь, -ют, to sow

хлеба́, cereals
рожь (*fem.*), rye
пшени́ца, wheat
ячме́нь (*m.*), barley
ове́с, oats
кукуру́за, maize
гречиха́, buckwheat
горо́х, peas

(The above cereals have no plural, they have a collective singular only.)

боб[ы́], bean[s]
ды́ня [н], pumpkin[s], melon[s]
са́ни (*pl.* only), sleigh
теле́га, cart, waggon
каре́та, carriage, coach
дро́жки, droshky
коля́ска, open carriage
в саня́х, in a sleigh
в теле́ге, in a cart
в каре́те, in a carriage
в коля́ске, in an open carriage
в дро́жках, in a droshky
развод-и́ть, -жу́, -ишь, ⎫
  -я́т   ⎬ to culti-
*разве-сти́, -ду́, -дёшь, ⎭ vate, to
  -ду́т   rear

не́вод [а́], big fishing net
сеть [и] (*fem.*), smaller fishing net
уда́ ⎱
у́дочка ⎰ fishing rod
охо́та, desire, inclination; hunt, chase
охо́-титься, -чусь, -тишься, -тятся, to hunt, to chase (за + *inst.*, or на + *acc.*)
охо́тник, volunteer; hunter
охо́тный, -ая, -ое, -ые, willing
охо́тно, willingly
лов-и́ть, -лю́, -ишь, ⎫
  -я́т   ⎬ to catch (see
*пойма́-ть, -ю, -ешь, ⎭ § 60, sub-
  -ют   section 3)

Exercises

Зимо́ю в Росси́и доро́ги, луга́ и поля́ покры́ты сне́гом; лю́ди е́здят в саня́х.

In winter the roads, meadows, and fields in Russia are covered with snow; people travel in sleighs.

Лётом лю́ди е́здят в те-
ле́гах, дро́жках, каре́тах
и коля́сках.

In summer people travel in
carts, droshkies, coaches,
and open carriages.

Зимо́ю ре́ки и озёра за-
мерза́ют.

In winter the rivers and
lakes freeze up.

В тече́ние [в продолже́ние]
трёх и́ли четырёх ме́ся-
цев они́ покры́ты тóл-
стым слóем льда.

For the duration of three or
four months they are
covered with a thick layer
of ice.

По льду е́здят и ката́ются
на конька́х.

On the ice people travel and
skate [on skates].

Доро́га по льду гла́дкая,
ро́вная. Е́хать легко́.

The road over the ice is
smooth and even. Travel-
ling is easy.

Ма́льчики и де́вочки лю́бят
ката́ться [с горы́] по
сне́гу и по льду на са́н-
ках.

Boys and girls like to slide
[downhill] over the snow
and ice in little sledges.

Ле́том они́ лю́бят гуля́ть
в лесу́ и в по́ле. Они́
собира́ют [набира́ют]
грибы́ и я́годы в лесу́
и рвут [нарыва́ют] цветы́
в по́ле.

In the summer they like to
stroll in the woods and in
the field. They gather
mushrooms and berries
and gather [pluck] flowers
in the field.

Зимо́ю на се́вере Росси́и
всегда́ о́чень хо́лодно. На
ю́ге да́же зимо́ю иногда́
быва́ет тепло́.

In the north of Russia it is
always very cold in winter.
In the south even in
winter it is sometimes
warm.

К восто́ку от Ура́льских
гор нахо́дится [лежи́т]
Сиби́рь.

To the east of the Ural
mountains lies Siberia.

К за́паду от Ура́льских
гор лежи́т Европе́йская
Росси́я.

To the west of the Ural
mountains lies European
Russia.

Погóда всё врéмя стоя́ла плохáя : шёл дождь, чáсто с грóмом и мóлнией.

The weather was [stood] bad all the time : rain, often with thunder and lightning.

Нéбо бы́ло покры́то тýчами [облакáми].

The sky was covered [overcast] with clouds.

Дул си́льный вéтер.

A strong wind was blowing.

Подняла́сь [начала́сь] бýря

A storm began.

Пáдал снег с грáдом [и град].

Snow fell with hailstones.

Шёл дождь с грáдом.

Rain fell with hailstones.

К нóчи начала́сь метéль.

Towards the night a snowstorm began.

Водá в бóчках и чáнах замёрзла и преврати́лась в лёд.

Water in barrels and tanks got frozen and turned to ice.

К веснé [веснóю] лю́ди копáют огорóд [зéмлю на огорóдах] зáступом.

Towards [in] spring people dig (their) gardens [the soil in the kitchen gardens] with spades.

Распáхивают [пáшут] поля́ сохóй и плýгом.

They plough up the fields with hand-plough and plough.

На огорóдах сáдят картóфель, капýсту, и сéют рéпу, моркóвь, рéдьку, реди́ску, огурцы́, бураки́, салáт и лук ; тáкже развóдят ды́ни и ты́квы.

In the kitchen garden people plant potatoes and cabbage, and sow turnips, carrots, radishes, black radishes, cucumbers, beetroot, lettuce, and onions ; they also cultivate melons and pumpkins.

Из буракóв и ботви́ньи в деревня́х вáрят борщ ; из капýсты вáрят щи.

From beetroots and beetroot-tops they cook borsch in the villages ; from cabbage—cabbage soup.

На полях сéют хлебá: [рáзные хлебá]: рожь, пшенйцу, ячмéнь, овёс, гречйху, кукурýзу.

In the fields they sow [are being sown] corn-crops [cereals] : rye, wheat, barley, oats, buckwheat, maize.

В садý растýт рáзные плодьí: яблоки, грýши, слйвы, вйшни, на яблонях, грýшах, слйвах и вйшнях.

In the orchard grow various fruits : apples, pears, plums, cherries, on apple trees, pear trees, plum trees, and cherry trees.

В садáх тáкже есть кустьí, на котóрых растýт : сморóдина, малйна, крыжóвник.

In the orchards there are also bushes on which grow : currants, raspberries, gooseberries.

В цветникáх растýт цветьí [цветóк].

In the flower beds grow flowers.

В лесý растýт рáзные дерéвья: сóсны [соснá], éли [ель] (*fem.*), дýбы [дуб], берёзы [а], осйны [а].

In the forest grow various trees : pines, fir trees, oak trees, birch trees, aspen trees.

В травé под дерéвьями растýт грибьí и ягоды : чернйка, бруснйка, землянйка.

In the grass under the trees grow mushrooms and berries : bilberries, red bilberries, wild strawberries.

В лесý всегдá прохлáдно и покóйно.

In the forest it is always cool and restful.

На лугý растёт травá.

On the meadow grows grass.

Травý [сéно] кóсят кóсами, сýшат и собирáют в стогй.

The grass [hay] is mown with scythes, dried and gathered into haystacks.

Сéном кóрмят скот : корóв, быкóв, лошадéй, овéц и коз.

With hay are fed cows, oxen, horses, sheep, and goats.

Корóвы, быкй, лóшади, óвцы, и кóзы — это домáшние живóтные.

Cows, oxen, horses, sheep, goats—these are domestic animals.

В деревня́х в хозя́йстве лю́ди разво́дят кур [ку́-рица], у́ток [у́тка], гусе́й [гусь], нидеек [нидейка].

Это дома́шние пти́цы.

Ку́ры, у́тки, гу́си и ни-де́йки кладу́т яйца.

В ка́ждом хозя́йстве есть соба́ки и ко́шки.

В Росси́и во мно́гих мес-та́х, осо́бенно на се́вере, в леса́х во́дятся [живу́т] ди́кие зве́ри : медве́ди, во́лки, лиси́цы [ли́сы].

На звере́й лю́ди охо́тятся [устра́ивают охо́ты] с ру́жьями и соба́ками.

В река́х и озёрах Росси́и мно́го ры́бы.

Ры́бу ло́вят невода́ми, се-тя́ми и у́дочками.

In the village households they rear chickens [hens], ducks, geese, turkeys.

These are domestic birds.

Hens, ducks, geese, and turkeys lay eggs.

In every household there are dogs and cats.

In Russia in many places, particularly in the north, in the forests there are [live] wild beasts : bears, wolves, foxes.

People hunt these beasts [arrange hunts] with gun and hounds.

In the rivers and lakes of Russia there is much fish.

The fish is caught with large and small nets, and fishing-rods.

APPENDIX I

Formation of the Conditional Mood

The conditional mood (see §§ 106, 132) is formed by the addition of the conditional particle бы [б] (a survival in modern Russian of an Old Slavonic verbal form) to any person of the past tense of the indicative mood of both imperfective and perfective verbs (see § 83). Although the conditional mood is expressed in the form of the past tense (with бы), it can refer *to any tense*, in accordance with the meaning of the sentence. The particle бы can either precede or follow the verb. Бы is often used with the conditional conjunction ёсли: если бы, if . . . had; if . . . did, etc. It can also be merged in the conjunction чтобы (see § 97), which is followed by a verb in the past tense if it introduces a subordinate clause of ' wish ' or ' request.' When used in the sense of a conditional mood бы means : should, would, might; should have, would have, might have. Чтобы means : that . . . might, that . . . should, that . . . would. But when чтобы is used as a conjunction of purpose (in the meaning of : in order to . . .), it is followed by an infinitive.

The conditional mood often serves the purpose of the subjunctive mood, for which there is no specific form in Russian :

Ёсли бы я знал [знай я] это раньше, я бы не продал коня.
Had I known this before I would not have sold the horse.

Я просил, чтобы мне дали разрешение ехать в Советский Союз.
I asked that a permit might be given me to go [travel] to the Soviet Union.

Я хочу, чтобы вы оставались здесь.
I wish that you should remain here.

Если бы я знал, что он поéдет в Лóндон, я бы послáл с ним
  кнúги.
Had I known that he was going [would go] to London I would have
  [might have] sent the books with him.

Ты бы что нибýдь[с]дéлал.
You should [might] do [have done] something.

APPENDIX II

Attributive [Long] Adjectives as Predicate

(Refers to §§ 103-104, pp. 184-185)

An attributive adjective can be used as the predicate of a sentence if the quality expressed by the adjective is a permanent one :

| дом был старый, | the house was an old one |
| сапоги были совсём новые, | the top-boots were perfectly new (ones) |

The adjective in these sentences is the name-part of a compound predicate. The long adjective as predicate is frequently used in popular speech. It is also in use in literary language, particularly when the adjective expresses an essential quality, such as colour, etc. :

| крыша была зелёная, | the roof was green [a green one] |
| день был пасмурный, | the day was dull [overcast] |

APPENDIX III

Notes left out in the body of the book

N.B.—The student is advised to insert cross-references in the pages to which these notes refer.

Note to § 63 (pp. 111-117).

The verb иттй [идтй], when preceded by a prefix, is contracted into йтй (dropping the т of the stem). Prefixes ending in a consonant take a euphonic o. In the conjugation of the present form the dropped т reappears as a д.

Note to § 64, *Group* 3 (p. 120).

In the past tense of вы́брать, разобра́ть, the accent *is not shifted* to the last syllable in the feminine; it remains on the same syllable as in the infinitive:

вы́брала, разобра́ла.

Note to § 64, *Group* 5 (p. 121).

In the past tense of добы́ть the accent can also fall on the vowel of the stem (ы) in masculine, neuter, and plural:

добы́л, добы́ло, добы́ли (but: добыла́ for feminine).

Note to § 64, *Group* 7 (pp. 122-124).

The imperative mood of the verbs in this group is formed by adding the terminations й, йте, respectively for singular and plural, to the stem of the perfective, and й, йте to the stem of the imperfectives.

Note to § 70 (p. 136).

If the first person singular of the present tense ends in y, the third person plural will end in ут; if the first person singular ends in ю, the third person plural will end in ют.

Note to § 78 (p. 146).

To this category belong also the verbs :

лиз-а́ть, to lick,	лиж-у́,	ли́ж-ешь,	-ут
пах-а́ть, to plough,	паш-у́,	па́ш-ешь,	-ут
пря́т-ать, to hide,	пря́ч-у,	пря́ч-ешь,	-ут
скак-а́ть, to gallop,	скач-у́,	ска́ч-ешь,	-ут
хлопот-а́ть, to hustle, to busy oneself,	хлопоч-у́,	хлопо́ч-ешь,	-ут
хохот-а́ть, to laugh (loudly),	хохоч-у́,	хохо́ч-ешь,	-ут

Note to § 81 (p. 150).

To this category belong also the verbs :

(a)	гляд-е́ть, to look (upon),	гляж-у́,	гляд-и́шь,	-я́т
	терп-е́ть, to suffer,	терп-лю́,	те́рп-ишь,	-ят
(b)	держ-а́ть, to hold, to keep,	держ-у́,	де́рж-ишь,	-ат
	дрож-а́ть, to shiver, to tremble,	дрож-у́,	-и́шь,	-а́т
	ворч-а́ть, to growl, to grumble,	ворч-у́,	-и́шь,	-а́т
	стуч-а́ть, to knock,	стуч-у́,	-и́шь,	-а́т
	звуч-а́ть, to sound,	звуч-у́,	-и́шь,	-а́т

(See also § 65.)

Note to § 123a (p. 203).

The infinitive of verbs used as an object-complement stands in the *imperfective aspect* if the preceding verb has the meaning of *starting, beginning, ceasing, finishing* :

он { стал / на́чал } проси́ть,   he began to ask

я { ко́нчу / ко́нчил } писа́ть,   { I shall finish / I finished } writing

он { переста́л / переста́нет } чита́ть,   { he stopped / he will stop } reading

Стать often serves as a substitute for the auxiliary verb быть for the formation of the compound future tense of an imperfective verb. (See § 57.)

APPENDIX IV

CONJUGATION OF VERBS

Auxiliary Verb быть

INDICATIVE MOOD

Singular

Present Tense
я есмь
ты еси
он, она, оно есть

Past Tense
я }
ты } был, -а, -о
он, она, оно }

Future Tense
я буду
ты будешь
он, она, оно будет

Plural

мы есмй
вы есте
они суть

мы }
, вы } были
они }

мы будем
вы будете
они будут

IMPERATIVE MOOD

будь (ты)
пусть он, она, оно будет

будьте (вы)
пусть они будут

CONDITIONAL MOOD

я }
ты } был бы, была бы, было бы
он, она, оно }

мы }
вы } были бы
они }

PARTICIPLE (ACTIVE)

Present: сущий, -ая, -ее; -ие
Past: бывший, -ая, -ее; -ие
Future: будущий, -ая, -ее; -ие [1]

GERUND (VERBAL ADVERB)

будучи [2]
быв [бывши] [3]

[1] Used as an adjective.
[2] being.
[3] having been.

FIRST CONJUGATION

IMPERFECTIVE ASPECT читáть (to read)	PERFECTIVE ASPECT прочитáть (to read through)

INDICATIVE MOOD

Present Tense

	IMPERFECTIVE ASPECT	PERFECTIVE ASPECT
Singular	я читá-ю ты читá-ешь он, -á, -ó читá-ет	(none)
Plural	мы читá-ем вы читá-ете они читá-ют	

Past Tense

	Singular		
	я ты он, -á, -ó	} читáл, -а, -о	я ты он, -á, -ó } прочитá-л, -ла, -ло
	Plural		
	мы вы они	} читáли	мы вы они } прочитáли

Future Tense

IMPERFECTIVE ASPECT	PERFECTIVE ASPECT
я бýд-у ты бýд-ешь } читáть он, -á, -о бýд-ет мы бýд-ем вы бýд-ете } читáть они бýд-ут	я прочитá-ю ты прочитá-ешь он, -á, -ó прочитá-ет мы прочитá-ем вы прочитá-ете они прочитá-ют

IMPERATIVE MOOD

IMPERFECTIVE ASPECT	PERFECTIVE ASPECT
читá-й (ты) читá-йте (вы) пусть они читá-ют	прочитáй (ты), -йте (вы) пусть они прочитá-ют

CONDITIONAL MOOD

	IMPERFECTIVE ASPECT		PERFECTIVE ASPECT
Singular	я ты он, -á, -о } читá-л бы -ла бы -ло бы	я ты он, -á, -о } прочитá-л бы -ла бы -ло бы
Plural	мы вы они } читá-ли бы	мы вы они } прочитá-ли бы

PARTICIPLE (ACTIVE)

Present	Past
читá-ющий, -ая, -ее; -ие	читá-вший, -ая, -ее; -ие
(none)	прочитá-вший, -ая, -ее; -ие

PARTICIPLE (PASSIVE)

Present	Past
читá-емый, -ая, -ое; -ые	чита-нный, -ая, -ое; -ые
читá-ем, -а, -о; -ы	читá-н, -на, -но; -ны
(none)	прочита-нный, -ая, -ое; -ые
	прочитá-н, -на, -но; -ны

GERUND (VERBAL ADVERB)

ACTIVE

Present	Past
читá-я	читá-в [-вши]
(none)	прочитá-в [-вши]

PASSIVE

Present	Past
(none)	быв чи́тан²
(none)	быв прочита-н,³ -на, -но; -ны

SECOND CONJUGATION

For the present tense (form) see § 70. The other moods and tenses are formed on the same pattern as verbs of the first conjugation. (See §§ 82, 83, 86a, 86b.)

¹ being read.   ² having been read.   ³ having been read through.

RUSSIAN INDEX

N.B.—*All references are made to pages.*

PREPOSITIONS

The literal English translations of Russian prepositions (see §§ 96-96e) will not always be the best guide for the student as to how they will fit into a Russian expression. Some prepositions have more than one English equivalent. The same can be said about English prepositions. Those Russian prepositions which are liable to some modification of meaning in the sentence are set out below with their respective English equivalents, as illustrated in phrases appearing in the Lessons-Section.

в, *at*, 254, 263-5, 271, 287, 294; в, *at* (*games*), 296; в, *in*, 244, 254-5, 264, 289, 302; в, *on*, 247, 263; в, *to*, 265, 271

для, *for* (*intended for*), 271

за, *at*, 247, 250, 285; за, *by*, 276; за, *during*, 280; за, *for*, 280; за, *to*, 279, 294-5

из, *of*, 271

к, *by*, 261, 263-4, 284; к, *for*, 247, 250, 263, 284; к, *to*, 247, 294-5; к, *towards*, 254, 264, 283

на, *at*, 255, 265, 289; на, *by*, 276; на, *in* [*during*], 262-3; на, *for*, 278; на, *on*, 244, 302; на, *to*, 265, 276-7, 294; на, *up*, 278

по, *after*, 279; по, *along*, 281; по, *at*, 281, 284; по, *by*, 281, 284; по, *in*, 281; по, *on*, 264, 272, 276, 279, 281; по, *to*, 276, 284

под, *on*, 285

с, *about*, 264, 278-9; с, *from* ... *on*, 264

у, *at*, 260-1, 269; у, *by*, 255; у, *from*, *of*, 272; у, *near by*, 269

The English prepositions given in the above list can be roughly translated as :

about, с; *after*, по; *at*, в, за, на, по, у; *by*, за, к, на, по, у·; *during*, за, на; *for*, для, за, к, на; *from*, с, у; *in*, в, на, по; *near*, у; *of*, из, у; *on*, в, на, по, под; *to*, в, за, к, на, по; *towards*, к; *up*, на.

ENGLISH INDEX

N.B.—All references are made to pages.

CPSIA information can be obtained
at www.ICGtesting.com
Printed in the USA
BVHW060351160223
658634BV00002B/33

9 781013 358333